Canadian Edition

m o s a i c s

Focusing on Sentences and Paragraphs in Context

Kim Flachmann
California State University, Bakersfield

Jane Maher
Nassau Community College

Elizabeth H. Campbell
GMI Engineering & Management Institute

Nancy Johnson
University of New Orleans

D.B. Magee
Texas Christian University

William Bunn
Mount Royal College

Beth Everest
Mount Royal College

Prentice
Hall

Toronto

Canadian Cataloguing in Publication Data

Mosaics : focusing on sentences and paragraphs in context

Canadian ed.
Includes index.
ISBN 0-13-988338-X

1. English language — Sentences — Problems, exercises, etc. 2. English language — Paragraphs — Problems, exercises, etc. 3. English language — Rhetoric — Problems, exercises, etc. I. Flachmann, Kim.

PE1408.M67 2001   808′.042   C00-930447-9

ISBN 0-13-988338-X

Vice President, Editorial Director: Michael Young
Executive Editor: David Stover
Senior Marketing Manager: Sophia Fortier
Signing Representative: Colleen Henderson
Associate Editor: Susan Ratkaj
Production Editor: Joe Zingrone
Copy Editor: Mary Bitti
Production Coordinator: Wendy Moran
Page Layout: April Haisell
Art Director: Mary Opper
Interior Design: Julia Hall
Cover Design: Julia Hall
Cover Image: Photodisc

1 2 3 4 5   05 04 03 02 01

Printed and bound in Canada.

CONTENTS

1   THE WRITING PROCESS   5

3   OBSERVING: THE WRITING PROCESS   45

7 ANALYZING   185

8

PERSUADING   222

9 PROBLEM SOLVING 251

I buy an old house and begin to paint—coats and coats of
white. (First draft, second draft, third?) The *living room* first.
I shall transform it from tacky darkness into light.
        —PHYLLIS WEBB, "UP THE LADDER: NOTES
                ON THE CREATIVE PROCESS"

To write is to communicate. While this statement seems to say the obvious, it is important to note that how and what we write communicate to our audience more than simply the words on the page. At the level of the essay, the paragraph and even the sentence, the words that we choose to use communicate our awareness of audience, our perspective on a specific topic, and our patterns of organization. These are some of the writing skills that we focus on in this text.

Words, sentences, and paragraphs are the primary focus for *Mosaics: Sentences and Paragraphs in Context*, the first in a series of two books that teach the basic skills necessary for effective written communication. Each book is divided into chapters, each highlighting one of eight primary purposes for writing: recalling, observing, explaining, investigating, researching, analyzing, persuading, and problem solving. Each contains both professional and student examples. Each examines the essay form, but *Mosaics: Sentences and Paragraphs in Context* specifically looks at how to write strong sentences and paragraphs.

The writer is one who writes. When we write, we speak with words. When we speak, we assume that there is a listener. The writer forms words into sentences, reads, and revises these sentences in an effort to best communicate with the intended audience. Reading and writing work together; they are a part of what we call the writing process. This process is not necessarily linear, with the writer moving from step to step to step in a specified order. Rather, it is a composite of activities that we return to again and again.

Cursive means running or flowing. *Recursive*, then, means to run or flow again. When we talk about the recursive process of writing, we mean that as we write, we run, we flow, back and forth through the tasks of reading, writing, and revising. We return to each of these tasks as needed, adding, deleting, and changing bits until we communicate what it is that we want to say.

Even accomplished writers go through similar acts of recursion as they work through drafts of their own writing, despite their personal approaches. For example, poet/novelist Robert Kroetsch is known to pin each printed page like a map so he can see the whole on his office wall; the late novelist W. O. Mitchell used to sit for endless hours in front of his typewriter tapping out inner thoughts as they came into his more conscious mind. These two writers have approached writing very differently, and both have been very successful writers and teachers of writing. What their approaches have in common, and what they have in common with the writing processes of other writers, is that they write and read, and rewrite and reread until they get the words exactly right. Your polished pieces of writing will undergo a comparable set of activities.

Rarely do we find good published writing that has not gone through this recursive process, the rhythmical modification of each draft, clarifying what is written and adding colour, like the painter brushing on layers and layers of paint until the house, the room, the page is transformed "from tacky darkness into light."

ASSUMPTIONS

This text is based on the following assumptions:

1. Writing is a recursive process.
2. Students learn best from discovery and experimentation.
3. Students must be able to transfer their writing skills to other areas of their professional and private lives.
4. Students profit from studying models of both professional and student writing.
5. Students profit from individual and collaborative learning.

HOW THIS BOOK WORKS

This book begins with a general introduction to the writing process in Chapter One. The eight chapters that follow are each divided into three carefully integrated sections:

The Writing Process

Focus on Sentences

Focus on Paragraphs

The afterword, on your own writing process, works as a summary to the text.

Reading and Writing for a Reason. Each chapter focuses on one of the eight primary purposes for writing: recalling (2), observing (3), explaining (4), investigating (5), researching (6), analyzing (7), persuading (8), and problem solving (9). The purpose is explained and then featured in both a professional essay and an essay written by a student before the readers are asked to compose essays of their own.

Learning from Published Writers focuses on a provocative professional essay with a controlled reading level in order to introduce students to a specific purpose for writing. Each essay was chosen for its high interest and moderate readability level and serves as a springboard in form and content for the rest of the chapter.

Learning from Your Peers walks students through the writing process using an actual student essay. Students witness the development of a peer essay that moves through the general recursive tasks of generating ideas, planning, developing, organizing, drafting, revising, editing. The revised draft is printed in each chapter with the student changes highlighted.

Writing Your Own Essay asks students to compose their own essays focusing on the purpose they have just studied. Following a brief review of the highlights of the chapter and the composing process, students are given at least four writing topics to choose from. After they draft, revise, and edit their essays, students are then asked some specific questions that require them to pause and reflect on their writing process before they start another chapter.

Focus on Sentences and Focus on Paragraphs. The second and third sections of each chapter, Focus on Sentences and Focus on Paragraphs, can be taught by themselves or in conjunction with the first section. The Focus on Sentences sections serve as brief but thorough reference guides to grammar and usage; they move from the most basic usage and syntactic problems to the more sophisticated writing conventions. Most importantly, they teach grammar in the context of the students' own work. The Focus on Paragraphs sections focus on the larger issues of paragraph development; they progress from fairly simple to more complex revision strategies. These Focus sections include instruction and exercises that are drawn from the professional and student essays featured in the chapter. Each of the Focus sections begins with a checklist summarizing the tasks to be covered and ends with collaborative work for individual, small group, or entire class projects.

UNIQUE FEATURES

Several unique and exciting features separate this book from other basic writing texts:

1. It moves students systematically from personal and academic writing.
2. It gives student writing more attention than professional writing.
3. It sees learning to write as recursive.
4. It illustrates all aspects of the writing process.
5. It teaches revising and editing through the student essays in each chapter.
6. It focuses on individual aspects of both the sentence and the paragraph.
7. It teaches grammar instruction in the context of process.
8. It features culturally diverse reading selections that are of interest to students.

ACKNOWLEDGMENTS

The authors would like to acknowledge the support of the people at Prentice Hall/ Pearson Education, Mount Royal College, their students, and especially their families.

CHAPTER ONE

The Writing Process

In writing there is an element of search—not pursuing anything
quite so tangible as oil or gas or their by-products—but the
search is an intense and continuing one . . . . Perhaps the
writer's work is more closely allied to the work of the refiner.
He separates and he combines until he has what he seeks.
                              —W. O. MITCHELL, *THE POETRY OF LIFE*

GETTING STARTED

The writing process begins before we actually begin drafting an essay. Many writers use
one or more of a series of activities to explore a subject, generate ideas, settle on a specific topic, establish a purpose, and analyze a potential audience. These activities are
also effective ways to write yourself out of corners when you feel stuck for things to say.
Remember that you can return to these activities at any time during the writing process.

Generating Ideas

Before you begin writing you need to have something to write about. This something is
called the broad topic. There are a number of ways that you can generate and explore a
broad topic. You can use a single one or a combination of any, but the important thing
is that while you are exploring possibilities, you write down everything you are thinking about. You want to let your mind run free to uncover some material to work with.
It is also useful to discuss your ideas with friends or classmates. Return to this list at any
time during the writing process if you feel the need to revisit or flesh out an idea.

Journal: The word *journal* means "a place for daily writing." Many
writers keep a notebook with them at all times, and others spend some
time each day jotting down remembrances, autobiographical reflections,
ideas, snatches of conversation, dreams, and descriptions of people,
places, or objects that catch their attention. Your journal can be paper or

electronic. Use whatever is comfortable and easy. Include in your journal thoughts about each of the essays that you read in this text, and ideas and plans for essays as they occur to you.

Reading: Often what we read calls us to respond in some way, to answer back to the writer. Sometimes we will jot notes in the margin of the text, or grab a scrap of paper that we will later transfer into another space. Any or all of these can later be developed into something interesting. You will want to return to the original source to cite the author appropriately. And, rereading the original might give new insights into your topic. Often writers have favourite pieces that they like to read just to get them in the right frame of mind for writing.

List: Many writers find it helpful to jot down a list of ideas about possible essay topics or ideas for expanding a chosen topic. Write down all the ones that you think about, even if they don't seem all that great at the time. You can always delete them. Seeing them on paper often generates more thought. You may find it helpful to share your list with classmates. Their lists may spark some new ideas for you.

Freewrite: Writing freely about anything that comes to your mind is the way to *freewrite*. The act of writing usually makes writers think of other ideas. Simply start writing anything and everything that you think of. Do not, at this stage, worry about correct sentences and punctuation. If you are writing on a computer, you might try writing with the screen turned off so that you can write without the interference of correctness. Try writing for a specified amount of time; start with five minutes. Each time you freewrite, increase the number of minutes. Soon you will be able to comfortably write for greater lengths.

Brainstorming: Like freewriting, *brainstorming* draws on random thoughts about a subject. Words or phrases trigger connections to other words and phrases, and often generate some very interesting essay topics. You can brainstorm alone, with a friend, or, best of all, with a group. Regardless of the method, write down *all* your ideas; you can later delete those that won't work.

Clustering: *Clustering* lets you map your ideas as fast as they come into your mind. To cluster, take a sheet of blank paper and write a key word, phrase, or sentence in the centre of the page, and draw a circle around it. Next, write down and circle any more ideas you have and connect them with lines to the thoughts they came from. This exercise usually lasts about five minutes.

Questioning: Journalists and many other writers routinely ask questions to generate ideas on a topic. Using some type of questioning technique can help you avoid omitting important details. Most often, the questions used to generate ideas and details on a topic are the five w's and one h: *Who, What, Why, When, Where,* and *How.*

Planning

Once you have generated some ideas and then chosen a broad topic, you need to make some decisions about the essay you are creating. These decisions will help you to limit your topic and provide a focus for your essay. Jot down short answers to each of the following questions:

What **size** will your essay be?

Knowing the size of your essay ahead of time will help you to determine the scope of your topic and the amount of material it is necessary to generate. For example, a 500-word essay on hockey limits the content more than a 2000-word essay does. Perhaps you would provide a description of the game for the former, and a short history for the latter.

What **content** (person, event, object, etc.) do you want to focus on?

Each of your essays should *focus* on a set of related details or ideas. Although this focus will become clearer to you as you write, make some general, preliminary decisions about your content before you begin to draft an essay. Jot down three to five main points that directly relate to your topic. Such decisions will help you to keep focused and detect any irrelevant material.

What is your **purpose**?

Your purpose is your *reason for writing* an essay. Purposes for essays in this text range from the personal through the practical to the persuasive. Your purpose could be to explore your own knowledge or feelings on a topic, to share information on a subject, to find ways to solve a problem, or to persuade a reader to share your views on a controversial issue.

Who is your **audience**?

Your audience consists of the *people you think will read your essay*. The more you know about these people, the more likely you will successfully get your ideas across. Information about your audience will help you to choose suitable language and determine how to tailor your comments so you have a good chance of convincing them to see your topic the way you do.

What **perspective** will you take toward your topic?

Perspective is *how you feel about your particular topic*. It is the stance that you take. For example, are you for or against jail sentences for young offenders? Or, how do you feel about a certain issue affecting your community? Or you personally? For the sake of consistency, once you choose a stance toward your topic, keep it for the entire essay.

Developing

When you have answered the questions related to planning the essay, you have already begun to make some commitments to the direction your essay will take. Now that you know the size, general content, purpose, audience, and perspective, you are ready to develop some specific topics that will make up the bulk of your essay. Reread each of your main points. Add three or four more related details. If necessary, return to the questions of the generating and planning phases. Use these to help you to flesh out your ideas and to rethink your more focused topic.

Organizing

After you generate some ideas on a topic, you need to plan the best way of presenting your ideas. What should come first? What next? Would a different way of organizing your ideas achieve your purpose better?

In the early paragraphs of an essay, you should supply your readers with the facts needed to understand the purpose in order to create a context for what they are about to read. By providing answers to basic questions the readers might have (*Who, What, Why, When, Where,* and *How*) or explaining the facts surrounding a particular event, you enable your audience to share your viewpoint as fully as possible.

Then, organize your material in a way that will be most interesting to your audience. What's the most striking detail or fact about your topic? You might want to start with that. What meaning or significance does the topic have for you? You might want to end with that. Remember that those aspects of your topic that interest you are what you are most likely to write about effectively.

Outlining

Many writers use an outline to set up the essays they write. An outline is a map. It tells the order or the structure of the essay; it lets you see in an organized fashion the ideas you already have and how they connect. From it, you can tell where you need further development or support. It is important to remember, though, that there are many roads to get to a destination, and that like your essay, you might want to update and revise your outline as you go.

Writers also often use outlines once they have completed an essay. By examining your main point in each paragraph and setting it up as an outline, you can determine whether your organizational pattern works as you had intended. This type of outlining is called *organizational analysis*.

Drafting

Drafting, as you may have guessed, means writing out a first draft. At this point, you have been working both by yourself and in class, generating, planning, developing, and organizing your ideas on your essay topic. You may want to spread out your journal, clusters, lists etc. A helpful trick is for you to write your main idea at the top of the page or tack a note to the top of your computer screen. This *working title* will help to guide you in writing your essay, and help you to keep focused.

Now you're ready to begin writing in complete or almost complete sentences. This early draft is what the business writer Peter F. Drucker likes to call the *zero draft*. First you need to get the words out; in successive drafts you will spend more time shaping your sentences and paragraphs. For this zero draft, as you write, try to keep a steady flow of words going. Put as much as you can on paper. Don't let grammar and spelling distract you; you'll deal with those later. For now, just keep writing. Say what it is that you want to say. The refining happens as you revise and edit.

Revising

W.O. Mitchell was fond of saying that writing is a conversation between the writer and the creative partner, the person who reads and brings the writer's words to life. As writers, we refine, separate, and combine until we find what it is that best communicates what we want to say to our listening partner. Each draft is like a practice speech, rehearsed again and again until we get the words exactly right and our imagined partner responds in the manner that we have intended.

Revising and editing are both very much a part of the drafting phase of the writing process. *Revising* means "seeing again" and that is exactly what you try to do—see your essay again from as many different angles as possible. To revise most effectively, a writer needs some distance from his or her first draft. Ideally, you should put your draft aside for at least a day before you begin revising it.

Revision is a task that focuses on improving content and organization. Your main goal in revising is to make sure that the purpose of your essay is clear to your audience. It is also necessary for your main ideas to be supported with enough details and examples. Read carefully through each paragraph. A quick visual check used by many editors is to see if all paragraphs are roughly the same size. In addition, you should check to be sure your organization is logical. The Focus on Paragraphs section in every chapter of this book will help you establish your own revising strategies.

Editing

Edit means "to prepare for publication." Whether you plan to submit your essay to be printed in a magazine or newspaper, or simply to present it to your classmates or instructor, you are making it public. While editing is something that writers tend to do in each and every draft, it is necessary to provide your essay with a final edit before you go public because your audience will have particular expectations about correctness.

When you edit, read your essay slowly and carefully to make sure no errors in grammar, mechanics, or spelling have slipped into your draft. The Focus on Sentences section of every chapter of this book will help you develop some of your own editing strategies. Once you are certain that your essay is error free, try a final strategy used by many professional editors: read your draft from back to front; often you will catch errors that you might otherwise tend to overlook, especially spelling errors. Reading aloud is another good method to catch errors and awkward phrasing.

HOW TO USE THIS BOOK

Each of the following chapters provides a look at one of the eight main purposes for essay writing: recalling (2), observing (3), explaining (4), investigating (5), researching (6), analyzing (7), persuading (8), and problem solving (9). Every chapter takes you through a professional essay and the writing process of a student before offering strategies for writing your own essay. At the end of each chapter are instructions and exercises to help you revise your paragraphs and edit your sentences. The text ends with an afterword asking you to reflect on your own writing process.

Recalling
Reading and Writing to Remember

I try to remember times in my life, incidents in which there
was the dominating theme of cruelty, or kindness, or
generosity, or envy, or happiness, or glee. Then I select one.
–**MAYA ANGELOU**

LEARNING OUTCOMES

This chapter will help you:
- Understand and write an essay about a past event;
- Recognize and shape a paragraph and its topic and supporting sentences; and,
- Recognize and punctuate complete sentences.

Although you may not realize it, you are recalling–remembering–all the time. Whenever you tell someone about something that has happened to you–what your day was like, how a job interview went, what you did with your holidays, or your last date–you are remembering. Memories are a rich source of writing material.

Memories are often included in essays. And when a writer includes memories, the writer usually wants the reader to experience the memory for him or herself as he or she reads. Most often, the writer wants the reader to "live" the same experience so the writer gives the reader details: what happened, how it smelled, felt, tasted, looked, and sounded.

In this chapter, you're going to use one of your memories to write an essay. What kind of memory would make a good subject for your essay? You don't need to try to remember something newsworthy, weird, or wacky. Ordinary memories can make your reader interested in what you have to say, too.

When you write about one of your memories, you don't need to try to remember everything–every detail about what happened. You only need to remember the general gist of things–the important things. You also don't need to include everything that has ever happened to you over the course of your entire life. Find a memory that deals with one whole story. You should be able to record your memory in enough detail to give your reader the idea of what happened and tell the reader why this memory is significant for you.

The significance of an event is how the event changed you, how it made you realize something new about yourself or someone else. It's a lot like telling a story to your friends. When you relate a story to your friends you almost always explain its significance. If you don't, you almost always confuse them. They may be wondering why you started to tell the story in the first place. So, when you write an essay about a memory, you need to do two things: one, you need to write the memory in enough detail to make it interesting and vivid for your reader; two, you need to explain why this memory is significant.

Here's a sample of a memory and its significance from Rose Borris. She recalls a time when she decided to return to school as an adult to learn to read and write:

> The first day I came at school, I was lost and nervous. I saw all around. The principal gave me a paper. I forgot the room and my names for one week. I was always thinking about my house and I felt stupid and crazy. I hated the teacher, the principal, and myself so much. Not now. I was thirty years at home. It was strange, when my teacher Susan talked to me I jumped. Here it is nice, because we have a private teacher every day in the library. Today I'm happy because I didn't stop my school. I read and I write today, I like my two teachers very much.

This story is clear, vivid, and it explains the significance in the last two sentences.

LEARNING FROM PUBLISHED WRITERS

Before You Read

Focus Your Attention

Before you read this story, take a few moments to respond to the following questions in your journal:

1. Can you recall a time when you felt embarrassment or discomfort in front of your classmates? What do you recall?

2. The story you are about to read is titled "Eleven." Eleven refers to the age of the girl in the story. Try to remember what your life was like when you were eleven years old–you would have been in the fifth or sixth grade at the time. Were you particularly sensitive or conscious of what you looked like? Were you conscious of what your friends thought of you? Were you popular or not? Have you become more or less sensitive to those issues as you have gotten older?

Expand Your Vocabulary

Spend some time reading the sentences around the following words and see if you can figure out what each word means without using a dictionary:

Rattling (paragraph 5)

Raggedy (paragraph 9)

Nonsense (paragraph 15)

Invisible (paragraph 19)

Runaway (paragraph 22)

Sandra Cisneros

Eleven*

What they don't understand about birthdays and what they never tell you is **1** that when you're eleven, you're also ten, and nine, and eight, and seven, and six, and five, and four, and three, and two, and one. And when you wake up on your eleventh birthday you expect to feel eleven, but you don't. You open your eyes and everything's just like yesterday, only it's today. And you don't feel eleven at all. You feel like you're still ten. And you are—underneath the year that makes you eleven.

Like some days you might say something stupid, and that's the part of you **2** that's still ten. Or maybe some days you might need to sit on your mama's lap because you're scared, and that's the part of you that's five. And maybe one day when you're all grown up maybe you will need to cry like if you're three, and that's okay. That's what I tell Mama when she's sad and needs to cry. Maybe she's feeling three.

Because the way you grow old is kind of like an onion or like the rings in- **3** side a tree trunk or like my little wooden dolls that fit one inside the other, each year inside the next one. That's how being eleven years old is.

You don't feel eleven. Not right away. It takes a few days, weeks even, **4** sometimes even months before you say Eleven when they ask you. And you don't feel smart eleven, not until you're almost twelve. That's the way it is.

Only today I wish I didn't have only eleven years rattling inside me like **5** pennies in a tin Band-Aid box. Today I wish I was one hundred and two instead of eleven because if I was one hundred and two I'd have known what to say when Mrs. Price put the red sweater on my desk. I would've known

Women Hollering Creek (New York: Vintage, 1991), pp. 6-9.

how to tell her it wasn't mine instead of just sitting there with that look on my face and nothing coming out of my mouth.

"Whose is this?" Mrs. Price says, and she holds the red sweater up in the air for all the class to see. "Whose? It's been sitting in the coatroom for a month."   **6**

"Not mine," says everybody. "Not me."   **7**

"It has to belong to somebody," Mrs. Price keeps saying, but nobody can remember. It's an ugly sweater with red plastic buttons and a collar and sleeves all stretched out like you could use it for a jump rope. It's maybe a thousand years old, and even if it belonged to me I wouldn't say so.   **8**

Maybe because I'm skinny, maybe because she doesn't like me, that stupid Sylvia Saldívar says, "I think it belongs to Rachel." An ugly sweater like that, all raggedy and old, but Mrs. Price believes her. Mrs. Price takes the sweater and puts it right on my desk, but when I open my mouth nothing comes out.   **9**

"That's not, I don't, you're not . . . Not mine," I finally say in a little voice that was maybe me when I was four.   **10**

"Of course it's yours," Mrs. Price says. "I remember you wearing it once." Because she's older and the teacher, she's right and I'm not.   **11**

Not mine, not mine, not mine, but Mrs. Price is already turning to page thirty-two, and math problem number four. I don't know why, but all of a sudden I'm feeling sick inside, like the part of me that's three wants to come out of my eyes, only I squeeze them shut tight and bite down on my teeth real hard and try to remember today I am eleven, eleven. Mama is making a cake for me for tonight, and when Papa comes home everybody will sing Happy birthday, happy birthday to you.   **12**

But when the sick feeling goes away and I open my eyes, the red sweater's still sitting there like a big red mountain. I move the red sweater to the corner of my desk with my ruler. I move my pencil and books and eraser as far from it as possible. I even move my chair a little to the right. Not mine, not mine, not mine.   **13**

In my head I'm thinking how long till lunch time, how long till I can take the red sweater and throw it over the school yard fence, or leave it hanging on a parking meter, or bunch it up into a little ball and toss it in the alley. Except when math period ends Mrs. Price says loud and in front of everybody, "Now, Rachel, that's enough," because she sees I've shoved the red sweater to the tippy-tip corner of my desk and it's hanging all over the edge like a waterfall, but I don't care.   **14**

"Rachel," Mrs. Price says. She says it like she's getting mad. "You put that sweater on right now and no more nonsense."   **15**

"But it's not—"   **16**

"Now!" Mrs. Price says.   **17**

This is when I wish I wasn't eleven, because all the years inside of me—ten, nine, eight, seven, six, five, four, three, two, and one—are pushing at the back of my eyes when I put one arm through one sleeve of the sweater that smells like cottage cheese, and then the other arm through the other   **18** and stand there with my arms apart like if the sweater hurts me and it does, all itchy and full of germs that aren't even mine.

That's when everything I've been holding in since this morning, since   **19** when Mrs. Price put the sweater on my desk, finally lets go, and all of a sudden I'm crying in front of everybody. I wish I was invisible but I'm not. I'm eleven and it's my birthday today and I'm crying like I'm three in front of everybody. I put my head down on the desk and bury my face in my stupid clown-sweater arms. My face all hot and spit coming out of my mouth because I can't stop the little animal noises from coming out of me, until there aren't any more tears left in my eyes, and it's just my body shaking like when you have the hiccups, and my whole head hurts like when you drink milk too fast.

But the worst part is right before the bell rings for lunch. That stupid   **20** Phyllis Lopez, who is even dumber than Sylvia Saldívar, says she remembers the red sweater is hers! I take it off right away and give it to her, only Mrs. Price pretends like everything's okay.

Today I'm eleven. There's a cake Mama's making for tonight, and when   **21** Papa comes home from work we'll eat it. There'll be candles and presents and everybody will sing Happy birthday, happy birthday to you, Rachel, only it's too late.

I'm eleven today. I'm eleven, ten, nine, eight, seven, six, five, four, three,   **22** two, and one, but I wish I was one hundred and two. I wish I was anything but eleven, because I want today to be far away already, far away like a runaway balloon, like a tiny o in the sky, so tiny-tiny you have to close your eyes to see it.

 ## QUESTIONS FOR CRITICAL THINKING

THINKING CRITICALLY ABOUT CONTENT

1. Why do you think Cisneros pays such close attention Rachel's age and to the fact that it is her birthday? What does age mean to Rachel?

2. What does Rachel mean when she says that although there will be a cake and candles and presents and singing that evening at her home, "It's all too late"?

THINKING CRITICALLY ABOUT PURPOSE

3. What do you think Cisneros's purpose is with this essay? Explain your answer.

4. How does Cisneros show that Rachel is far more sensitive and intelligent than her teacher, Mrs. Price, thinks she is?

THINKING CRITICALLY ABOUT AUDIENCE

5. What type of audience do you think would most understand and appreciate this recollection?

6. Does the writer succeed in making the audience feel the pain and hurt of an eleven-year-old girl? How does she accomplish this?

THINKING CRITICALLY ABOUT PERSPECTIVE

7. Does it sound like an eleven-year old is saying these words? How would the story be different if Rachel was an adult remembering what had happened to her on her eleventh birthday?
8. The whole story is told from Rachel's perspective. Try and rewrite the story from Mrs. Price's perspective expressing her frustration with Rachel.

LEARNING FROM YOUR PEERS

When you write your own recollections, you need to identify and emphasize details that interest other readers so you can help them understand why particular incidents are so important to you or why they played a role in shaping your life.

Craig's Writing Assignment: Recalling

This is the topic Craig's instructor assigned:

This first essay is about a memory. Think back to a time when something happened to you that changed your life. It can be something nice to remember or something not so nice. When you write out your memory, remember to include why it was important to you (significance) because that helps make it important to your readers.

Generating Ideas, Planning, And Developing

In Craig's case, he worked with several activities to help him think, plan, and develop his essay all at the same time. He worked this way because he found that this was the way he preferred to write. He wrote his best papers this way.

Make a list. Craig's first reaction was that he couldn't think of an interesting memory to write about. He twiddled his pen around his fingers for a while. He thought about making a list. He wondered if he had any interesting memories he could write about. So, he decided to write down all the memories he had of his childhood.

Eating goldfish with Sam

Cycling home from Grandpa's

Ice cream at Phillip's on Sundays

He relaxed for a moment, unhappy with the ideas he generated. As he wrote this list, he happened to be wearing a hockey jersey. He examined the shirt. It was worn. He loved hockey. He still played. Suddenly, he realized he had a possible topic. He added these words to his list:

Hockey games

Hockey equipment

As he wrote down the last item, he recalled getting ready for a game. Suddenly he was inspired. He didn't have a clear idea of where he was going, but he knew he wanted to start writing about hockey.

Freewrite on your topic. He flipped over a page on his notepad and started to write. He wasn't worried about spelling or punctuation. He just wanted to get the ideas out and on the paper.

He wrote a paragraph and realized he didn't have enough to write about.

So he fell into frustration again and started to doodle all over his paragraph. He drew a picture of a hockey stick.

Cluster ideas around a topic. He remembered that he had several techniques to help him generate more ideas. So he picked the clustering idea and turned to a fresh page. He put the word "hockey" in the middle of the page and drew a big circle around it. He drew another picture of a hockey stick next to it. As he thought about what he wanted to say he doodled some tape onto the stick. Then a puck. He relaxed and waited for the ideas to hit.

He generated a few more ideas, but nothing "clicked" the rest of the evening. Craig put his writing away. He knew he could work on it a little more in class the next day.

Discuss possible topics with others. The next day he took what he had written to class. He spent time working with his classmates to generate ideas. Most of the group felt that the hockey stick was the most interesting part of what he had so far. A couple of other people in his group had played hockey, and the whole group ended up talking about the game until class ended. As Craig talked and listened, he picked up a few more ideas for his paper. Another student said, "I know hockey is important to you, and it's kind of interesting to me, but why would I want to read your essay? How is your essay going to be different than all the others I've seen?" It was a tough question, but one Craig knew he had to answer, though he didn't have the answer right then. He added a few comments, ideas, and questions to his notes and brought them home again to work on it.

Cluster ideas around the topic again. Craig still didn't feel like he had all he needed to write the essay. So, that evening Craig added the comments and suggestions to the cluster after he reread his freewrite.

Ask questions about your topic. Then he spent some time thinking about hockey. What was so great about hockey? He wrote his answers down.

The dressing room

Getting up early

Getting to the arena

Taping the sticks

Craig began to see that he didn't just love the game, he liked getting ready for it, and finishing it off afterward. As he thought about what came before the game and what happened afterwards, he realized he had a few things to write about. He listed all of the things he could think of that he noticed and enjoyed before and after a game.

Brainstorm for details. In the next class, the instructor said that he wanted to help the class add important detail to the memories so far. Craig's instructor asked the class to write other versions of the same memory. First, he asked them to rewrite their memories as if they were blind. Craig began to think about what his memories would be like if he was blind. He heard the sound of the hockey tape. He smelled the locker room. He heard the sound of his blades cut the ice. Then the instructor asked the class to imagine that they were only able to tell the reader what they touched and how it felt, and that had to be enough to help the reader figure out what the memory was. Craig thought for quite a while and tried to imagine details about how things felt. After a few more exercises, the instructor asked the class to pick out favourite details that could help the reader "live" the experience.

Craig found he had lots to say—much more than he needed to reach the number of words required for the assignment.

Now that he had all he needed, he could organize it and revise it.

Organizing

Organize your words for best effect. He cut out each of the little pieces of his freewrite and began to play with what order he wanted to place them in. He played around until he had a pretty good idea of what he wanted to do, then he taped all the pieces back together and took a separate piece of paper and wrote up the outline. He thought about what he had written and who he was writing for. What should he write about first? What would give his audience the best impression of his memories? What should he end with? Should he combine some of the points?

Discuss your paper with others. In class the next day, Craig explained his essay in more detail and how he thought he would structure it. His group helped him think about his audience, and who he was trying to reach with his essay. They looked at what he had written and tried to help him think about its strengths and weaknesses.

Drafting

Craig has spent time thinking, planning, developing, and organizing. Now he is ready to begin writing the first version of his paper. We call this drafting. He writes best late at night, when everything is quiet. He spreads out his class notes, his journal, his clusters, and his taped outline. He pulls a Coke out of the fridge and he begins to write his paper from beginning to end.

Craig's Essay: First Draft ....

Game day has arrived and I head to the arena prepared and ready for battle. Nervous excitement running through my body and like a vice, gripping my stomach. The arena is now within my sights and all the strategies and plays I have learned throughout the many previous practices flash through my mind having arrived, I throw my equipment up on my shoulder, grip my sticks in my free hand, and proceed towards the arena entrance. I pull open the door and head down the hallway to my team's designated dressing room.

Greeted by my teammates, I enter the dressing room and find a stall in the room where I will dress. The air is moist with steam from the showers of the previous team, and filled with an aroma of sweaty equipment, bags of equipment litter the floor, and the room echoes with the laughter and the sound of unrolling tape, as my teammates and I prepare our sticks. It is now time to put on my gear and the sound of the room changes from loud and rowdy to more focused and calm. Once again, thoughts and strategies race through my head, trying not to leave out the smallest detail, so my reactions will seem second nature during the game.

The game now only ten minutes away. My team and I are ready and waiting with our skates laced up and our jerseys on, the coach then enters the room and gives the team one final pep talk and an overview of the game plan. Emotions soar as my team hears the zamboni leave the ice, and everyone puts on his helmet and gloves. On the command of the coach everyone hurries out of the room. Skates clatter as the team walks down the hallway towards the ice, and in the distance I hear the crowd shout louder as they sight the first of my teammates.

I skate round my zone briefly, feeling my blades cut over the ice as I warm myself up before the game begins. The referee sounds his whistle and all but the teams' starting two lines head to their designated bench "home" or "visitors." In this case it was the "home" bench I headed for, and took my position in the line up amongst my teammates the puck is dropped and fans cheer as the teams battle for possession of the puck with hopes of achieving the first goal. My turn on the ice comes closer as my teammates become tired and need to be changed. I watch and listen to the coach and hear all the noises of hockey as I wait for my moment.

My time has come as one of my teammates skates off the ice. I accelerate out of the box and stride into the play. I get a chance to change and head to the bench for a brief rest before I am back out crashing and banging again.

My team prevails in the end, and we head out of the bench and towards the goal crease to congratulate our goalie for a job well done, before we all head back into the dressing room. Excited from our victory, I sit down in the same stall I began in and take my sweat-drenched equipment off.

In the dressing room, my teammates and I talk to each other about the good and bad points of the game and laugh with each other once again. Steam then fills the air again as myself and my teammates show and redress before we all head home to conclude another day at the rink.

Revising

Craig completed the first draft of his essay, but he knew he still had a lot of work ahead of him. At this point, his instructor wanted every student to focus on the meaning of each sentence in his or her essay. The instructor explained that controlling meaning at the sentence level makes the whole essay stronger and more effective.

Craig reviewed the Checklist for Recognizing and Developing Sentences (p. 36) at the beginning of the Focus on Sentences section of this chapter. His instructor explained to the class that revising means focusing on content, not grammar—concentrating on whether the sentence says exactly what the writer intends it to say. Craig did all the exercises and learned how to recognize a sentence. He decided to return to his essay draft to make sure each sentence was a whole sentence and that each sentence was marked with a capital letter at the beginning and a period at the end.

He also learned to expand some of his points by adding detail so the reader can better understand what he is trying to say. He had a friend go over the essay and mark the places where he needed to explain things in more detail.

COLLABORATIVE WORK

PEER GROUP ACTIVITY

After you read the portions of the Focus on Sentences section, turn to Craig's first draft (p. 19) and complete the following tasks in small groups.

1. Underline the parts of Craig's draft you think need to be developed.
2. Mark the parts of the essay that relate a memory and the parts that explain the significance.

Compare your marks to ones your instructor will show you. Where do your marks differ from your instructor's? What do you need to review before writing your own essay?

CLASS ACTIVITY

As an entire class, look at the underlined portions of Craig's revised draft (p. 22) to see how he changed each sentence.

1. Did you identify the revision problems that Craig corrected?
2. Discuss his changes. Do you think his changes are good ones?

Editing

Once the sentences in Craig's draft were as fully developed as he could make them, he needed to do some final editing and proofreading before handing in his essay. The instructor told the students that they needed a working knowledge of the sentence to help them catch errors as they proofread. Craig shifted his focus from the content of his sentences. He read the Focus on Paragraphs section in this chapter to learn about paragraphs. After he finished the assigned exercises he went through the questions in the Checklist for Recognizing Paragraphs (p. 27) and revised his essay.

COLLABORATIVE WORK

PEER GROUP ACTIVITY

After you read Focus on Sentences, turn again to Craig's first draft and complete the following tasks in small groups.

1. Put every subject and predicate in brackets.
2. Underline any sentence fragments.
3. Highlight any sentences that are missing a period or a capital letter.

Compare your group's work with your instructor's. Where do your marks differ from your instructor's? What do you need to understand before you write your own essay?

CLASS ACTIVITY

As an entire class, look at the underlined portions of Craig's revised draft to see how he changed each sentence.

1. Did you identify the editing problems that Craig corrected?
2. Do you think his changes are good ones? Why or why not?

Craig's Revised Essay ....

Game Time

Game day has arrived and I head to the arena prepared and ready for battle. Nervous excitement ~~running~~runs through my body and like a vice, ~~gripping~~it grips at my stomach. The arena is now within my sights and all the strategies and plays I have learned throughout the many previous practices flash through my ~~mind having~~mind. Having arrived, I throw my equipment up on my shoulder, grip my sticks in my free hand, and proceed towards the arena entrance. I pull open the door and head down the hallway to my team's designated dressing room.

Greeted by my teammates, I enter the dressing room and find a stall in the room where I will dress. The air is moist with steam from the showers of the previous team, and filled with an aroma of sweaty ~~equipment, bags~~equipment. Bags of equipment litter the floor, and the

room echoes with the laughter and the sound of unrolling tape, as my
teammates and I prepare our <u>sticks.</u>

It is now time to put on my gear and the sound of the room
changes from loud and rowdy to more focused and calm. Once again,
thoughts and strategies race through my head, trying not to leave out
the smallest detail, so my reactions will seem second nature during
the game.

The game <u>is </u>now only ten minutes ~~away. My~~<u>away, and my</u> team
and I are ready and waiting with our skates laced up and our jerseys
~~on, the~~<u>on. The</u> coach then enters the room and gives the team one
final pep talk and an overview of the game plan. Emotions soar as my
team hears the zamboni leave the ice, and everyone puts on his
helmet and gloves. On the command of the coach everyone hurries out
of the room. Skates clatter as the team walks down the hallway
towards the ice, and in the distance I hear the crowd shout louder as
they sight the first of my teammates.

I skate round my zone briefly, feeling my blades cut over the ice
as I warm myself up before the game begins. The referee sounds his
whistle and all but the teams' starting two lines head to their
designated bench "home" or "visitors." In this case it was the "home"
bench I headed for, and took my position in the line up amongst my
~~teammates the~~<u>teammates. The</u> puck is dropped and fans cheer as the
teams battle for possession of the puck with hopes of achieving the
first goal. My turn on the ice comes closer as my teammates become
tired and need to be changed. I watch and listen to the coach and hear
all the noises of hockey as I wait for my moment.

My time has come as one of my teammates skates off the ice<u>,
tired, and calling to be changed</u>. I accelerate out of the box and stride
into the play. I <u>hear my skates carving, the fans shouting, the
crashing of the boards, the shooting and passing of the puck, and the</u>

talking on the ice as I skate. As my shift continues, my breathing becomes stronger, and as I work harder a thin vapour appears in my line of vision on my hockey visor. I get a chance to change and head to the bench for a brief rest before I am back out crashing and banging again.
~~again.~~

My team prevails in the end, and we head out of the bench and towards the goal crease to congratulate our goalie for a job well done, before we all head back into the dressing room. Excited from our victory, I sit down in the same stall I began in and take my ~~sweat drenched~~sweat drenched equipment off.

In the dressing room, my teammates and I talk to each other about the good and bad points of the game and laugh with each other once again. Steam then fills the air again as myself and my teammates shower and redress before we all head home to conclude another day at the rink.

 # COLLABORATIVE WORK

PRACTISE OUTLINING

Spend time as a class thinking, planning, developing, and organizing a potential recalling essay.

1. Spend about 10 minutes sharing a few memories.
2. Once three or four have been suggested, choose one or two for the subject of a potential essay. What makes one idea better than another idea?
3. Decide on the audience and the purpose.
4. Brainstorm this memory's possible significance to the audience. Have someone write ideas on the overhead or blackboard.
5. Develop the ideas to give a sense of what a person could write if he/she were to write this essay.
6. Organize the ideas so they appear in the best order for the best effect.

Could you write this essay? How long would it take you to finish this essay?

WRITING YOUR OWN RECALLING ESSAY

So far you have seen an essay from a professional writer and from a fellow student. You have also worked as a class to build most of an essay. As you've spent time in this chapter you've followed the writing process of another student from first to final draft, and you absorbed ideas and ways of explaining those ideas in words. All of these activities have prepared you to write your own essay focusing on one of your own meaningful memories.

What Have You Discovered?

Before you begin your own writing, let's review what you have learned in this chapter so far:

> Don't pressure yourself to choose a spectacular event for your essay topic. Ordinary events can be as powerful as dramatic ones. Craig's essay demonstrates the power of an ordinary memory.

> Learn as much as possible about your readers. You'll find it's easier to write if you know who you're speaking to.

> Include enough detail to help your memory come to life for your readers. Craig's essay develops several key details for his readers.

> Organize (reorganize) your ideas to be sure they are in the most effective order.

> Select techniques to help you overcome obstacles in the writing process. There is no "correct" way to write. If a writing technique helps you keep writing, then it's a good one.

Your Writing Topic

Choose one of the following topics for your recalling essay:

1. Reflect on your own childhood and recall an incident or event that made you feel happy, sad, angry, joyful, powerful, weak, afraid, or proud. It doesn't have to be a major memory. It can be an ordinary one: walking with a grandparent, losing a favourite possession, fighting with a best friend, or being 11 years old. Write an essay to explain this memory to someone who was not with you.

2. Your old high school's newsletter editor has asked you to submit an essay recalling a job or volunteer experience that you enjoyed. The editor wants to show current high school students some options for volunteer and paid work.

3. The members of your English class are putting together a collection of essays paying tribute to people who encouraged them to go to college. Who gave you the

courage and determination to pursue your education–a teacher, a relative, a supervisor at work? Was there a memorable event or conversation that helped you decide to continue your schooling? Record that memory and why it was important to you.

4. Create your own topic and consult your instructor about it.

When you select one of these topics, you begin to work through your own writing process. As you write, keep track of what you do to finish a final draft that you're proud to hand in.

Reflect On Your Writing Process

Once you hand in your essay, take some time and reflect on what you did to complete it. You'll want to become familiar with what you need and like to do to write well. In a single page, write a short version of what you did to write your essay. Include how and where you got your ideas, right up to the finished essay you handed in.

Once you've documented your writing process, would you like to change anything about it for your next essay? Write a short paragraph explaining parts of the writing process that you'd like to change.

Recognizing Paragraphs

Checklist For Recognizing Paragraphs

✓ Will your reader recognize when your paragraphs start and end?
✓ Does each body paragraph have a controlling idea or topic sentence?
✓ Is each sentence in a body paragraph related to the paragraph's topic sentence?
✓ Are there enough details in each paragraph to support the controlling idea and make it interesting?

Imagine yourself chatting with someone about the good and bad sides of income tax. In the middle of the conversation, you remember that you wanted to invite this person to a gathering. How do you change topics in your conversation?

Most often, you will finish the income tax topic and then pause. After the pause, you could ask your friend to attend the gathering. The pause you'd use is longer than the pause used for a period. The pause simply tells the listener that you're going to change topics. The paragraph mark asks the reader to pause long enough to tell the listener to expect a change of topic.

It might help to think of the paragraph as a kind of punctuation like a period. When you end one paragraph, the pause before you start the next one is roughly the same length as three period-length pauses. To try out the paragraph pause, try reading the following two sentences out loud with a normal period pause in between. Then read the same two sentences, but at the end of the first sentence put a paragraph-sized pause.

I'm afraid of the dark. I need to see a doctor.

They sound different, don't they? More importantly, they mean different things. What's the difference in meaning between the two?

To become an effective writer and reader, you need to recognize when topics start and end, and how they are typically organized in essays.

Basic Features Of The Paragraph

A paragraph is one topic or aspect of a topic with one main idea supported with descriptive, explanatory, or factual details. Well-developed paragraphs have distinguishing features that make them easy to recognize.

Just as a capital letter signals a complete sentence to a reader, an indentation from the margin (or extra space between blocks of text, or other markers) indicates the beginning of a paragraph. This indentation signals a change in topic: the new paragraph will develop another idea related to the essay's subject. We as readers expect this idea to be developed in a series of related sentences.

Types Of Paragraphs: Introductory, Body, And Concluding Paragraphs

Most essays contain three different types of paragraphs: introductory, body, and concluding. The first paragraph is often the introduction of an essay; the last paragraph is usually its conclusion; and the paragraphs that fall between the introduction and the conclusion are called body paragraphs. A short essay usually consists of one introductory paragraph, several body paragraphs, and one concluding paragraph. In the rest of this chapter, we will focus on body paragraphs.

Do Your Body Paragraphs Have Topic Sentences?

You probably won't want to write with the parts of the paragraph in mind. You'll want to use this information to help you revise your paragraphs to make sure they're communicating clearly to your readers. Try to implement the following suggestions about paragraphs AFTER you've written a draft of your essay.

Body paragraphs fall between the first paragraph (the introduction) and the last paragraph (the conclusion). One characteristic of a successful body paragraph is that it has a main or controlling idea, a specific idea it states and supports in the essay. The controlling idea of a body paragraph is usually stated in a topic sentence. In Sandra Cisneros's essay, "Eleven," the topic sentence is the first sentence of the paragraph:

> <u>That's when everything I've been holding in since this morning, since when Mrs. Price put the sweater on my desk, finally lets go, and all of a sudden I'm crying in front of everybody.</u> I wish I was invisible but I'm not. I'm eleven and it's my birthday today and I'm crying like I'm three in front of everybody. I put my head down on the desk and bury my face in my stupid clown-sweater arms. My face all hot and spit coming out of my mouth because I can't stop the little animal noises from coming out of me, until there aren't any more tears left in my eyes, and it's just my body shaking like when you have the hiccups, and my whole head hurts like when you drink milk too fast.

Does Your Topic Sentence Summarize The Rest Of The Sentences In The Paragraph?

A topic sentence expresses all that the entire paragraph says in one sentence. Look at the underlined sentence in the paragraph above: it summarizes the entire paragraph. It clearly says what the whole paragraph is about.

Is Your Topic Sentence The First Sentence In The Paragraph?

Usually the topic sentence is the first sentence of a paragraph, but writers sometimes vary the placement of their topic sentences in the paragraph or let the supporting sentences in the paragraph suggest the main idea. Generally your writing will be its clearest if you make the topic sentence the first sentence in each paragraph. That way your readers will understand what the paragraph is about before they read the rest of the paragraph.

Cisneros's paragraph is made up of five sentences. The first sentence, the topic sentence, announces the controlling idea: she's crying in front of everyone. The sentences that follow explain this idea with more details about crying in front of everyone: the narrator's embarrassment about crying and what her body does when she cries.

Craig's essay is about what it's like to prepare for and play a hockey game. He introduces and explains different aspects of the hockey game. Each time he wants to talk about one part of his game, he must introduce the idea, and then support it with detail. Paragraph four is about the last minutes before the team moves out to the ice. As Craig read it over, he realized that none of the sentences really summarized the whole paragraph. In other words, he noticed that this paragraph didn't have a topic sentence.

> The game is now only ten minutes away, and my team and I are ready and waiting with our skates laced up and our jerseys on. The coach then enters the room and gives the team one final pep talk and an overview of the game plan. Emotions soar as my team hears the zamboni leave the ice, and everyone puts on his helmet and gloves. On the command of the coach everyone hurries out of the room. Skates clatter as the team walks down the hallway towards the ice, and in the distance I hear the crowd shout louder as they sight the first of my teammates.

As he looked over the paragraph, he tried to come up with a sentence to summarize all the detail in the paragraph. He tried a few sentences and came up with this one:

> It's almost time to leave the dressing room and hit the ice for the warm-up skate.

Craig wanted his writing to be clear, so he made his new topic sentence the very first sentence in this paragraph:

> It's almost time to leave the dressing room and hit the ice for the warm-up skate. The game is now only ten minutes away, and my team and I are ready and waiting with our skates laced up and our jerseys on. The coach then enters the room and gives the team one final pep talk and an overview of the game plan. Emotions soar as my team hears the zamboni leave the ice, and everyone puts on his helmet and gloves. On the command of the coach everyone hurries out of the room. Skates clatter as the team walks down the hallway towards the ice, and in the distance I hear the crowd shout louder as they sight the first of my teammates.

As he looked it over, he noticed that it was easier to read. Then he proceeded to work through the rest of his paragraphs.

Exercise P2-1

Underline every topic sentence in Craig's revised essay (p. 22). Then, review Craig's first draft and look for paragraphs without topic sentences. Are the paragraphs with topic sentences easier to read? Where are topic sentences usually placed in Craig's essay?

Exercise P2-2

State the controlling idea in paragraphs 9, 10, and 11 of Sandra Cisneros's essay (p. 13).

pporting Sentences

Topic sentences, though they summarize the entire paragraph, are usually not enough to make the point effectively. That's why the rest of the sentences in the paragraph are important. They add detail, and help you explain or prove your point. You may need a long paragraph to make your point clear and strong. You may need a short one. It depends on how much information your readers need or want.

The best paragraphs use supporting sentences to provide relevant, specific details that describe or explain the controlling idea. In the previous section, we saw how the details in paragraph 19 of Sandra Cisneros's essay describe her crying in front of everyone, the paragraph's controlling idea (see p. 15).

Do You Have The Right Number Of Sentences In Your Paragraph?

If you want your ideas to be effective, you need to consider if you've included enough detail to explain your idea. Craig looked at paragraph six in his first draft and decided he needed more detail to make his point clear. He wanted to give his readers a sense of the game:

> My time has come as one of my teammates skates off the ice. I accelerate out of the box and stride into the play. I play for a while. Then when I'm tired, I get a chance to change and head to the bench for a brief rest before I am back out crashing and banging again. My team prevails in the end, and we head out of the bench and towards the goal crease to congratulate our goalie for a job well done, before we all head back into the dressing room. Excited from our victory, I sit down in the same stall I began in and take my sweat-drenched equipment off.

Since this essay is about a hockey game, Craig realized that he could include a few more details to help the reader imagine the game.

> My time has come as one of my teammates skates off the ice. I accelerate out of the box and stride into the play. I play for a while. Then when I'm tired, I get a chance to change and head to the bench for a brief rest be-

fore I am back out crashing and banging again. My team prevails in the end, and we head out of the bench and towards the goal crease to congratulate our goalie for a job well done, before we all head back into the dressing room. Excited from our victory, I sit down in the same stall I began in and take my sweat-drenched equipment off. <u>I hear my skates carving, the fans shouting, the crashing of the boards, the shooting and passing of the puck, and the talking on the ice as I skate. As my shift continues, my breathing becomes stronger, and as I work harder a thin vapour appears in my line of vision on my hockey visor. I realize my helmet's visor is loose in one spot. It's bugging me.</u>

Craig was fairly happy with the extra detail he added. But he knew the paragraph needed more work so he asked another question about this paragraph.

Are Your Supporting Sentences All On The Same Topic?

When Craig checked his paragraphs for topic sentences, he also checked each paragraph for supporting sentences. He examined one paragraph and couldn't see if he had one paragraph or two:

My time has come as one of my teammates skates off the ice. I accelerate out of the box and stride into the play. I play for a while. Then when I'm tired, I get a chance to change and head to the bench for a brief rest before I am back out crashing and banging again. My team prevails in the end, and we head out of the bench and towards the goal crease to congratulate our goalie for a job well done, before we all head back into the dressing room. Excited from our victory, I sit down in the same stall I began in and take my sweat-drenched equipment off. I hear my skates carving, the fans shouting, the crashing of the boards, the shooting and passing of the puck, and the talking on the ice as I skate. As my shift continues, my breathing becomes stronger, and as I work harder a thin vapour appears in my line of vision on my hockey visor. I realize my helmet's visor is loose in one spot. It's bugging me.

As he looked at the paragraph, he noticed that he was really talking about the game as it's being played and the end of the game. These are two different ideas, so he separated both ideas and made them into two separate paragraphs:

My time has come as one of my teammates skates off the ice. I accelerate out of the box and stride into the play. I play for a while. Then when I'm tired, I get a chance to change and head to the bench for a brief rest before I am back out crashing and banging again. I hear my skates carving, the fans shouting, the crashing of the boards, the shooting and passing of the puck, and the talking on the ice as I skate. As my shift continues, my breathing becomes stronger, and as I work harder a thin vapour appears in my line of vision on my hockey visor. I realize my helmet's visor is loose in one spot. It's bugging me.

My team prevails in the end, and we head out of the bench and towards the goal crease to congratulate our goalie for a job well done, before we all head back into the dressing room. Excited from our victory, I sit down in the same stall I began in and take my sweat-drenched equipment off.

This revision gives the essay a much more effective conclusion.

e There Any Irrelevant Sentences?

Craig also checked his paragraphs for irrelevant sentences. Irrelevant sentences are those that do not help to explain the controlling idea of a paragraph: they're off topic. Craig found that the paragraph didn't have a clear topic sentence and the rest of the paragraph contained a couple of off-topic sentences that did not add to the paragraph's main idea (they're underlined).

My time has come as one of my teammates skates off the ice. I accelerate out of the box and stride into the play. I play for a while. Then when I'm tired, I get a chance to change and head to the bench for a brief rest before I am back out crashing and banging again. I hear my skates carving, the fans shouting, the crashing of the boards, the shooting and passing of the puck, and the talking on the ice as I skate. As my shift continues, my breathing becomes stronger, and as I work harder a thin vapour appears in my line of vision on my hockey visor. <u>I realize my helmet's visor is loose in one spot. It's bugging me.</u>

Craig deleted the irrelevant sentences and wrote a topic sentence (it's underlined):

<u>The game slowly moves into a steady rhythm.</u> My time has come as one of my teammates skates off the ice. I accelerate out of the box and stride into the play. I play for a while. Then when I'm tired, I get a chance to change and head to the bench for a brief rest before I am back out crashing and banging again. I hear my skates carving, the fans shouting, the crashing of the boards, the shooting and passing of the puck, and the talking on the ice as I skate. As my shift continues, my breathing becomes stronger, and as I work harder a thin vapour appears in my line of vision on my hockey visor.

Now Craig's paragraph has a topic sentence that clearly states the paragraph's main idea: the rhythm of the hockey game. And the rest of the sentences in the paragraph develop that idea.

Are Your Sentences In The Right Order?

All the sentences are on topic. The paragraph has enough detail. However, it still doesn't read very well. The sentences could be in a more effective order. The topic sentence is in the right place: at the beginning of the paragraph. The rest of the sentences need to be rearranged:

> <u>The game slowly moves into a steady rhythm.</u> My time has come as one of my teammates skates off the ice. I accelerate out of the box and stride into the play. I play for a while. Then when I'm tired, I get a chance to change and head to the bench for a brief rest before I am back out crashing and banging again. I hear my skates carving, the fans shouting, the crashing of the boards, the shooting and passing of the puck, and the talking on the ice as I skate. As my shift continues, my breathing becomes stronger, and as I work harder a thin vapour appears in my line of vision on my hockey visor.

Craig pulled the sentences apart and experimented with their order. After tinkering for a while, he came up with this order:

> The game slowly moves into a steady rhythm. My time to play has come as one of my teammates skates off the ice. I accelerate out of the box and stride into the play. I hear my skates carving, the fans shouting, the crashing of the boards, the shooting and passing of the puck, and the talking on the ice as I skate. As my shift continues, my breathing becomes stronger, and as I work harder a thin vapour appears in my line of vision on my hockey visor. I play for a while. Then when I'm tired, I get a chance to change and head to the bench for a brief rest before I am back out crashing and banging again.

Do Any Sentences Repeat Information?

As he rearranged the sentences, Craig noticed that one sentence repeated something he had already said (it's underlined below). The detail he added tells the reader he's playing hockey, so he decided to delete it:

> The game slowly moves into a steady rhythm. My time to play has come as one of my teammates skates off the ice. I accelerate out of the box and stride into the play. I hear my skates carving, the fans shouting, the crashing of the boards, the shooting and passing of the puck, and the talking on the ice as I skate. As my shift continues, my breathing becomes stronger, and as I work harder a thin vapour appears in my line of vision on my hockey visor. <u>I play for a while.</u> Then when I'm tired, I get a

chance to change and head to the bench for a brief rest before I am back out crashing and banging again.

His final paragraph looks like this:

The game slowly moves into a steady rhythm. My time to play has come as one of my teammates skates off the ice. I accelerate out of the box and stride into the play. I hear my skates carving, the fans shouting, the crashing of the boards, the shooting and passing of the puck, and the talking on the ice as I skate. As my shift continues, my breathing becomes stronger, and as I work harder a thin vapour appears in my line of vision on my hockey visor. Then when I'm tired, I get a chance to change and head to the bench for a brief rest before I am back out crashing and banging again.

Happy with this paragraph, Craig worked through the rest of the paragraphs in his essay.

Exercise P2-3

List any questions that paragraph two of Craig's first draft (p. 19) leaves in your mind.

Exercise P2-4

Read the paragraph below and eliminate the sentences that are not relevant to the controlling idea of the paragraph.

Any student's first day at a new school can be both tough and exciting. The buildings are unfamiliar, and it is easy to lose your way and be late. My cousin Amy got lost in a strange mall one time and got locked in. Planning a trip to a new school before the first day of classes can eliminate the lost feeling. Not knowing anyone can be intimidating, but the prospect of new friends and activities can be attractive. My cousin Seth is a member of a lot of clubs at his school. Joining clubs and volunteering is a good way to make friends. Trying out for school sports is another way. I really don't like baseball and track, but I like volleyball. If you extend yourself, others will help you.

Exercise P2-5

The following paragraph lacks specific supporting details. Supply supporting details from your own experience.

Many people today choose to go to college. They think that college will help them get what they want. I chose to go to college for many reasons, not just money.

COLLABORATIVE WORK

After writing a draft of your own recalling essay, exchange papers with a classmate, and do the following tasks:

A. Underline the controlling idea for each body paragraph. If the controlling idea is implied, note in the margin what you think it is. Mark with a paragraph symbol (¶) any places where you think paragraphs should be divided so that each new paragraph focuses on only one controlling idea.

B. Put a check mark next to any paragraphs that need more supporting sentences; cross out any irrelevant sentences; and circle any sentences that should be in another paragraph.

C. Jot down any questions you have that a paragraph does not answer.

Then return the paper to its writer and use the information in this section to revise your draft.

Recognizing And Developing Sentences

Checklist For Recognizing And Developing Sentences

✓ Does every sentence end with a period?
✓ Does every sentence begin with a capital letter?
✓ Does each sentence contain a subject and a predicate?

Writing an essay is a little like assembling a building. You think about what you want to do before you pick up the hammer, and you start with the smallest bits of construction material. You nail the pieces together carefully knowing that they will stick together. You want to build something that's not going to fall apart and will suit your purpose. You might be able to build a little shack with four bare walls to house your dog, but you wouldn't want to live in it yourself. You'd probably prefer something with more to it, something with heat, water, and electricity.

Instead of lumber and nails, essays work with basic building blocks: the sentence. Not only do your sentences need to be grammatically complete, they need to develop your ideas, to make your meaning strong and clear. You'll certainly want your essay to hold together. The strength of every sentence depends on how you treat the most important parts of the sentence: the subject and the verb. How you build and arrange your sentences depends on who you're writing for and what you want to do.

In the next sections you will learn to recognize a sentence, a subject, a predicate, and a verb. And, you'll learn when to use a period.

Recognizing Sentences

If the basic building block of our essays is the sentence, then it makes a good deal of sense to find out what a sentence is and get some idea of how to recognize one. It sounds easy, but it might be more difficult than you first think.

Complete sentences always contain two elements: a subject and a predicate. The subject tells you what the sentence is about, and the predicate makes a comment about the subject.

Subject	Predicate
I	Head to the arena prepared and ready for battle.

In this example you can see that the sentence's topic is "I" and that the predicate gives us a comment on the subject telling us that it "head(s) to the arena prepared and ready for battle."

To make the sentence clear to our readers we give them some clues that what we have just written is a sentence. To show our readers that we are beginning a sentence we capitalize the first letter of the first word in the sentence. To show our readers that we are ending a sentence we put a period, a question mark, or an exclamation mark at the end.

I head to the arena prepared to do battle.

We will confuse our readers if we don't have a complete sentence, but we begin it with a capital and end it with a period.

Head to the arena prepared to do battle.

This example looks like a sentence, but it isn't. If we look for a subject and a predicate, we discover that the subject is missing.

And, we can confuse our readers if we don't show them where sentences start and end.

I head to the arena prepared to do battle nervous excitement runs

through my body.

If you look at the sentence carefully you'll discover that there is a subject and a predicate followed by another subject and predicate. There are, in fact, two sentences, but these two sentences only have one capital letter and one period. Because of these signals, the reader will try to treat these two sentences as one sentence, and it will confuse him or her. You never want to confuse your reader.

How To Find A Subject

A subject names the topic of the sentence. It has to be a person, place, or thing–the name of something. To find the subject, ask yourself this question: what or who is this sentence about? Here's a sentence. Let's see if we can find the subject.

I head to the arena prepared to do battle.

Let us ask the subject question: what or who is this sentence about? You might be tempted to say "the arena." But the subject usually comes at the beginning of the sentence. What is at the beginning of this sentence? The word "I" is first. "I," then, is the subject of the sentence. This sentence is about "I." Let's try this with another sentence:

Nervous excitement runs through my body.

What or who is this sentence about? "Nervous excitement" comes first in the sentence, and it is the subject of the sentence. Try these sentences:

The arena is now within my sights.

All the strategies and plays I have learned throughout the many

previous practices flash through my mind.

Who or what is each sentence about? In the first sentence, the words "the arena" are the subject. In the second sentence the subject is "All the strategies and plays I have learned throughout the many previous practices."

Finding a subject is usually simple, but there are a few sticky parts. There are four kinds of subjects a sentence can have. A subject can name a person, place, or thing; a group of persons, places, or things; a feature of a person place or thing; the name of an idea; or, it can name an activity. Here are some examples of each kind of subject.

Sentences can name a person, place, or thing.

Person

John likes to feed his hamster.

Place

Canada is a country with multiple personalities.

Thing

Super glue won't solve every problem.

A Group of People Places or Things

People

The audience moshed as the band played.

Places

Tropical countries are great places to live.

Things

That flock of sheep is the wrong colour.

Televisions are difficult to fix.

A Feature of a Person, Place, or Thing

John's ugliness is something of a wonder.

Susan's anger flares up when she drives.

An Idea

Communism never understood love.

Frank's view of a good time frightens me.

An Activity

Writing isn't easy.

Jogging makes me tired.

Sentences can replace subjects with words designed to act like subjects and nouns (for more information on nouns, see p. 67). These words are called pronouns. In some sentences you encounter, you may find a pronoun acting as the subject of the sentence. Here are some examples.

Instead of this sentence:
Steve and Ruth think that is stupid.

We can write this sentence:
They think that is stupid.

"They" is a pronoun and it replaces "Steve and Ruth" from the previous sentence. That's what pronouns do.

These are some of the most common pronouns:

I, my, mine, me, we, our, ours, us, you, your, yours, he, his, him, they, their, theirs, them, she, her, hers, it, its.

Tricky Subjects

Most sentences will be easy to figure out, but some are more difficult. Sometimes subjects may be taken out of the sentence, or words that seem like a subject might not actually be the subject.

Sometimes the sentence has a subject but the subject isn't written down—it's implied or understood by the reader. If you were to ask what or who these sentences are about, you couldn't answer the question easily.

Recycle!

Pay attention!

These sentences do have a subject—the subject is "you." They're commands and the reader understands the subject automatically. We could rewrite these sentences to include the subject:

You recycle!

You pay attention!

Sometimes, sentences are addressed to a specific person, place, or thing. Whoever or whatever the sentence is addressed to is not the subject of the sentence.

Person

John, *the car* has been blown to bits.

Place

Oh Canada, *we* stand on guard for thee.

Thing

Computer, *I* need some information.

In the first sentence, "John" is not the subject; "the car" is. In the second example, "Canada" is not the subject of the sentence; "we" is. In the third sentence, "Computer" is not the subject of the sentence; "I" is.

Keep an eye out for sentences that have more than one subject. A sentence can have two or more parts to the subject. Look at these examples:

Susan and Patsy moved to Sudbury yesterday.

Canada and the U.S. signed the accord.

Hard bread and molasses make a good combination.

There is one last tricky thing you need to understand. The subject most often appears at the beginning of a sentence. But, there are times when it can be moved to other places within a sentence. Here's an example:

To the arena prepared to do battle, I head.

In this case the end of the sentence has been moved to the front. The subject is still "I," but it has moved in the sentence. Even though the subject is now in a different position within the sentence, the question will still work.

Who or what is the sentence about? Is it about "to the arena prepared to do battle"? That doesn't make too much sense. Is it about "head"? That doesn't make much sense either. The sentence, then, is still about "I." If you encounter a sentence that doesn't begin with the subject, you can usually take the information at the beginning of the sentence and move it to the end of the sentence like this:

To the arena prepared to do battle, I head.

I head to the arena prepared to do battle.

When you move the extra information to the end of the sentence, it's much easier to see what the subject is.

How To Find A Predicate

Every complete sentence has a predicate to explain what the subject is or does. The predicate often sounds like a comment about the subject. It finishes the thought the subject introduces.

One way to find the predicate is to find the subject first. If you find the subject of the sentence the rest of the words form the predicate. Here are some samples from Craig's first draft:

I head to the arena prepared to do battle.

Nervous excitement runs through my body.

The arena is now within my sight.

All the strategies and plays I have learned throughout the many

previous practices flash through my mind.

"I" is the subject of the first sentence, so the words "head to the arena prepared to do battle" must be the predicate. "Nervous excitement" is the subject of the second sentence, so "runs through my body" is the predicate. "The arena" is the subject of the third sentence, so "is now within my sight" is the predicate. The fourth sentence is a little more difficult: "All the strategies and plays I have learned throughout the many previous practices" is the subject.

Whatever is not the subject is the predicate. The predicate will become more important as we look at verbs in Chapter 4's Focus on Sentences (p. 102).

Understanding Sentence Fragments

If a group of words is missing a subject or a predicate, we call it a sentence fragment. The word "fragment" describes sentences that aren't complete—they're pieces of a whole sentence. Most of the time, sentence fragments are easy to detect. The easiest way to figure out if you have a sentence fragment is to read the sentence out loud. You can hear that it's missing something. Then, when you examine the sentence in detail, you will notice that the subject or the predicate is missing. Read the following sentences out loud and try to call each sentence either complete or a fragment:

1. Exercising daily helps improve general health.
2. Apples for my love.
3. Jane Urquhart, a woman who won a Governor General's Award.
4. March!
5. Love is a lovely word.

If you think you've found a sentence fragment, look for a subject and a predicate. Mark the sentence if you can't find one or the other: it's a fragment.

Exercise S2-1

Underline the predicates in the following paragraph.

The purpose of college is to educate students. The best education combines classroom instruction with a social exchange. The educational process occurs in classrooms and social situations throughout the college years. Asking students to memorize information and spit it out again is not education. Education means learning how to learn. To this purpose, we are called.

Exercise S2-2

On a separate sheet of paper write four sentence fragments and four complete sentences. Rewrite the sentences and mix them up. Trade papers with someone else. Identify the four sentence fragments on their sheet of paper. Rewrite those sentences to make them complete. Rewrite the complete sentences and make them into sentence fragments.

Exercise S2-3

Draw one line under the subject and two lines under the predicate for every sentence in paragraph one of Craig's first draft (p. 19). If you find any sentences with more than one subject or predicate, make note of them. We'll return to this kind of sentence in the next chapter (p. 45).

Exercise S2-4

Draw one line under the subject and two lines under the predicates in paragraph one of Sandra Cisneros's essay (p. 13).

Understanding The Period

Punctuation marks are the road signs of writing. Punctuation tells the reader when to slow down, when to turn, and when to stop. Punctuation helps the reader move through your words the way you want them to so they can arrive at the destination your writing wants to take them to: your main point. Without punctuation, your readers are less likely to understand what you say because they don't know how you want them to read things. Your reader will have a difficult time figuring out what you are saying. Read the following lines out loud:

What does Joe do he is a garbage collector his job is full time and he walks to work he lives near the dump there he goes now

How easy are these lines to read? You probably read the lines several times because you didn't know where the sentences started and stopped. Try these sentences:

What does Joe do? He is a garbage collector. His job is full time, and he walks to work. He lives near the dump. There he goes now!

This collection of sentences is much easier to read: you know when to start and stop as you read. The punctuation helps you understand what is being said.

What A Period Does And How To Read It

There are three punctuation marks you can use to end a sentence: the period (.), the question mark (?), and the exclamation mark (!). The period is the most frequently used punctuation mark. A period is like a stop sign. It asks the reader to pause–to stop reading for a moment. The pause, when a person is speaking out loud, tells the listener that one thought has ended and another one is going to begin. When you see a period it means that what is before the period is one complete sentence on one topic. One of the best ways to get a sense of how a period works is to read out loud.

When To Use A Period

Put a period after each complete sentence. What is a complete sentence? The smallest complete sentence must have a subject and a predicate. You can add extra subjects and predicates to a sentence or expand the subject and predicate, but every sentence must have at least one of each. We can also call this subject and predicate a sentence or an independent clause.

You probably already have a sense of how to use a period. If you were to speak a sentence out loud, you'd have a sense of when a period is necessary.

Reading Aloud

Find a partner and read the following paragraph out loud to each other. Begin by putting a long pause between sentences. Shorten your pauses until it sounds right.

It's difficult to say what made Biju choose that kind of life. His enthusiasm for climbing mountains in the middle of winter probably helped. But, his biggest influence was his father. His father always enjoyed climbing in dangerous conditions. His father's love of adventure seems to have rubbed off on Biju. So, I'd have to say that Biju became what he is because of his father.

Exercise S2-5

Have another person read the first two paragraphs of your essay out loud to you. Do your sentences sound right? Is it easy to read and understand each sentence?

Exercise S2-6

The following paragraph has no punctuation. Read it out loud and try to put punctuation where it belongs:

my time has come as one of my teammates skates off the ice tired and calling to be changed I accelerate out of the box and stride into the play I hear my skates carving the fans shouting the crashing of the boards the shooting and passing of the puck and the talking on the ice as I skate as my shift continues my breathing becomes stronger and as I work harder a thin vapour appears in my line of vision on my hockey visor I get a chance to change and head to the bench for a brief rest before I am back out crashing and banging again

Observing
The Writing Process

Writing well is very much like building a good stone wall. If
you think of words and thoughts as stones for the essay/wall,
you can see my meaning. First there is the gathering and
selection of rocks. Some, no matter how beautiful they appear
on their own, just will not hold up under the weight and have
to be discarded in favour of the larger structure. . .

—JANICE MACDONALD

LEARNING OUTCOMES

This chapter will help you:
- Understand and write about what you observe;
- Identify and use nouns, pronouns, and modifiers; and,
- Compose focused and specific topic sentences.

How aware are you of what is happening around you right now? Your answer depends on how careful an observer you are. Your ability to observe is not limited to what you can see, however. **Observing** means receiving impressions on many levels and involves all the senses: seeing, hearing, touching, smelling, and even tasting. Your senses help you gather the material you will need—facts, details, descriptions, and impressions—to write a clear, accurate, and convincing account of an event or person in your environment.

When you write an observation, however, simply recording literally what you see isn't enough. You must use your writing skills to help your readers see your observation *through your eyes*. You should give your readers enough information to let them share the impact of your experience—how it changed you or perhaps how it helped you discover something about yourself, about other people, about society, or even about the world.

Of course, writers cannot possibly write down everything they observe about a person, place, incident, or object. The result would be an endless, confusing (and boring) list of everything the writers saw, heard, tasted, smelled, or touched. Therefore, writers must decide on a **dominant impression**, the feeling or mood that they wish to create. In his published workbook, Canadian novelist Timothy Findley writes his observation of what it is like to walk through the deep mud on his property in Cannington, Ontario:

> There was a good deal of puddling there and everywhere the cattle have walked, they have churned up the earth, creating a kind of stew made of stones and clods of weed and mud. In the lane, I had already lost a boot and fallen on my knees so that now my trousers were soaked and one of my socks was sodden and the bottoms of both my sleeves were freezing against my wrists.

If Findley had simply told us, his readers, that he walked down the lane and it was muddy, his observations would mean little to us. Instead, he provides us with specific detail that allows us to virtually experience the scene. Notice some of the words that he chooses to use: *puddling, stew,* and *sodden.* These words are unusual, but they help to create the precise image and feeling that Findley wishes. As a result of his word choice and selection of detail, we can imagine what it would be like to be in this mud. Perhaps we are also reminded of our own experiences of muddiness.

Findley later uses these observations to help him picture what it must have been like for the soldiers in the Flanders campaign of the First World War, where his own grandfather fought and so many Canadian soldiers died. He reworks this information when he writes his novel *The Wars.* He begins a scene by exploring the word *mud* in relation to what it must have been like on the battlegrounds:

> The mud. There are no good similies. Mud must be a Flemish word. Mud was invented here. Mudland might have been its name. The ground is the colour of steel. Over most of the plain there isn't a trace of topsoil: only sand and clay.

Findley says that there is no simile, no comparison to help describe the mud, yet he goes on to explain the soldiers as they might experience the mud:

> . . . the water rises at you out of the ground. It rises from your footprints–and an army marching over a field can cause a flood. In 1916, it was said that you "waded to the front." Men and horses sank from sight. They drowned in the mud. Their graves, it seemed, just dug themselves and pulled them down.

Findley creates the dominant impression of being sucked in by the mud. The reader is able to feel this experience even before he tells us that it "pulled them down." Findley does not include every detail, but carefully selects those most important in providing an experience for the reader.

In Chapter Two of *Mosaics,* we talked about including the significance, the reason why we are telling the story. Findley ends the mud scene with the following sentences: "Now it was a shallow sea of stinking grey from end to end. And this is where you fought the war." The final comment provides the significance for the description, the author's comment on why so many lives were lost in this part of the war.

As a writer observing, you must draw on both objective and subjective details. *Objective details* are factual descriptions such as "colour of steel," and "it rises from your footprints." *Subjective details* enable the reader to feel the mood or conditions that existed, such as graves that "just dug themselves," and "shallow sea of stinking grey." By concentrating on the essential objective and subjective details, the writer can create a dominant impression that enables the reader to see through the writer's eyes.

LEARNING FROM PUBLISHED WRITERS

In the following essay, Collette Russell's detailed and accurate descriptions enable readers to "observe" for themselves the actions and events. Russell uses her own experiences as a homeless person to observe and describe the daily activities, joys, frustrations, and humiliations that the homeless endure both in shelters and on the streets. Notice how Russell is able to create a dominant impression by limiting her observations to one location and one day. Less than two years after Russell wrote this essay, she returned to the streets. Nine months later, she died alone in a motel room.

Before You Read

Focus Your Attention

Before you read this observation essay, take a few moments to respond to the following questions in your notebook:

1. If you were a homeless person forced to carry everything you own with you, what of your possessions would you keep? Make a list.
2. In the essay you are about to read, the writer describes in precise detail her daily routine. If you were homeless, where would you go and what would you do in order to satisfy your need for food, shelter, and comfort?

Expand Your Vocabulary

Find each of the listed words in the following essay. After reading the words in context (what they appear to mean in the sentence), write down a definition for each.

Ablaze (paragraph 1)

Invariably (paragraph 2)

Garment (paragraph 7)

Assembled (paragraph 12)

Severance pay (paragraph 18)

Collette Russell

A Day in the Homeless Life*

"Good morning ladies. It's 5 a.m. Time to get up." Ceiling lights were suddenly ablaze. This message boomed repeatedly until nearly everyone was out of bed.   **1**

Two toilets and three sinks for 50 women; no toilet paper in the morning, invariably. Three tables with benches bordered by beds on two sides were our day room, dining room and lounge.   **2**

Breakfast usually arrived at 5:45 a.m., too late for those who were in the day-labor van pools. They went to work on empty stomachs, and they were the ones needing food the most.   **3**

Breakfast generally consisted of rolls and sausages and juice until it ran out. The coffee was unique: It didn't taste like coffee but that's what we had to drink.   **4**

At 6:30 a.m. we were ordered to go down to the lobby, where we joined 50 other women either standing or sitting on wooden benches awaiting the light of day. Some talked to themselves. Some shouted angrily. Some sat motionless. Some slept sitting up. Some jumped up and down, walking away and then returning. Some chain-smoked.   **5**

All of us had our belongings with us. Carrying everything every step of the way every day was hard on the arms, and I felt that it was a dead giveaway that I was homeless.   **6**

At 7:30 a.m. the clothing room opened. It was shocking to be told "Throw away what you're wearing after you get a new outfit." No laundry, just toss out yesterday's garments. We were allotted five minutes to paw through racks looking for articles that fit.   **7**

I was always happy to see 8:30 a.m. roll around. Grabbing my bags, I headed down Berkeley Street away from the jam-packed, smoke-filled "holding cell." Always I felt guilty about not going to work like everyone else who hurried by as I approached the business district.   **8**

The main library was my daily stop. I positioned myself at a table where I could watch the clock: We had to return to the shelter before 4 p.m. to get in line for a bed, otherwise we might miss out.   **9**

Reading was the high point of the day. Escape into a book. There was relative privacy at a library table. It was heavenly. I hated to leave.   **10**

The clock signaled the task of trudging back, at 3:45 p.m., with even heavier bags. The bags, of course, were no heavier; they just seemed heavier.   **11**

*Collette Russell's "A Day in the Homeless Life."

Back in the "yard" I joined the group already assembled. Some women **12** never left the grounds, staying all day in the small yard by the building. God forbid. With the appearance of a staff member, we would form a line as the staffer prepared a list of our names and bed requests.

I was always glad when the lights went out at 9 p.m. and I could climb **13** into bed (a bottom sheet and a blanket—no top sheet) and close my eyes and pretend I wasn't there but back in my apartment on the West Coast.

Twice I was robbed. Once a bag was taken. Another time my new blue **14** underpants disappeared out of one of my bags. Who knew they were there?

Even if I were to do day labor at $4 per hour and clear $28 or so a day, **15** how many weeks would it take to save enough for first and last month's rent on an apartment plus deposit and enough to pay for initial utilities? I was too depressed to even try to work and took frequent breaks to sit down while doing kitchen volunteer work. I was tired all the time.

The true stories I heard were heartbreaking. Which was the sadder? **16**

One young woman with no skills and no job training had been OK finan- **17** cially until her CETA job ended—the program was abolished—and the YWCA raised its weekly room rate. She couldn't afford a room and couldn't find a job. She'd been in shelters for three or four years. I marveled that she was still sane. She did crossword puzzles while waiting everywhere.

Another older lady had held the same job for 10 years and would still **18** have been working had not the corporation, without notice, closed up shop. She was 59 years old and out of a job, with little severance pay and no help to find new work. She tried but was unsuccessful in finding a new job. She exhausted her savings after her unemployment ran out. One June day in 1987 she found herself homeless. No money for rent.

Both of these women are intelligent, honest, pleasant, clean, and neatly **19** dressed. And both are penniless and homeless. How will they escape the shelters? Will they?

I got by, all right, by keeping my mouth shut around the staff and talking **20** with only two or three women whom I knew to be sane and sociable. I was lucky. Two and a half months after I'd first gone into a shelter my son rescued me. I was on the verge of madness, so hungry for a little privacy and peace that I was afraid I'd start screaming in my sleep and be shunted off to a mental ward.

Now I've got a job paying more than I've ever earned. But I remember **21** those days and nights.

No one should have to live like that. Too many do. And will, I fear, un- **22** less and until we who have homes and jobs help them end their eternal, living nightmare.

QUESTIONS FOR CRITICAL THINKING

THINKING CRITICALLY ABOUT CONTENT

1. What are some of the details the writer includes to help her readers fully sense what it is like to be homeless? Note which of the five senses she uses, and state whether the details are objective or subjective.

2. Why do you think the writer describes the lives of other homeless women in addition to her own? How would homeless life be different for a man?

THINKING CRITICALLY ABOUT PURPOSE

3. What attitude do you think Russell wants her readers to have about homeless people? On what details do you base your answer?

4. Why do you think the writer tells her readers how long it would take her to save enough money to rent her own apartment?

THINKING CRITICALLY ABOUT AUDIENCE

5. This essay was originally published in a magazine for the homeless. Do you think the writer would have included the same details and information if her primary readers were going to be the general public? Why? How would it be different?

6. Who or what does the writer blame for making the lives of homeless people so difficult? What impact does this information have on her readers? Do you think it will change their opinions and attitudes about homeless people?

THINKING CRITICALLY ABOUT PERSPECTIVE

7. How do you think Russell feels about her subject matter. What details show this? Note also the final three paragraphs. Is what Russell suggests positive or negative? Does she offer homeless people a sense of hope?

8. Could someone who has never been homeless write a good essay about homelessness? How would it be different from this essay? Write the first paragraph of an essay about homelessness from your own perspective.

LEARNING FROM YOUR PEERS

Careful observing of the world around us is one of the most important ways we learn. Whether your intent is to learn more about human nature or about the natural processes in the environment, you will benefit from looking with a writer's eye for details that will help you communicate your experience to your audience. To help you see how an observing essay takes shape from the very beginning, we are going to follow the writing of a student named Choi Sau Foon.

Choi Sau Foon's Writing Assignment: Observing

Choi Sau Foon's instructor asked the class to think about a place that evoked a particularly strong atmosphere for them. It could be a place that is peaceful, beautiful, or busy; it could involve people or a particular person. It could be a place of employment or worship, a quiet place to study, a scenic park, or the neighbourhood video arcade. They were to think also about the significance of that particular place, and then describe the place for someone who has never been there, showing readers the sights, sounds, tastes, smells, and textures that make it so significant.

Sau Foon goes through the writing process outlined in Chapter One: generating ideas, planning, developing, organizing, drafting, revising, and editing.

Generating Ideas

The topic is an easy one for Sau Foon. Since she now lives in Canada, her Chinese experiences seem to stand out even more starkly. The difficult thing for her will be to choose one experience and focus only on it. Sau Foon likes to do much of the planning in her head, but she jots down her general ideas so that she has a record of all of them.

She spends several minutes brainstorming, and then decides that she will keep a small notebook with her so that each time she comes up with an idea she will jot it down. She tries to think of things that will be interesting to a primarily non-Chinese audience. By the end of the day, she has several possibilities. She calls a classmate and talks about some of the ideas, and together they come up with one that will reveal a part of Chinese culture yet still be understandable to Sau Foon's peers. She will write about a particular experience of communicating with the dead. Before she writes anything, however, she likes to let the ideas percolate inside her head for a few days.

Planning And Developing

Planning and developing work together for Sau Foon's. Since English is not her first language, she finds it easier to fully remember the experience as one might remember a series of paintings or a film. She tries to come up with all of the colours and textures that she can remember being there. She knows that she will have to rely very much on her imagination to recreate the dominant impression. Her fear is that she will not find enough English words to fully capture the atmosphere and the importance of the experience.

Sau Foon begins to list all of the qualities of the scene.

Sights:

    Old building

    Shoddy looking

    Mostly dark; only a bit of light; a red light

    Cracked and peeling paint

Smells:

Dust; musty; damp

Smoke

Incense

Sounds:

Chanting

Mumbling

Words faster and faster

Tastes:

?

Textures:

Sitting on the hard floor

Warm? Cold?

Organizing And Drafting

Because Sau Foon has gone over in her head so many times what she wants to say, she finds that the details seem to organize themselves as she writes. She knows that she can change anything around when she wants. She turns on her computer and freewrites a first draft.

Sau Foon's Essay: First Draft

Main idea: For some, an important part of Chinese culture is communicating with the dead.

Many things can't be explained in Chinese culture. Every country has its own traditional beliefs and superstitions. Chinese people have some beliefs that are not grounded in reason. Some of the elderly believe people can communicate with dead people. My grandma is one of them who believes that this works. Actually, this is an ancestral secret, and no one can prove if it is a truth or not. However, a wired experience happened when I was ten years old.

I still remember it happened when my grandfather died almost a year ago. One day, my grandma brought me to a very old shoddy looking building with only a little bit of light. The paint was cracking and peeling. There was a dusty smell in the air. We had to walk up five floors to reach an apartment.

A pretty old and short woman opened the door. She brought us into a room where there were some red lights and which was very smoky because a lot of Chinese incense sticks had been lit. When lit, incense was a form of respect towards ancestors and helped to satisfy their hunger in the underworld. I heard from my mother that Chinese incense sticks were for feeding ancestors or dead relatives.

My grandma and I sat down on the floor with the woman sitting opposite us. She asked about my grandfather. After a moment, she closed her eyes and repeatedly called my grandfather's name. Suddenly, she started shaking her hands and body and mumbling under her breath. She gradually spoke faster and faster, so I couldn't hear what she said. A minute later, she stopped shaking but spoke with a wired deep voice that was unlike her previous voice. My grandma said that this was because the woman could communicate with my grandfather's spirit, and his spirit had entered into the body of the woman in order to contact us. My grandma was very emotional and said, "How are you? I miss you very much. Did you receive the money and clothes we sent you?" It is a Chinese custom for people to burn some money, clothes or even cars that are made out of paper for their dead relatives, so the relatives can use them in the underworld. The woman answered, "I am fine. I received the money and the clothes. You don't have to worry about me. You have to take care of yourself." After the conversation, the woman shook her body again and spoke with her own voice. She looked very tired, and there was a lot of sweat on her face.

I am not quite sure whether the ability to communicate with dead people is real or not, but I am very amazed that it happened. I'm not sure if it was really my grandfather's spirit, or just the woman pretending to be him in order to make money. Does the woman really have the power to communicate with the spiritual world? I think that is a secret only the woman knows. For me, the important point is that my grandma feels very happy after she knows my grandfather is fine, and she thinks that he will always be here to bless my whole family.

Revising

Sau Foon remembers her instructor's emphasis on the importance of feeling comfortable expressing ideas as fully as possible in sentences before turning to the larger features of the essay. She rereads her draft and decides that her descriptions could be stronger if she adds more sensory detail, especially those using the sense of taste and texture, because the picture that she sees in her head is more complete than the one she has put on paper. She thinks that she can do a more thorough job at describing, particularly the atmosphere in the room where the communication takes place. She wants also to further build up the tension she felt in the room. She marks all of the areas that she feels could use some revising and then leaves the draft until the next day.

In class the following day, her instructor talks about the importance of topic sentences in each paragraph. Together the class works through the Focus on Paragraphs section in this chapter, and does the exercises that the instructor assigns. That night, Sau Foon revisits her essay, and makes sure that each of her paragraphs has a controlling idea. She rewords some of the ideas, and now feels that she is ready to focus in on individual sentences

 ## COLLABORATIVE WORK

PEER GROUP ACTIVITY

After you read the Focus on Paragraphs section, turn to Sau Foon's first draft and complete the following tasks in small groups.

A. Put a caret (^) at points in the essay where you think Sau Foon needs more detail. What kinds of detail should she include?

B. Use an asterisk (*) to indicate the points at which Sau Foon could use stronger controlling ideas for her paragraphs.

Compare the marks your group records with those your instructor shows you. Where do they differ? What do you need to review before writing your own essay?

Class Activity

As an entire class, look at the underlined portions of Sau Foon's essay to see the changes she makes.

A. Did you identify the **revision** problems that she corrects?

B. Do you think the changes are good ones? Discuss them.

Editing

Sau Foon knows exactly what she needs to do to make her essay more descriptive. She now turns to the Focus on Sentences section of this chapter so that she can get some tips on correct use of modifiers, nouns, and pronouns. She takes this information and applies it to the areas in her essay that she has identified as needing further detail. She uses the section on pronouns to make her sentences sound more concise.

 ## COLLABORATIVE WORK

Peer Group Activity

After you have read the portions of Focus on Sentences that your instructor assigns, turn to Sau Foon's first draft and complete the following tasks in small groups:

A. Circle all of the modifiers in the first couple of paragraphs. Draw arrows to the words that they modify.

B. Draw a box around the pronouns. With arrows, connect the pronouns to the nouns that they replace.

Compare your answers with those from another peer group. Where do your answers differ from theirs? What do you need to review before writing your own essay?

Class Activity

As an entire class, look at the portions of Sau Foon's revised draft to see how she changed each sentence.

A. Did you identify the editing problems that Sau Foon corrected?

B. Do you think her changes are good ones? Discuss her changes.

Sau Foon's Revised Essay ....

Secrecy

~~Many things can't be explained in Chinese culture.~~ There are so many things in this world that can't be explained, and it seems that every country has its share of beliefs and superstitions that are rooted in tradition. ~~Every country has its own traditional beliefs and superstitions.~~ Chinese people have some beliefs that are not grounded in reason. For instance, some people, especially the elderly ~~Some of the elderly~~ believe certain people have the power to ~~can~~ communicate with the dead ~~people.~~ My grandma is one ~~of them~~ who believes that this works. Actually, this is an ancestral secret, and no one can prove if it is true ~~a truth or not.~~ However, ~~a wired experience happened~~ when I was ten years old, I had a weird experience.

~~I still remember it~~ It happened ~~when my grandfather died almost a year ago~~ almost a year after my grandfather had died. It was a hot, muggy day, the day that ~~One day,~~ my grandma brought me to a very old and shoddy looking building. ~~with only a little bit of light. The~~ I looked long and hard at that building, and I wasn't sure whether I wanted to go further. Paint was cracking and peeling. There was a dusty smell in the air. Inside it was dark, with only a little bit of light from a single window high up the stairwell. We ~~had to walk~~ climbed up five flights of rickety stairs ~~floors~~ to reach an apartment.

I felt that something unusual but also somehow familiar was about to happen. A ~~pretty old and short~~ stooped old woman opened the door almost before we knocked. She must have heard us coming. She brought us into a room where the air was thick and sweet with incense. The air seemed to glow with ~~where there were some~~ red lights. ~~and which was very smoky because a lot of Chinese incense sticks had been lit. When lit,~~ Lighting incense ~~was a form of~~ showed respect towards ancestors and dead relatives, and helped to satisfy their hunger in the underworld. ~~I heard from my mother that Chinese incense sticks were for feeding ancestors or dead relatives~~ The weird experience was about to begin.

My grandma and I sat down on the floor with the old woman sitting opposite us. She asked about my grandfather. After a moment, she closed her eyes and repeatedly called ~~my grandfather's~~ his name.

Suddenly, ~~she started shaking~~ her hands and body started to shake and ~~she mumbled~~ ~~mumbling under her breath~~ almost inaudibly. ~~She gradually spoke~~ And then, faster and faster she spoke, so fast that ~~so~~ I couldn't ~~hear~~ understand what she said. A minute later, she stopped shaking but now she spoke with a ~~wired~~ weird deep voice that was unlike ~~her previous~~ any voice I had previously heard her use. My grandma said that this was because the woman could communicate with my grandfather's spirit, and his spirit had entered into the body of the woman in order to contact us.

My grandma was very emotional and said, "How are you? I miss you very much. Did you receive the money and clothes we sent you?" ~~It is a Chinese custom for people to burn some money, clothes or even cars that are made out of paper for their dead relatives, so the relatives can use them in the underworld.~~

The woman answered, "I am fine. I received the money and the clothes. You don't have to worry about me. You have to take care of yourself."

It is a Chinese custom for people to burn some money, clothes or even cars that are made out of paper for their dead relatives, so the relatives can use them in the underworld. Apparently, my grandfather received the gifts, and was pleased.

I guess that was all that my grandfather wanted to communicate, and now he was ready to leave. There was silence a.After the conversation, and the ~~woman shook her body~~ woman's body went all shaky again. Now, though, she ~~and~~ spoke with her own voice. She looked very tired, ~~and there was a lot of sweat on her face~~ her face beaded with sweat. She had finished the communication. We paid her the fee that she demanded, and left the dark building. The sun was brightly shining.

I am not quite sure whether the ability to communicate with dead people is real or not, but I am very amazed that ~~it~~ this

<u>experience</u> happened. I'm not sure if it was really my grandfather's spirit, or just the woman pretending to be him in order to make money. ~~Does~~ <u>Could</u> the woman really have the power to communicate with the spiritual world? I think that is a secret only the woman knows. For me, the important point is that my grandma feels very happy ~~after~~ <u>because</u> she knows my grandfather is fine, and she thinks that he will always be here to bless my whole family.

PRACTISE OUTLINING

As a class, spend time thinking, planning, developing, and organizing a potential observing essay.

1. Spend five minutes brainstorming a few memories of strong observations.
2. Choose five for the subject of a potential essay. Discuss what makes one idea better than another. Choose the best one.
3. Decide on the audience and the purpose.
4. Draw a cluster of this memory's possible significance to the audience.
5. Develop the ideas to give a sense of what a person might potentially write.
6. Organize the ideas so they appear in the best order for the best effect.
7. Could you write this essay? What would be the main topics for each paragraph?

WRITING YOUR OWN OBSERVING ESSAY

You have seen a professional writer and fellow student at work describing an observation or experience that was significant to them. Reading Russell's published essay and Sau Foon's writing-in-process has prepared you to write your own essay focusing on an observation that is significant to you.

What Have You Discovered?

- Observe accurately and carefully to produce interesting writing.
- Draw on all five senses to write a good observing essay.
- *Show* rather than *tell* readers what you have seen or experienced.
- Choose the best details to communicate a dominant impression.
- To present your observation effectively, logically organize your ideas.

- To help you shape your essay, learn as much as possible about your readers.

- Before you write a draft, decide on a perspective toward your subject.

- After you write a draft, revise your essay for meaning and organization.

- After you revise your essay, edit for grammar, usage, and sentence structure.

Your Writing Topic

Choose one of the following topics for your observing essay:

1. Think about a place where you spend a lot of time, an activity you engage in often, or a person whom you know very well. You can choose something or someone you are very fond of, or something or someone you don't like very much—just as long as you are familiar with your subject as, for example, Collette Russell was with homelessness. Write an observation that will enable your readers to know and understand the place, the activity, or the person you are observing as if they could see the thing or person you are describing.

2. Many places seem to have particular atmospheres, such as hospitals, churches, graveyards, and greenhouses. Choose one that evokes a particularly strong memory for you. Describe that experience. Use as many sensory details as are necessary to provide a dominant impression as, for example, Sau Foon does in "Secrecy."

3. A national travel magazine is asking for honest descriptions (positive or negative) of places people have visited or lived in for extended periods of time. They are offering payment for all essays chosen. You may decide to write about a marvelous beach or about a dreadful place you were forced to live in because of circumstances beyond your control. Choose your details carefully.

4. Create your own observing topic, and write an essay in response to it. You might like to check this one with your instructor.

When you begin writing, you will work through your own writing process. Although how you specifically write may differ from other writers, you need to go through all parts of the writing process. Compare the process you go through to the one Sau Foon took to complete her essay. Keep track of what you do to finish a final draft.

Composing Topic Sentences

Checklist For Composing Topic Sentences

✓ Are your topic sentences clear?
✓ Are they focused?
✓ Are they specific?

In school clubs, business firms, and the military, people are organized in a chain of command to conduct the group's daily activities as well as to determine its procedures and goals. The president of a corporation, for instance, sets its overall goals; the other officers plan specific projects and assign the detail work to specific workers. In a similar way, the title of an essay generally states its overall subject, the thesis statement (usually in the first paragraph) provides the controlling idea that shapes and directs the entire essay, and topic sentences introduce the controlling idea for each body paragraph. Topic sentences, like middle managers of a business, give shape and direction to the middle paragraphs of an essay. The supporting sentences of each paragraph are the workers that take care of specific tasks.

Clear Topic Sentences

A **topic sentence** should clearly express the main idea in its paragraph. A topic sentence should usually be the first or last sentence in a body paragraph, and it should set out the idea that the rest of the paragraph develops. Unlike the title—which can be a single word, phrase, or clause—a topic sentence, like all the sentences in an essay, should be complete. It should have a subject, a predicate, and a complete thought. For example, the title of Sau Foon's essay is "Secrecy," and she develops the idea of secrecy by looking at a specific personal incident that exemplifies its importance in one area of Chinese culture. Each paragraph in her essay contains a controlling idea, an idea that shows the reader what is being developed in that particular paragraph.

Look at paragraph two as an example. First, notice how the opening sentence relates directly back to the final thought in the previous paragraph. *It happened* is an extension of *a weird experience*. There is a strong transition from one paragraph to the next. Secondly, we know that the writer is going to tell us about the experience because her topic sentence tells us this. The topic sentence makes a statement about the contents of the paragraph. The rest of the paragraph describes the setting of the experience.

> **It happened almost a year after my grandfather had died.** It was a hot, muggy day, the day that my grandma brought me to a very old and shoddy looking building. I looked long and hard at that building, and I

wasn't sure whether I wanted to go further. Paint was cracking and peeling. There was a dusty smell in the air. Inside it was dark, with only a little bit of light from a single window high up the stairwell. We climbed up five flights of rickety stairs to reach an apartment.

This rich description is set up by the controlling idea of the paragraph. *It could only come about as a result of the grandfather's death.* The description evokes for the reader the sights and smells that the author remembers, and Sau Foon's details take the reader right to the door of the apartment. The reader assumes, then, that the events in the next paragraph will begin at the apartment door.

As Sau Foon revises her observing essay, she decides that her topic sentence for the paragraph is awkwardly phrased, and it does not clearly lead into the content of the paragraph.

First Draft: I still remember it happened when my grandfather died almost a year ago.

Revision: It happened almost a year after my grandfather had died.

In her first draft, the topic sentence sets up the grandfather's death almost a year ago. In the revision, the weird experience is emphasized—as a result of the grandfather's death a year prior to the experience. Her revised topic sentence directs her readers' focus to the weird experience, and the details set up the dominant impression of the atmosphere of the experience.

Exercise P3-1

State the controlling idea for paragraph six of Collette Russell's "A Day in the Homeless Life." More fully develop the paragraph by adding details that you imagine she might have included.

Exercise P3-2

Reread paragraph three of Sau Foon's first draft. Divide it into paragraphs and provide each paragraph with a clear topic sentence. Add details where needed.

Exercise P3-3

Underline any of the following topic sentences that could be developed in one paragraph.

1. Children who watch television every day are exposed to the highest-pressure advertising in mass media.

2. I have tried several relaxing hobbies.

3. The University of Windsor in Ontario was the best choice for me.

4. Universities often have different areas of strength and weakness.

5. I learned one easy way to make friends.

6. Cats make better pets than dogs.

7. There are several ways to avoid being disappointed in love.

8. Lasting relationships are built on a foundation of mutual interests and mutual respect.

9. I will never forget the day I got my driver's licence.

10. Riding Mountain National Park is a great place for a holiday.

Exercise P3-4

Compose a topic sentence for the following paragraph.

For example, we spent a great deal of time generating ideas about something or someone we had observed closely. Then, we chose the idea that we felt we could develop with a great many relevant details. After settling on a controlling idea for the essay, we planned the body of the paper.

Focused Topic Sentences

Remember the story of Goldilocks and the three bears? She was searching for porridge that was "just right." This principle can be applied to topic sentences. A topic sentence should state an idea that can be adequately developed in one paragraph. The topic sentence thus offers shape and direction to the details in the paragraph.

As Sau Foon began revising her observing essay, she found that the second to last paragraph was unwieldy. First she decided what details belonged together, and then she began to shape the paragraphs. She moved some of the sentences around. She knew that the details of the woman returning to her former self should be some of the last ones in the essay because they made up the end of the story, but there weren't enough to make up a complete paragraph. In the end, she realized that the new small paragraph lacked focus. What it needed was a topic sentence to direct the reader's attention to the change, and to provide a transition from the previous paragraph. She reworded some of the sentences and added details to make the sentences much clearer and the paragraph complete.

First Draft: Suddenly, she started shaking her hands and body and mumbling under her breath. She gradually spoke faster and faster, so I couldn't hear what she said. A minute later, she stopped shaking but spoke with a wired deep voice that was unlike her previous voice. My grandma said that this was because the woman could communicate with my grandfather's spirit, and his spirit had entered into the body of the woman in order to contact us. My grandma was very emotional and said, "How are you? I miss you very much. Did you receive the money and clothes we sent you?" It is a Chinese custom for people to burn some money, clothes or even cars that are made out of paper for their dead relatives, so the relatives can use them in the underworld. The woman answered, "I am fine. I received the money and the clothes. You don't have to worry about me. You have to take care of yourself." After the conversation, the woman shook her body again and spoke with her own voice. She looked very tired, and there was a lot of sweat on her face.

Revision: My grandma and I sat down on the floor with the old woman sitting opposite us. She asked about my grandfather. After a moment, she closed her eyes and repeatedly called his name. Suddenly, her hands and body started to shake and she mumbled almost inaudibly. And then, faster and faster she spoke, so fast that I couldn't understand what she said. A minute later, she stopped shaking but now she spoke with a weird deep voice that was unlike any voice I had previously heard her use. My grandma said that this was because the woman could communicate with my grandfather's spirit, and his spirit had entered into the body of the woman in order to contact us.

My grandma was very emotional and said, "How are you? I miss you very much. Did you receive the money and clothes we sent you?"

The woman answered, "I am fine. I received the money and the clothes. You don't have to worry about me. You have to take care of yourself."

It is a Chinese custom for people to burn some money, clothes or even cars that are made out of paper for their dead relatives, so the relatives can use them in the underworld. Apparently, my grandfather received the gifts, and was pleased.

I guess that was all that my grandfather wanted to communicate, and now he was ready to leave. There was silence after the conversation, and the woman's body went all shaky again. Now, though, she spoke with her own voice. She looked very tired, her face beaded with sweat. She had finished the communication. We paid her the fee that she demanded, and left the dark building. The sun was brightly shining.

These revisions sort out the details and provide a strong focus for the reader. Note, especially, the strength of the highlighted topic sentence.

Exercise P3-5

Review Sau Foon's revision above. Which of the revised paragraphs could still use a clearer topic sentence which focuses the paragraph details? Write topic sentences for those paragraphs.

Exercise P3-6

Write a topic sentence that would give shape and direction to a paragraph developing each of the subjects listed below:

1. The best feature of my college.
2. The ideal spot to study.
3. The most entertaining sport.
4. The sport that is the best to participate in.
5. The most misleading advertising claim.
6. The most clever ad on television.
7. Choosing an outfit.
8. My favourite musicians.
9. My least favourite foods.
10. A good book.

Exercise P3-7

Write a topic sentence for the following paragraph to make the controlling idea as clear as possible.

At Olds College, classes are small enough for your instructors to know you personally, yet the college has enough students to offer a wide variety of courses. Because Olds is in a rural setting, peace and quiet surround you; however, Calgary, a major city housing several colleges and a university, is only an hour's drive away. Olds' students are motivated to achieve without feeling pressure to compete.

Specific Topic Sentences

The words in topic sentences should be chosen carefully so that the controlling idea is plain to the reader. The topic sentence in this excerpt from Amy Tan's book *The Joy Luck Club* is a good example: "On the wall opposite the bed was a big wooden clock with a forest and bears carved into it." Note that this is the second sentence in the paragraph, surrounded before and after by specific details.

> While thinking this, I was startled by a sudden clang! clang! clang! followed by music. **On the wall opposite the bed was a big wooden clock with a forest and bears carved into it.** The door on the clock had burst

open, and a tiny room full of people was coming out. There was a bearded man in a pointed cap seated at a table. He was bending his head over and over again to drink soup, but his beard would dip first in the bowl and stop him. A girl in a white scarf and blue dress was standing next to the table, and she was bending over and over again to give the man more of this soup. And next to the man and the girl was another girl with a skirt and short jacket. She was swinging her arm back and forth, playing violin music. She always played the same dark song. . . .

Without the clear statement in the second sentence referring to a clock, readers might easily believe they are reading about a bearded man and a real girl ladling soup, not the carved figures emerging from the clock when the hour strikes.

All words in a topic sentence should be as exact as possible. In revising the topic sentences in her essay, Sau Foon realizes that, again, she has details in some of her paragraphs that do not seem to belong to the topic sentence. She takes this as a sure sign that the paragraph needs to be split into two or more with their own topic sentences. Take a look at the third paragraph of her first draft. It is a good example.

First Draft: A pretty old and short woman opened the door. She brought us into a room where there were some red lights and which was very smoky because a lot of Chinese incense sticks had been lit. When lit, incense was a form of respect towards ancestors and helped to satisfy their hunger in the underworld. I heard from my mother that Chinese incense sticks were for feeding ancestors or dead relatives My grandma and I sat down on the floor with the woman sitting opposite us. She asked about my grandfather. After a moment, she closed her eyes and repeatedly called my grandfather's name.

Revision: **I felt that something unusual but also somehow familiar was about to happen.** A stooped old woman opened the door almost before we knocked. She must have heard us coming. She brought us into a room where the air was thick and sweet with incense. The air seemed to glow with red lights. Lighting incense showed respect towards ancestors and dead relatives, and helped to satisfy their hunger in the underworld. The weird experience was about to begin.

My grandma and I sat down on the floor with the old woman sitting opposite us. She asked about my grandfather. After a moment, she closed her eyes and repeatedly called his name. . .

Now Sau Foon's details are more clearly ordered, and the separate topics flow from one to the next. Notice how well the topic sentence leads specifically into the details that follow.

Exercise P3-8

Take a look at all of the topic sentences in Sau Foon's essay. Which ones still need specific details to make them strong? Rewrite the ones that could use changes. Share your changes with your peers.

Exercise P3-9

Rewrite the following sentences using specific, descriptive words from your own experience so that your reader gets a better picture of your controlling idea for the paragraph that might follow.

1. My first pet was cute.
2. My favourite class seems to go quickly.
3. One of my friends seems very unusual.
4. Our neighbours are noisy.
5. I like to relax.

Exercise P3-10

Compose five topic sentences using specific words and phrases for paragraphs that you might write to fulfill your observing assignment.

 ## COLLABORATIVE WORK

After writing a draft of your own observing essay, exchange papers with a classmate and complete the following tasks:

A. Underline each topic sentence.
B. Put brackets around any topic sentences that do not make the controlling idea clear.
C. In the margin, suggest changes to make the topic sentences clearer and more meaningful.

Then return the paper to its writer and use the information in this section to revise your draft.

Nouns, Pronouns, And Modifiers

Checklist For Identifying And Using Nouns, Pronouns, And Modifiers

✓ Does each noun name something?
✓ Is each noun in its correct form for its position in the sentence?
✓ Does each pronoun clearly refer back to the noun that it replaces?
✓ Is each pronoun in its correct form for its position and function in the sentence?
✓ Is each modifier positioned to emphasize the noun or verb to which it refers?

A *noun* is a word used as a name. Nouns are the doers in a sentence; they name persons, places, things, emotions, or qualities that tell who or what is involved in the action or state of being.

Persons:	Since my **brother Frederick** moved away, I never see him.
Places:	When I first went to my brother's **hometown** in **Nova Scotia**, I thought it would be a great place to visit.
Things:	I imagined wearing a large yellow fishing **hat** and eating **lobster** fresh from the **ocean**.
Emotions:	I told him about the **excitement** I felt, but also the **trepidation**.
Qualities:	Although he went to further his **ambitions,** I knew that I would miss his **friendship.**

Nouns can appear in various places in the sentence, and their forms may change depending on how they are used.

He is a good **friend** (noun as object).

His **friendship** is something I value (noun as subject).

Because of his **friendliness**, he meets many people (noun expressing quality).

There are three basic types of nouns:

Common nouns name any one of a class of persons, places, or things. Some examples are as follows: politician, city, animal. Emotions and qualities also fit into this category.

Proper nouns name particular persons, places, or things. Note that they usually begin with a capital letter. Some examples are as follows: Jean Charest, Moosejaw, Sniffy the Rat.

Collective nouns are common nouns whose singular form names a collection or group of individuals. Some examples are as follows: herd, audience, majority.

Clues For Identifying Nouns

1. Look for the articles *a*, *an*, and *the*. A noun is sure to follow.

   Examples: a car, an apple, the cats (concrete nouns).

                              a recession, an appreciation, the challenge (abstract nouns).

2. Look for words that end in common noun suffixes such as -age, -ance, -dom, -ence, -er, -ian, -ice, -ism, -ist, -ity, -ment, -ness, -ship, -sion, -tion, and -ure.

   Examples: postage, grievance, kingdom, existence, runner, librarian, practice, socialism, nudist, gravity, shipment, kindness, friendship, mansion, pollution, and failure.

3. Look for words that begin with capital letters. Not all words that begin sentences are nouns. However, most capitalized words found within sentences are proper nouns.

Exercise S3-1

Copy out and double space Sau Foon's first paragraph. Underline each of the nouns and identify the type.

Exercise S3-2

Fill in each of the following blanks with an appropriate noun.

1. My _____ raises _____ on his farm.

2. The _____ bought a new _____ yesterday.

3. Our _____ bark wakes us up every _____.

4. The _____ end made me wish for more.

5. The _____ of caribou is constantly threatened by _____.

6. During our trip to _____ , we stayed in a small _____ that overlooked a _____ .

7. Each time we go to _____ we spend more _____ than we planned, usually on _____ .

8. My friend _____ has been working out seven days a week for the past six months preparing for a body-building _____ .

9. His _____ is a _____ in the shoe department at
_____ .

10. I had to take my _____ to the _____ because it hadn't
been working correctly for the past few _____ .

Exercise S3-3

Write one sentence using each of the following nouns:

1. outfit
2. image
3. responsibility
4. reward
5. accent

Pronouns

A **pronoun** is a word used in place of a noun to avoid repetition of a noun. It can do anything in a sentence that a noun can do. Read the following sentence aloud:

> **The woman** went to **the woman's** room because **the woman** was going to use **the woman's** skill as intermediary to communicate with the dead.

The sentence is awkward and monotonous. When we substitute pronouns for the noun, we have a much better sentence.

> The woman went to **her** room because **she** was going to use **her** skill as intermediary to communicate with the dead.

Note that there are different forms that the pronoun can take. This depends on where the pronoun appears in the sentence and how it functions (as a subject or an object, or to show possession). The most important pronouns are the personal pronouns. These pronouns are the ones that will give you the most trouble unless you understand how they work. The other types of pronouns will be discussed in a later chapter.

Personal Pronouns

Subjective Pronouns appear in place of the subject or follow linking verbs. They work exactly like the subject does. They simply replace the subject.

Examples: She is the priest at our church.

The priest at our church is **she**.

Objective Pronouns serve as objects of the sentence; that is, they receive the action of the sentence.

Examples: Grandmother sent **us** boxes of bagels and cookies.

By way of Canada Post, Grandma sent **them** to us.

Possessive Pronouns indicate ownership. Note how the form of the pronoun changes according to the role it plays.

Examples: These are **her** gloves; she forgot them at **your** house.

The dog lost **his** collar when he caught it on **our** fence.

Their house is being built next to **yours**.

The form a pronoun takes also depends on whether you are referring to one person or thing, or more than one person or thing (singular or plural). The following chart shows all of the forms that the personal pronouns can take.

	Subjective	**Objective**	**Possessive**
Singular	I	Me	My
	You	You	Your, yours
	She, he, it	Her, him, it	Her, hers, his, it
Plural	We	Us	Our, ours
	You	You	You, yours
	They	Them	Their, theirs

Exercise S3-4

Choose the correct pronoun for each of the following sentences.

1. George bought bagels for Grandma and (I , me).
2. Shiobhan and (I, me) spent the summer at Gull Lake.
3. The money belongs to (they, them).
4. It is (she, her) who will try out for the Canadian hockey team.
5. It is just (we, us) and (they, them).

Modifiers

Modifiers are words that restrict, qualify, or supply additional meaning to another word or group of words. Usually when we think of modifiers, we think of words that describe, such as *adjectives* or *adverbs*. Like verbs and nouns, adjectives and adverbs have different forms.

Adjective Forms

Adjectives are words that describe or modify nouns or pronouns. Adjectives normally come before the nouns or pronouns they modify, adding specific information that makes the sentence more colourful and interesting. The following example comes from Sau Foon's revised draft:

> It was a **hot, muggy** day, the day that my grandma brought me to a very old and shoddy looking building.

Note the comma between the adjectives. Here, the word *and* could have been inserted between the two words. In fact, Sau Foon does this in the second half of the sentence with *old and shoddy*. In the first half, a comma doesn't exactly replace the *and*, but because the author is making a list, in this case about the qualities of the day, she can omit the *and* and still have the sentence make sense. Although she could have also done this with *old and shoddy*, she chooses not to so that the sentence has more variety of sound.

Adjectives can also appear after the noun they modify. Note the changes in the following sentences:

> It was a day, **hot and muggy**, that my grandmother brought me to a very old and shoddy looking building.

> It was a hot, muggy day, the day that my grandmother brought me to a building, **very old and shoddy looking**.

Exercise S3-5

Read aloud the following variations to see which sound better to you. Notice which words are emphasized in each.

1. It was a **hot and muggy** day, the day that my grandma brought me to a very **old and shoddy** looking building.

2. It was a **hot, muggy** day, the day that my grandma brought me to a very **old, shoddy** looking building.

3. It was a **hot, muggy** day, the day that my grandma brought me to a very old and shoddy looking building.

4. It was a **hot and muggy** day, the day that my grandma brought me to a **very old, shoddy** looking building.

5. It was a day, **hot and muggy**, that my grandmother brought me to a very old and shoddy looking building.

6. It was a hot, muggy day, the day that my grandmother brought me to a building, **very old and shoddy looking**.

FOCUS ON SENTENCES

Exercise S3-6

Underline the adjectives in the following sentences and draw an arrow to the word or words they modify.

1. They have just bought a new cabin on the shores of Lac La Biche.
2. I received a very attractive offer from PetroCanada.
3. Vancouver is a large and hospitable city.
4. I saw an excellent movie last night.
5. The tired, old man on the park bench suddenly sat bolt upright.

Exercise S3-7

Supply adjectives to complete each of the following sentences.

1. The _____ day seemed _____ .

2. A _____ turtle sat in the _____ street.

3. We went to the _____ fair and saw _____ exhibits.

4. Elena has _____ brothers and _____ sisters who all live together in a _____ house.

5. Frank selected a _____ shirt and _____ jeans for his _____ date.

Exercise S3-8

Write sentences incorporating the following adjectives.

1. greasy
2. dramatic
3. colourful
4. upset
5. remarkable

Comparative Adjective Forms

When we are using adjectives to compare anything, such as the heights of different mountains, we need to know which form of the adjective to use. Look at the following examples:

Mount Athabasca is high.

(Mount Athabasca is not being compared to any particular mountain.)

Mount Alberta is higher.

(Mount Alberta is being compared to one other mountain.)

Mount Robson is the highest.

(Mount Robson is being compared to more than two other mountains.)

As in the examples above, most short adjectives consisting of one or two syllables add -er and -est at the end to form their comparative adjective. Longer adjectives, composed of three syllables or more, add the words *more* and *most* (or *less* and *least*) before them to form their comparative adjective.

Examples: Charlene is **more** agreeable

Andrea is the **most** agreeable

Katelyn is **less** patient

Ian is the **least** patient

Some adjectives can form their comparatives either way, like *lovely* (*lovelier* or *more lovely*; *loveliest* or *most lovely*). Other adjectives cannot be compared at all. For example, if something is *dead*, how can it be *deader* or *deadest*? The following adjectives have no degrees of comparison:

complete	favourite	vertical
empty	pregnant	round
endless	finite	square
equal	horizontal	unanimous
eternal	impossible	unique
	parallel	

Here's a word of caution: adjectives should not be doubly compared. If an adjective takes an -er or -est ending, you should not use *more* and *most* or *less* and *least* with the comparative form. Likewise, if you can add *more*, *most*, *less*, or *least* before an adjective, you should not add the -er or -est endings.

Irregular Forms Of Adjectives

Adding the endings -er and -est and the words *more*, *most*, *less*, and *least* are ways to form comparisons for regular adjectives. Some adjectives, however, are irregular, meaning they change spelling to form their comparative forms. Here are the most common irregular adjectives.

bad	worse	worst
good	better	best
many, much	more	most
little	less	least

Exercise S3-9

Choose the correct comparative adjective form for each of the following sentences.

1. Of the two men, I consider Soichi the (better, best) worker.
2. Tegan is much (healthier, more healthy) than her sister.
3. Of all of the students, Bryan is the (less, least) attentive.
4. This room is less noisy than (any, any other) room in the house.
5. This photograph is the (beautifuller, more beautiful) of the two.

Exercise S3-10

Return to Collette Russell's essay. Underline adjectives and draw arrows to the nouns that they modify.

Adverb Forms

While adjectives are associated with nouns, pronouns, and linking verbs, most **adverbs** modify action verbs. They tell us something about the verb: how, when, where, to what extent, and in what manner. Sometimes they will modify adjectives, other adverbs, and in some cases, entire sentences. Here are some examples from Sau Foon's essay:

She **repeatedly** called his name.

(*Repeatedly* modifies the verb *called.*)

The sun was **brightly** shining.

(*Brightly* modifies the verb phrase *was shining*, and appears between parts of the verb.)

She mumbled **almost** inaudibly.

(*Almost* tells us to what degree she was inaudible, and *inaudibly* tells us in what manner she mumbled.)

Now she spoke with a weird deep voice.

(*Now* tells us when she spoke.)

Adverbs do not always immediately follow the verb. They do, however, work most effectively if they appear close to the word that they modify. Otherwise, they might appear to modify the wrong word.

Exercise S3-11

Read the following sentences aloud, and note the change in meaning and emphasis when the adverb is moved about in the sentence.

1. She mumbled almost inaudibly.
2. She almost mumbled inaudibly.
3. She mumbled inaudibly, almost.
4. Almost inaudibly, she mumbled.

Exercise S3-12

Underline the adverbs in the following sentences and draw an arrow to the word that each adverb modifies.

1. Have you ever visited Saskatoon?
2. He will remain in Canada temporarily.
3. She plays tennis well.
4. We have been rather busy selling tickets to tonight's NHL game.
5. The canola tasted bad.

Exercise S3-13

Fill in the blanks with adverbs that will logically complete the sentences.

1. Paul _____ misses a day of school.
2. I _____ hope that the obnoxious guests will leave _____ .
3. During the time trials Laura types _____ .
4. The mail often arrives _____ .
5. Carmelita _____ placed the baby on the bed.

Exercise S3-14

Write sentences using the following words as adverbs.

1. harshly
2. rather
3. more energetically
4. normally
5. down

COLLABORATIVE WORK

After you revise your observing essay, work with a classmate on the following tasks.

A. As you read the essay, circle any words that are unusual or appear to be used incorrectly.

B. Choose one paragraph and read it for its descriptive content. Suggest places where the writer might use more detail to create a dominant impression.

C. Choose another paragraph and underline all adjectives and adverbs. Discuss whether the writer has achieved a balance between careful observation and selection of detail.

Then return the paper to its author and use the information in this section to edit your draft.

CHAPTER FOUR

Explaining

The writer should strive to be clear rather than coy. . . . I also
believe . . . the author . . . should "care" or "feel" deeply
about his subject.

ALISTAIR MACLEOD

LEARNING OUTCOMES

This chapter will help you:

- Understand and write an essay that explains a topic to the audience;
- Recognize and order paragraphs with the various patterns of organization; and,
- Recognize and use verbs effectively.

Have you ever found yourself in a situation where you want to explain yourself? You might be tempted to give someone an explanation when you're late to class or work, when someone doesn't understand why you acted in a certain way, or when you want to teach someone a task that you're familiar with. Explaining is an important part of most kinds of communication.

Explaining is also something we do when we write essays. When we explain we are trying to accomplish one of two things: one, we may be trying to offer reasons for why things are the way they are (justifying); two, we may be trying to explain something we know to someone else (procedures and process descriptions). Here's a diagram of the different kinds of explaining and how they fit together:

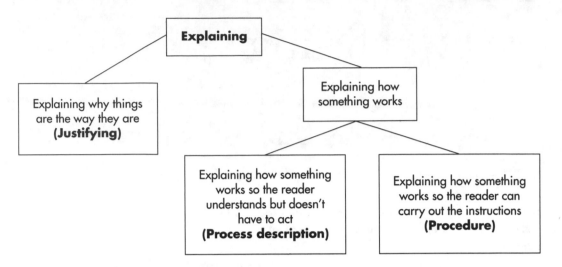

If you're writing a *justifying* essay, you're trying to explain why something has happened, or why you acted in a certain way: why you didn't pay the rent on time, why you chose to go to school, or why fossil fuels endanger the ozone. You need to explain yourself to your readers to help them understand what you know about a topic, how you feel about it, and why you feel the way you do. Your readers may not agree with what you're saying, but at least they will understand why you are saying it.

For example, in his book *All I Really Needed to Know I Learned in Kindergarten*, author Robert Fulghum writes that he enjoys doing laundry. If the rest of his paragraph did not explain this statement, his readers would wonder why he likes to wash and dry dirty clothes. Instead, Fulghum explains the feeling of satisfaction he gets from performing various tasks related to doing the laundry:

> I like sorting the clothes—lights, darks, in-betweens. I like setting the dials—hot, cold, rinse, time, heat. These are choices I can understand and make with decisive skill. I still haven't figured out the new stereo, but washers and dryers I can handle. The bell dings—you pull out the warm, fluffy clothes, take them to the dining-room table, sort and fold them into neat piles. I especially like it when there's lots of static electricity, and you can hang socks all over your body and they will stick there. . . .

Robert Fulghum reveals that doing the laundry is a task he understands, unlike new technology. He explains and describes how he launders his clothes and explains why this is important to him. Fulghum's readers do not have to agree with him—in fact, they can have the opposite feeling about washing clothes—but his explanation helps his readers understand his position on the subject. Fulghum is writing to *justify* his viewpoint.

When you're writing a justifying essay, there is no set order of things you can follow. These kinds of essays can be ordered in a number of different ways. You'll have to rely on your sense of how your ideas can be most effectively organized.

If you're writing an explaining essay, you might try to explain how something should be done, or how something works: changing a tire, planting a tree, or how paper is made. In this kind of writing you try to make sure the reader understands a process description or procedure and each stage or step along the way. Sometimes you'll want to explain how something happens in a general way, so your readers will understand but they won't have to do it themselves. We'll call this a **process description**. Other times, you'll want to explain how to do something in specific detail so your reader will understand how something happens and they'll know how to do it him or herself. We can call this a **procedure**.

Process descriptions give the reader a general sense of how something happens, but the reader doesn't have to complete the process him or herself. If you were to read an essay called "How a Mosquito is Born" you would realize that you are supposed to understand the process a mosquito goes through in order to be born. You aren't supposed to undertake the steps yourself. Here are some other examples: "How a Car Engine Works;" "How the Canadian Justice System Works;" and, "How Glass is Recycled in Ontario." This kind of writing explains something in a general way. Here's a small sample of a process description:

> Quality coffee is roasted, not in big batches, but small 30- to 70-pound batches by a professional master roaster. The beans drop into the roaster for a gentle 12- to 18-minute roast to coax out their character. After the beans roast, they need to cool down quickly to halt the roasting process and protect them from absorbing other flavours and aromas. The beans drop into an air-cooling tray to allow them to return to room temperature.

When you explain a procedure, you want your reader to carry out your instructions. You might want someone to be able to drive a standard-shift car, or make a pizza. You have been reading examples of explaining a process all of your life in the form of instruction manuals, maps, menus, and directions for assembling products. Here is a typical example from a recipe book:

> You'll need a mixing bowl, a mixing spoon, measuring utensils, and a 9-inch square pan. In the mixing bowl, mix the following ingredients in the order given, mixing after adding every ingredient:
>
> 1 egg
> 1 cup of sugar
> 1 teaspoon of soda
> 1 teaspoon of vanilla
> 1 1/2 cups of flour
> 2 cups of fruit cocktail and syrup
> 1/2 cup of chopped nuts
>
> Stir the batter until most of the lumps have disappeared. Then, pour into a 9-inch square pan. Sprinkle 1/4 cup of brown sugar on the top. Bake at 350 degrees Fahrenheit for 45 minutes.

You can tell that these instructions are supposed to be carried out. The reader is expected to use this writing to complete a task.

Process descriptions and procedures follow a typical pattern. Both begin, most often, by introducing the process or task. In the introduction, the writer helps the reader understand what the situation is like before the process or task begins. The next part of process descriptions and procedures shows, stage by stage or step by step, how the process or task moves to completion. Finally, both end by explaining what the situation is like once everything has been completed. You need to make sure you explain yourself carefully enough that you answer any and all of your readers' questions before they arise.

As you can see, there are three kinds of explaining we can use. Each kind is useful depending on what you're trying to get your reader to do.

LEARNING FROM PUBLISHED WRITERS

The essay you are about to read, written by Edna Weber, is an unusual example explaining why things are the way they are—what we now call **justifying**. Ms. Weber explains how her son died and her own confusion about it. You may not agree with what she is saying, but you will understand why she feels the way she does.

Before You Read

Focus Your Attention

Before you read Weber's explanation, take a few moments to respond to the following questions in your journal:

1. Think back over the last month or two and try to recall some of the stories you've heard on the news. Pick one story and write down the details you remember. Why do you think you feel so strongly about that story?

2. Can you imagine saying something to a parent or friend that would make them avoid you for a long time?

Expand Your Vocabulary

In order to understand the story properly, you need to understand everything about it. Here are some words you may not know. Spend some time reading the sentences around the word and see if you can figure out what it means without using a dictionary.

Shunning (paragraph 7)

Streaming (paragraph 2)

Arresting (paragraph 6)

Prowler (paragraph 8)

Jest (paragraph 13)

Edna Weber

For They Know Not What They Do*

This Easter Sunday will mark the 25th anniversary of the night my second-oldest son died. Did he die for his own sins? Or did he die for the sins of others? You tell me.

My late husband, Arnott, and I knew early on that Kenneth was definitely something special, over and above his three brothers. We could see it at home, and his teachers confirmed that observation. Back in the late fifties and early sixties, when schools encouraged excellence via "streaming," Kenny completed 12 grades in 10 years, graduating from Grade 12 with a 90-plus average at the age of 16.

We were told that his IQ placed him in the top 1 percent of the population. When he graduated three years later with an honours bachelor of commerce degree, well, my goodness, but weren't we proud! Arnott was even talking about the possibility of having a lawyer in the family.

But there were other ways in which Kenny was "different" from his brothers: Larry, Bruce, and Brian. He was not athletic; he was not extraordinarily handsome; nor did he make friends easily, especially girlfriends. I mentioned this once to one of his high-school home-room teachers. He said not to worry, that it was because all of the students Ken attended classes with were, to him, "big kids."

But that teacher was wrong. My son was not only a 1-percenter intellectually, he was, or thought he was, a 2-percenter psychosexually. Shortly after his father's death, 26 years ago, he told me that he was a homosexual. He said that he was tired of living a lie to himself and everybody else and that he wanted very much for me to understand and accept this fact before he told anyone else.

Of course, I was absolutely shocked and horrified! I didn't know what to do or to say. I asked him why he was telling me this now, rather than having discussed it with his dad while he was still alive. He laughed and replied, "If I'd told Dad, either the news would have killed him, or he would have killed me." (That was probably true.)

Still all at sea over this astonishing occurrence, I did what all Christians do when they don't know what to do: I fell back on the Bible. I read to my son from Leviticus 20:13: "If a man also lie with mankind, as he lieth with a woman, both of them have committed an abomination; they shall surely be put to death. . . ." Then I went on to suggest that maybe his teacher had been right and that his abnormal academic schedule had resulted in arrested

1

2

3

4

5

6

7

*From *The Globe and Mail*, "Facts And Arguments," Wednesday, April 8, 1998

social development; maybe he needed psychiatric help. I offered to pray with him for guidance. But none of this was what my son wanted to hear, and he shook his head sadly and walked out.

After he left, I did something I have regretted ever since: I called the **8** other boys over, told them the whole thing and asked what they thought could or should be done. We talked it over and decided that the old Anabaptist practice of "shunning" might be helpful. We would treat Ken as if he didn't exist until he gave up his wicked and perverse notion and commenced living like a decent, proper young man. And that's what we did for just over a year.

On the evening of Easter Sunday, Bruce and I were watching television **9** in the living room, and his girlfriend Susan was in the kitchen cleaning up dishes. Suddenly, she came into the living room and said, "Mrs. Weber, you must have left a light on in your garage." Well, I knew there had been no one in that garage for over a week; so I told Bruce to go out and see if we had a prowler on the place.

Bruce went and the first thing he saw, through the window, was the front **10** of Ken's car. Then, almost immediately, he realized that he was also seeing thick swirls of exhaust smoke. Dashing for the door, he threw it open and saw his brother lying peacefully on the floor, hands folded over his chest, with his face directly under the exhaust pipe. He quickly dragged Ken outside and began giving him artificial respiration. But it was too late. The boy whom we had treated as if he didn't exist now really didn't exist.

We buried Kenny at the Beechmount Cemetery, not far from where **11** Arnott lies, on the afternoon of the following Wednesday. It was a chilly, windswept, unpleasant day, and everyone left as soon as it was over. Not much was said on the way home; I think we were all just trying to make some sense of out of the whole thing. But there was no sense to be made of it.

Larry, my oldest, who paid for the funeral, said, "I just spent $6,000 to **12** bury a guy I wouldn't have loaned $6 to the day before he died."

No—no sense at all. **13**

In the intervening years since my son's death, I have read dozens of arti- **14** cles in newspapers and magazines that discuss what we now call "gays." Are they born that way? If so, is it the cruelest imaginable jest of God? . . . Or does the Lord select special people to face special trials? I don't know.

I do know, though, that when I think back to that cheerful, friendly little **15** blond-haired boy, so eager to please his dad and me with those wonderful report cards, or the brilliant young man with limitless opportunity stretching out before him . . . well, something very wrong happened back in 1972 and 1973.

What do the other kids think now? I don't know that either. We have **16** never spoken about it since the day of the funeral, and somehow I don't think we ever will.

❓ QUESTIONS FOR CRITICAL THINKING

THINKING CRITICALLY ABOUT CONTENT

1. Do you think it would have been harder for Kenneth to confess to his mother in 1972 than it would be today? Why?

2. What is Weber trying to explain to her readers?

3. Do you agree with her views? Do you respect her viewpoint? Why?

THINKING CRITICALLY ABOUT PURPOSE

4. If Weber's family isn't going to discuss this incident, why do you think she writes about it and publishes it in the newspaper?

5. What do you think Weber hopes her essay will do to her readers? Does this essay work for you?

THINKING CRITICALLY ABOUT AUDIENCE

6. Do you think this essay would interest only Christians or the gay community? Who is she trying to talk to with her essay? Prove your answer with clues from the text.

7. Do you think she had other readers in mind as well? What aspects of the essay make you think that the writer had other readers in mind?

THINKING CRITICALLY ABOUT PERSPECTIVE

8. How would this essay change if Weber was writing about something she read in the newspaper instead of something that had happened in her life?

9. How does Weber feel about what she's explaining? Support your answer with her essay.

LEARNING FROM YOUR PEERS

Learning how to explain something without leaving out important details is a skill that most people need to improve. For students in college, it is essential. In papers and tests, you are often asked to explain the causes of a war or economic depression, how a chemical process works, or why a certain person was elected to office. For insight into one person's experience with an explaining essay, we are going to follow the writing activities of a student named Ramsey Paul.

Ramsey's Writing Assignment: Explaining

This is the topic Ramsey's instructor assigned:

All of us can point to experiences in our lives that have changed our thinking in some way. Maybe we lost a home or possessions as a result of a fire or tornado or earthquake; maybe we were robbed or mugged; maybe someone helped us when we desperately needed help; maybe an argument with a friend taught us to look at another person's point of view more closely; maybe working in a nursing home helped us feel more sympathetic toward people who need help on a daily basis; maybe we or those close to us were injured in an automobile accident; maybe the experience of waiting on customers in a restaurant has made us more generous in the tips we leave to others who wait on us. Write an essay that explains how a single incident changed your thinking and/or behaviour.

Ramsey wrote the essay and encountered problems as he wrote using the methodology outlined in Chapter One: thinking, planning, developing, organizing, drafting, revising, and editing.

Thinking

Ramsey's first problem was that he had no idea what he wanted to write about. Fortunately, the entire class was spending some time to help generate essay ideas. Ramsey's writing group was given some time to talk about possible topics during class. At first no one had any essay ideas, but some students decided to make lists of five major events in their lives. They passed the lists around their circle, asking each member of the group to point out the two most interesting topics and then ask one question about each of those topics.

Ramsey's list looked like this:

1. High school graduation.
2. Got driver's licence.
3. Had car accident.
4. House burned down.
5. Broke leg in football game.

The group passed their list of five events to each other and wrote questions about each other's list items. Ramsey's group members added several comments and questions to his list:

1. High school graduation.

    What changed your thinking at graduation?

    Did you think about adult responsibilities?

2. Got driver's licence.

3. Had car accident.

   What happened?

   Was it your fault?

   This must have been scary.

   Did anyone get injured or die?

   Was your car totaled?

4. House burned down.

   I've never known anyone whose house burned down.

   Did your parents build it back in the same place?

   Did all of your belongings burn up in the fire?

   If you lost things, is there one thing that you would like to get back?

   I was in a tornado once, and I still remember how awful it was.

   Were you in the house when it started burning?

5. Broke leg in football game.

   How bad was the break?

   How did it happen?

When Ramsey looked at the list, he saw that most of the comments and questions were about the fire. Now he had a topic.

Ramsey still didn't really know what he wanted to say about the fire. That night he began to think about the fire, and he decided to do some freewriting about the experience. He replayed his experience in his thoughts, reliving it again. He remembered his heart beating and the sour smell of the smoke as the fire hoses doused the flames. He found himself not wanting to dwell on the experience or the things he lost. He wrote down as much as he could until he felt tired. Then, he headed to bed.

Planning

As soon as Ramsey settled into bed, he realized in a flash what he wanted to focus on in his essay—his quilt. It was one of the best things that came out of the fire. The quilt reminded him of their kind neighbour, Mrs. Wilson. She let his whole family stay with her. As he drifted off to sleep, he began making a mental list of all the good things that happened as a result of the fire.

Developing

The next morning after breakfast, Ramsey sat at his desk with a hot cup of coffee and tried to remember the mental list he made as he fell asleep the night before:

1. The sight of the house in flames, the police car, the fire trucks.
2. Talking to my mother. Seeing the dog.
3. Knowing immediately that the fire was bad.
4. Mrs. Wilson coming out of nowhere and inviting us to her house.
5. Being in a daze, sleeping in a strange house, having nightmares.
6. Grabbing on to the quilt to help me sleep. Because I thought I was too old to go looking for my mom and dad in the night.
7. Going home again.
8. Taking the quilt with me.

He also decided to list what he did not want to include:

1. The sadness that I still feel when I think of my baseball-card and comic-book collections.
2. The fear every time I smell smoke and don't know where it's coming from.
3. I still wake up 20 times every night to make sure everything is okay.

Organizing

Ramsey decided to start his essay with the most dramatic scene—the house on fire. He thought most of his readers would want to know how he felt when he realized his house was on fire and how the fire has affected him. He looked at the list of things he wanted to talk about and added a few more details.

1. The sight of the house in flames.
2. The police car.
3. The fire trucks.
4. Smoke coming out the kitchen window.
5. SLOW MOTION.
6. Talking to my mother.
7. Seeing the dog.
8. The dog shaking and whimpering.
9. Mom's hands over her eyes.
10. Knowing immediately that the fire was bad.
11. Being glad no one was hurt.
12. Saying thank goodness, thank goodness, over and over again.
13. Mrs. Wilson coming out of nowhere and inviting us to her house.
14. How huge that house seemed.

15. Being in a daze.

16. Sleeping in a strange house.

17. Having nightmares.

18. Waking up all night.

19. Grabbing on to the quilt to help me sleep.

20. Because I thought I was too old to go looking for my mom and dad in the night.

21. Going home again.

22. Hating to leave the quilt.

23. Taking the quilt with me.

24. Glad to be home again.

Drafting

Now Ramsey had enough ideas to begin writing. He spent some time thinking, remembering, planning, developing, and organizing his essay. He wasn't worried about spelling and punctuation. He knew he could fix that later. Here is Ramsey's first draft.

Ramsey's Essay: First Draft

Main idea: Although the fire in my house was the most horrible experience in my life, a few good things resulted from it.

When I was in Ms. Temple's sixth grade class, I came home from school one day to find fire engines in front of my house, which was the third one from the corner, and smoke pouring out of the kitchen window. There was a police car, and I could see my mom and my dog. Sitting in the back of the car. My mom was holding one hand over her mouth and the dog with her other hand I couldn't look at the house. I just ran to my mom. Like it was slow motion. It seemed like it took forever. To get to the police car. When she saw me, she put her arm around me. Kept hugging the dog with her other arm. The dog was shaking and whining. In a sad, quiet way.

Mom told me everyone was okay, no one else was at home. She said I might not have all my toys and stuff when I go in there. She said the fire had a pretty good start when she got home from work it was an electrical fire. Electrical problems cause a lot of fires. Anyway, she looked at me and told me that my bed and my toys might be ruined. I told her I knew that. I was just happy that everyone was okay, especially her and the dog.

When the fire was put out, the neighbours all said we could come and sleep at their houses. One lady had a big house and lots of beds. Mrs. Wilson, who wore a big smile and a long apron. She said we could stay there and watch our house until it was fixed. Houses always get broken into when they are being worked on. My parents were glad about that.

I had a nice, soft bed in that house, my favourite thing there was a special quilt. Something I still have. It belonged to the lady, Mrs. Wilson she let us all go up in her attic to pick out blankets and sheets and pillows for our beds. The quilt was buried on the bottom. I picked out this quilt, which someone had probably pieced together a long time ago, because it was very soft. When I went to sleep. I could put my hands through a worn spot in the lining. It kept my hands warm and made me feel good. If I woke up with a nightmare. I could get a handful of the stuffing and hang on to it. After a bad experience, all children need something like a quilt to comfort them.

One day when I came home from school, my mom said to me, "Guess what. It's time to move back home again." I was really glad, and school was almost over for the year too. The house was almost like new. But I didn't know what to do about the quilt. I wanted to take it home with me, and Mrs. Wilson was really nice, but I was scared to ask her about the quilt. I just packed up my clothes and stood by the bedroom door. My mom said to fold all the bedding and put it on a pile on the bed it wasn't ours. Then Mrs. Wilson came upstairs. I said, "Thank you for letting us stay here. You were very kind." I really was happy to go home. I turned around to take my suitcase down the stairs. The stairs were steep. There was Mrs. Wilson, smiling. She said, "Here. I think you forgot your quilt." I said, "Oh no, it belongs to you."

She said, "I don't remember it at all. It must be yours." "Thank you," I said again. I suddenly remembered I had a loose tooth. I smiled and went home with the quilt tucked under my arm. When I got home, I gave the quilt a big hug before I spread it across my bed.

The house fire was scary. I am glad no one was hurt. But the most important thing I learned was that sharing with people is important, especially when they are a little scared or a little sad. I regret that I never told Mrs. Wilson how very much that quilt meant to me, the quilt gives me a warm feeling each time I see it and feel its soft fabric. Even now, sometimes I wake up with a nightmare. Then I grab ahold of that quilt and hang on tight.

Revising

Ramsey felt good about his first draft. As he put his innermost feelings and thoughts about this tragic time in his life on paper, he was surprised it was not as painful as he imagined. Instead, writing about these events gave him a sense of relief. He knew he still had to revise his work.

At this point in the term, Ramsey's instructor had asked the class to focus on **unity** and **support** in their writing. If the student writers make sure now that their work is unified and supported with details and examples, they can build on this ability as their writing gets more and more complex.

Ramsey reviewed the Focus on Sentences section at the end of this chapter. The instructor wanted the students to build more complex sentences, and to concentrate on the relationship of ideas to one another.

Ramsey learned that only ideas related to each other can be linked together in sentences. So Ramsey took his essay apart sentence by sentence, looking for related ideas he could join together into longer sentences. He found problems in both areas and set out to improve each sentence to make a stronger essay.

 ## COLLABORATIVE WORK

PEER GROUP ACTIVITY

After you have read the Focus on Sentences section, turn to Ramsey's first draft (p. 87) and complete the following tasks in small groups:

A. Put in brackets any information that is not related to the main idea in its sentence.

B. Underline the portions of Ramsey's sentences that your group believes are not adequately supported.

Compare the brackets and underlining your group recorded with those your instructor will show you. Where do your marks differ from your instructor's? What do you need to review before writing your own essay?

CLASS ACTIVITY

As an entire class, look at the underlined portions of Ramsey's revised draft (p. 90) to see how he changed each sentence.

A. Did you identify the revision problems that Ramsey corrected?

B. Do you think his changes are good ones? Discuss his changes.

Editing

After Ramsey built stronger sentences, he needed to do some final proofreading and editing before handing in his essay. The instructor helped the students see the importance of choosing strong, clear verbs for each sentence. So Ramsey shifted his focus from joining sentences together to strengthening his verbs. He read the Focus on Paragraphs section in this chapter. He learned how to recognize a verb and then he learned how to choose stronger verbs.

Ramsey's Revised Essay ....

The Fire Quilt

When I was in Ms. Temple's sixth grade ~~class~~, I came home from school one day to find fire engines in front of my house, which was the third one from the corner, and smoke pouring out of the kitchen window. There was a police car, and I could see my mom and my ~~dog. Sitting~~dog sitting in the back of the car. My mom was holding one hand over her mouth and the dog with her other hand<u>.</u> I couldn't look at the house <u>because I was afraid that I might see one of my family still inside.</u> I just ran to my mom. ~~Like it was slow motion. It seemed like it took forever. To got to the police car.~~ When she saw me, she put her arm around me. Kept hugging the dog with her other arm. The dog was shaking and ~~whining. In~~whining in a sad, quiet way.

Mom told me everyone was ~~okay, no~~okay. No one else was at home. She said I might not have all my toys and stuff when I go in there. She said the <u>electrical</u> fire had a pretty good start when she got home from work ~~it was an electrical fire~~. Electrical problems cause a lot of fires. <u>50 percent of the fires in our area.</u> Anyway, she looked at me and told me that my bed and my toys might be ruined. I told her I knew that. I was just happy that everyone was okay~~, especially her and the dog~~.

When the fire was put out, the neighbors all said we could come and sleep at their houses. ~~One lady had a big house and lots of beds.~~<u>Our next-door neighbor, Mrs. Wilson, lived alone in a five-bedroom house that had enough beds for all seven of my family.</u> Mrs. Wilson, who wore a big smile and a long apron. She said we could stay there and watch our house until it was fixed. ~~Houses always get broken into when they are being worked~~<u>We had a place to stay.</u> ~~on. My parents were glad about that.~~

I had a nice, soft bed in that ~~house, my~~<u>house. My</u> favorite thing there was a special ~~quilt. Something~~<u>quilt, Something</u>something I still have. It belonged to the lady, Mrs. ~~Wilson~~ <u>she</u>Wilson. <u>When we arrived, she</u> let us all go up in her attic to pick out blankets and sheets and pillows for our beds.~~The quilt was buried on the bottom.~~ I picked out this quilt, which someone had~~probably~~ pieced together a long time ago, because it ~~was very soft. When I went to sleep. I could put my hands through a worn spot in the lining. It kept my hands warm and made me feel good.~~<u>somehow reminded me of my old house.</u> If I woke up with a nightmare. I could ~~get a handful of the stuffing and hang on to it. After a bad experience, all children need something~~<u>wrap myself up in the blanket and it made me feel safe.</u>

~~like a quilt to comfort them.~~

One day when I came home from school, my mom said to me, "Guess what. It's time to move back home again." I was ~~really glad, and school was almost over for the year too.~~<u>glad, to move back into our own house with our own things and have our own routine again.</u> The house was almost like new. <u>My room was painted and all the furniture had been cleaned or replaced.</u> But I didn't know what to do about the ~~quilt.~~quilt because I wanted to take it home with~~me, and Mrs. Wilson was really nice, but~~me. I was scared to ask ~~her~~Mrs. Wilson about the quilt. I ~~just packed~~remember packing up my clothes and ~~stood~~standing by the bedroom door. ~~My mom said to fold~~I had folded all the bedding and put it on a pile on the ~~bed it wasn't ours. Then~~bed. When Mrs. Wilson came upstairs. I said, "Thank you for letting us stay here. You were very kind." ~~I really was happy to go home. I~~ turned around to take my suitcase down the stairs.~~The stairs were steep.~~ There was Mrs. Wilson, ~~smiling.~~smiling.

She said, ~~"Here. I think you~~"You forgot your quilt."

~~I said, "Oh no,~~"But, it belongs to ~~you."~~you," I said. She said, "I don't remember it at all. It must be yours."

"Thank you," I ~~said again. I suddenly remembered I had a loose~~replied.

~~tooth.~~I smiled and went home with the quilt tucked under my arm. When I got home, I gave the quilt a big hug before I spread it across my bed.

The house fire was ~~scary. I am glad no one was hurt. But~~a frightening experience for a boy in grade six. And, the most important thing I learned was that sharing with ~~people is important, especially when they are a little scared or a little sad. I regret that I never told Mrs. Wilson how very much that quilt meant to me,~~people, the way Mrs. Wilson shared with me, can help people recover from dark moments of their lives. It sounds a little silly to say that a blanket makes a grown man feel good, but the quilt gives me a warm feeling each time I see ~~it~~ it. It's come to mean everything I've ever loved about my home

~~and feel its soft fabric. Even now, sometimes I wake up with a nightmare. Then I grab ahold of that quilt and hang on tight.~~

COLLABORATIVE WORK

PRACTISE OUTLINING

Spend time as a class thinking, planning, developing, and organizing a potential explaining essay.

1. Spend about 10 minutes sharing a few ideas.
2. Once three or four have been suggested, choose one or two for the subject of a potential essay. What makes one idea better than another idea? What are we looking for?
3. Decide on the audience and the purpose.
4. Brainstorm this explaining topic's possible significance to the audience. Have someone write ideas on the overhead or blackboard.
5. Develop the ideas to give a sense of what a person could write if he/she were to write this essay.
6. Organize the ideas so they appear in the best order for the best effect.

Could you write this essay? How long would it take you to finish this essay? How long did it take you?

WRITING YOUR OWN EXPLAINING ESSAY

So far you have seen a professional writer and a fellow student at work trying to explain an experience or process they felt was worth talking about. As you read the published essay and followed the writing process of another student from first to final draft, you absorbed ideas and ways of giving those ideas a form of their own. These reading and writing activities have prepared you to write your own essay explaining an experience or process that is meaningful to you.

What Have You Discovered?

Before you begin your own writing task, let's review what you have learned in this chapter so far:

- Explaining falls into two categories: (1) justifying, and (2) explaining how something works.
- There are two ways to explain how something works: process description, or procedure.

- Explaining in writing is more difficult than explaining in speech because you cannot get immediate feedback from readers about the clarity of your message.

- To present your explanation effectively, organize your ideas carefully.

- To help you shape your essay, learn as much as possible about your readers.

- Before you write a draft, decide on a perspective toward your subject.

- After you write a draft, revise your essay for meaning and organization.

- After you revise your essay, edit its grammar, usage, and sentence structure.

Your Writing Topic

Choose one of the following topics for your explaining essay:

1. Think about something you enjoy—a sport, a hobby, a job, a project—and write an essay explaining this activity so completely and precisely that your reader could actually do the activity.

2. Explain an incident that made you appreciate your own life and circumstances more deeply. This event may have been something that happened to you personally, an event in the news, or portions of a novel or film that have changed your perspective. Explain the incident and your response to it so your classmates can understand its impact on your life.

3. Have you ever taken on a project or a job that required organization and specific skills? You may have decorated a room, planted a garden, or constructed a model ship or airplane. You may have had a job that required you to learn a special method of doing things. Write an essay in which you explain the methods and skills you learned in completing your project. Your reader won't have to do what you're suggesting. He or she will only need to understand it. (Some examples of what not to do might help make your point with your readers.)

4. Create your own explaining topic (with the assistance of your instructor), and write a response to it.

When you have selected one of these topics, begin your writing process in the same way Ramsey did. (You may find his experience helpful in giving you ideas.) This time your purpose is to write your own explaining essay. If some tasks occur out of order, that adjustment is probably part of your personal writing process. Follow your instincts, and mold your own writing process. But make sure you've worked through all the stages by the time you complete your final draft.

Organizing Sentences In Paragraphs

Checklist For Organizing Paragraphs

✓ Are the sentences in your paragraphs organized in an effective way: general-to-specific order, specific-to-general order, time order, space order, or movement from one extreme to another?

✓ Do you use a combination of paragraph organization methods when appropriate?

When you've finished doing something for the first time, you often have an idea of how you could have done it better. You look back on it and discover you could have been more efficient or just had more fun. Writing is all about looking back and improving. This section is all about organizational patterns you can use to look back at paragraphs you've already written to see if you can make them stronger.

The sentences in successful paragraphs tend to be organized in a few recurring patterns. The most common ways of organizing paragraphs are (1) general-to-specific order, (2) specific-to-general order, (3) time order (or reverse time order), (4) space order, and (5) movement from one extreme to another.

General-to-Specific Order

General-to-specific order will probably be the most useful method of organization. Paragraphs arranged in this way usually begin with a general statement, then move to specific details to develop that statement.

The general-to-specific order works well if your readers know the topic well and will agree with most of what you say. Plus, it promotes clear writing because it announces what the paragraph is about before it begins.

The following paragraph from Edna Weber's essay, "They Know Not What They Do" uses a general-to-specific organization to describe what she means when she says "Kenny was 'different'":

> But there were other ways in which Kenny was "different" from his brothers: Larry, Bruce, and Brian. He was not athletic; he was not extraordinarily handsome; nor did he make friends easily, especially girlfriends. I mentioned this once to one of his high-school home-room teachers. He said not to worry, that it was because all of the students Ken attended classes with were, to him, "big kids."

Exercise P4-1

1. *Organize the following sentences to reflect the pattern we've just talked about.*

Travis had been fighting with his sister about some missing money, and he became enraged and pushed her down the stairs. He knew that he had given up hope of having a normal life, so he gave himself excuses for treating others in what he now sees as inexcusable ways. For example, he kept borrowing money from family members and never paid any of it back. When they stopped loaning him money, he started stealing from them. He said he was unable to go anywhere else and steal to support his habits because his getaway vehicle was too easy to identify. He said he had never heard of any paraplegic bank robbers. His mother told him that she did not want another crippled child, so he had to learn to resolve his differences with his sister without resorting to violence.

Do the changes you've made improve the paragraph? How can you tell?

2. *Find another example of a general-to-specific paragraph in this book.*

Specific-to-General Order

When you reverse the first method of organization, you arrange your paragraph so that it proceeds from specific statements to a general one. If you feel a topic may be hard for your audience to understand or difficult for readers to agree with, you may choose to use specific-to-general order. Or, if you want to heighten your reader's curiosity, then this organization helps. This kind of paragraph is often used as an introductory paragraph.

The following paragraph from Ezra Long's essay "Why I am a Luddite" (the student essay in Chapter Six), describes a scene, beginning with details and ending with a general statement:

A small group of men bask in the light of a weaving machine on fire. They're not trying to save the machine, they are enjoying watching it burn. They are happy because for a moment, they have beaten back the effects of technology. This is revenge. Their employer had a choice between paying labourers or buying a machine. The employer chose the machine.

Exercise P4-2

1. *Organize the following sentences to reflect the pattern we've just talked about.*

Finally, a combination of his mother's tough love and an honest look at his own behaviour convinced Travis that he had to change his life. He is a drug and alcohol counselor at a local rehabilitation clinic. He started drinking at the age of 15 and soon found himself a paraplegic after jumping off a diving board into the deep end of an empty swimming pool. "That ended one night of drinking," he said, but it led to many more nights and days trying to escape reality by using and abusing drugs and alcohol. "You might say that I dove right into my career," said Travis Lawrence.

Do the changes you've made improve the paragraph? How can you tell?

2. *Find another example of a specific-to-general paragraph in this book.*

Time Order

Time order (also called chronological order) is a third way to organize the material in your paragraphs.

Time order makes the most sense if you're relating a story or an event. You probably used this method in your recalling essay, which discussed a past experience; you may have also used it in your explaining essay if you described a process or a procedure.

In paragraphs arranged according to a time sequence, words that express time indicate to your reader the order in which events occurred or the order in which they should be performed.

The following paragraph, taken from Edna Weber's essay "They Know Not What They Do," is organized according to time:

> On the evening of Easter Sunday, Bruce and I were watching television in the living room, and his girlfriend Susan was in the kitchen cleaning up dishes. Suddenly, she came into the living room and said, "Mrs. Weber, you must have left a light on in your garage." Well, I knew there had been no one in that garage for over a week; so I told Bruce to go out and see if we had a prowler on the place.

Exercise P4-3

1. *Organize the following sentences to reflect the pattern we've just talked about.*

> He realized that his anger at his paralysis was being misdirected, and he decided to get some counseling. That very night he looked at himself honestly for the first time. For years, everybody had been trying to get him to wise up. Finally, he, too, saw that he was not going anywhere. After thinking about himself, he then realized how important his family was and how badly he had treated them.

Do the changes you've made improve the paragraph? How can you tell?

2. *Find another example of a time-ordered paragraph in this book.*

Space Order

Space order, or organizing details in a paragraph using their relationship to each other in space, helps you describe how something looks—an outfit, a room, or a trip you took to Ontario or B.C. The following paragraph is taken from Ramsey's essay, "The Fire Quilt," in this chapter:

> When I was in Ms. Temple's sixth grade class, I came home from school one day to find fire engines in front of my house, which was the third one from the corner, and smoke pouring out of the kitchen window. There was a police car, and I could see my mom and my dog. Sitting in the back of the car. My mom was holding one hand over her mouth and the dog with her other hand.

Here's another paragraph that orders the information around space:

> My can of Pepsi sits on the same kitchen table where I do most of my writing. On my left is the oven clock that I have to avoid eye contact with if I want to keep my ideas flowing. Straight ahead of where I am sitting at the table is a wall with some pictures on it of various family events; these are great to stare at when I need new ideas or inspiration for whatever I am writing. The pictures bring back lots of memories for me to draw from. To my right is the door to the living room and the rest of the house. I do my best writing when I can hear but not talk to people in the house. Behind me is the refrigerator where I go for snacks when I am having serious writer's blocks. I don't know why, but I always walk to the refrigerator when I am really stuck on a paper. Then I'm always convinced some junk food will get me through the temporary crisis.

Exercise P4-4

1. *Write a paragraph about what you see around you right now. You might want to organize it in a similar way to the previous sample paragraph.*

2. *Find another example of a time-ordered paragraph in this book.*

Movement From One Extreme To Another

Another method of organizing details in a paragraph, movement from one extreme to another, can follow any line of reasoning that makes sense of the details you have chosen for your essay. You might explain how to choose a dog, for example, by moving from most important to least important considerations. For a city apartment, the most important feature would be the dog's size and exercise needs. (For instance, a Dalmation needs running space while a Lhasa Apso is quite content in a 10-by-12-foot room.) Least important to an apartment dweller would be a dog's hunting ability or usefulness in herding sheep. You can also reverse the order and begin with the least important; this is a good method to use in persuasive writing because readers often remember best the information they read last.

The following paragraph is from Sharmen Sorsdahl's essay "Cultures," in Chapter Five:

> Society believes it is moving away from the skinny model stereotype, and is becoming more accepting. Unfortunately Cathy says, "if they were to pick up a magazine, it will always feature a skinny model or celebrity."

Exercise P4-5

1. *Organize the following sentences to reflect the pattern we've just talked about.*

    That very night he looked at himself honestly for the first time. He along with his mom was able to find a clinic that let him stay for a month and learn all about the disease of alcoholism and how to overcome it. Most of the month's stay was an eye-opening experience. After thinking about himself, he then realized how important his family was and how badly he had treated them. He realized that his anger at his paralysis was being misdirected, and he decided to get some counseling. One of the most important things he learned was that he was responsible for his own moods and that "getting high" was almost inevitably followed by "getting low." He told me, "The problem with drinking is it is like a roller-coaster ride. You can only go so high, and then you come crashing down. After being through so many highs and lows, I was ready for some level ground." For years, everybody had been trying to get him to wise up. Finally, he, too, saw that he was not going anywhere.

Do the changes you've made improve the paragraph? How can you tell?

2. *Find another example of a movement-between-extremes paragraph in this book.*

 ## COLLABORATIVE WORK

After writing a draft of your own explaining essay, exchange papers with a classmate and do the following tasks:

A. Look at each paragraph and decide whether it is organized in a logical way or could be improved through another method of organization.

B. Mark the paragraphs that need revising and make suggestions for new methods of organization in the margin.

Then return the paper to its writer and use the information in this section to revise your draft.

Understanding And Identifying Verbs

Checklist For Editing Verbs

✓ Are verbs in their correct forms?
✓ Are verbs in their correct tenses, changing to show differences in time?
✓ Are nouns used correctly according to case?
✓ Are adjectives close to the words they modify?
✓ Are comparative adjective forms used correctly?
✓ Are adverbs located near the words they modify?
✓ Are comparative adverb forms used correctly?

If you want to improve your writing, you need to understand verbs. Some writing instructors say that the most important part of the sentence is the verb: it is the best chance you have to make an interesting sentence. Every other word in the sentence depends on it in some way. Writers build sentences around verbs, just as you build an outfit around a flashy shirt or a favourite pair of jeans.

Most writers and instructors agree that the chances of making errors with verbs are higher than with almost any other part of a sentence. If you want to look like you know what you're doing, you need to understand verbs.

You'll discover as you work through this section that you already know a lot about verbs. This section will help you understand and clarify what you already know.

What Verbs Do

Verbs are important for several reasons. First, every complete sentence must have a verb. Second, verbs communicate the action of the sentence. Verbs are the life, the muscle, the fizz of the sentence. Third, verbs tell time. They tell the reader when something happened. The verb tells the reader that something happened in the past, something is happening at the moment, or something is going to happen.

Frank baked the beans. (Past)

Frank is baking the beans. (Present)

Frank will bake the beans. (Future)

In each of these sentences you have an idea of when Frank bakes the beans because of the verbs.

What Verbs Can Talk About

Every sentence has at least one verb. The verb can communicate one of two kinds of information. It can communicate an action—something that is happening. The verb tells the reader what's going on in the sentence. Or, if there's no real action in the sentence, the verb describes what someone or something is like: something about its existence, condition, or appearance. These kinds of verbs communicate a "state of being."

Action Verbs	The Player raced down the court.
	The government filed the documents.
State of being—existence	I am. (A verb can tell us that something or someone exists.)
State of being—condition	I feel happy. (The verb tells us the condition of a person or thing.)
State of being—appearance	I look happy. (A verb can report on the appearance of a person or thing.)

Kinds of Verbs

All verbs fall into one of two categories: **action** verbs or **linking** verbs.

Action Verbs

Action verbs are like the verb in the first sentence of the previous examples: *raced* is an action verb. Action verbs express what something or someone does, has done, or will do. Writers often strive to use action verbs because these words help their writing become lively and descriptive.

Linking Verbs

Verbs like *is*, *feel*, and *looks* are linking verbs. These verbs don't express action. Instead they express states of being—information about a person or thing's existence, condition, or appearance—describing or renaming the verb's subject. Linking verbs also serve as connectors, joining words that come before and after them.

The scenery was gorgeous and green.

Her name is Amy.

The verb in the first example, *was*, serves as a bridge between the subject *scenery* and *gorgeous*. The verb helps the sentence report on the "state of being" of the scenery. In the second example, the linking verb *is* connects the subject *name* with the word *Amy*, a word that restates the subject.

Most linking verbs are forms of the verb *be*: be, being, been, am, is, are, was, and were. Other verbs like *appear*, *become*, *feel*, *grow*, *look*, *seem*, *smell*, *sound*, and *taste* can also function as linking verbs.

Here's a partial list of some of the most common linking (helping) verbs:

Be	Do	Have	Can	Shall
Am	Does	Has	Could	Should
Is	Did	Had	May	Will
Are			Might	Would
Was			Must	
Were				

How To Identify Verbs

The first step in understanding verbs is being able to identify them.

The verb is part of the predicate. You already know the first step in identifying a verb: find the predicate (p. 36).

Locate The Action

There are two questions you can use to help you find the verb. First, find the subject of the sentence (p. 36) and ask yourself this question: what is the subject doing? If you can point to the word or words that answer this question, you're probably pointing to the verb.

Change The Verb Tense

To make sure you have the verb, ask yourself another question: do these words tell me when the event occurred: past, present, or future? The verb is the only part of the sentence that controls when the action happened. We call the verb's ability to indicate time *tense*. Since the verbs are the only words that use a tense, you can change the tense of the sentence by changing the verbs.

Azmina honked her horn at the man.

The president said she could not attend Wednesday's meeting because she was sick.

Honked and *said* are the main verbs of the sentences. Both verbs tell you the action, and also communicate when the action occurred. To make sure, we'll rewrite the first sentence and change the event from the past to the present.

Azmina honked her horn at the man.

Azmina **honks** her horn at the man.

Honked is the word we had to change to change the tense. Therefore, *honked* is the verb.

Linking verbs are harder to spot. The first question won't work. Use this second question (technique) to help you locate the verb. The second question, though, will help you identify the verb because a linking verb, though not a strong action, always helps to tell you when the event occurred.

> Jurgen's voice is soothing and mellow.
>
> Vince is taking a course at the college.

Is and *is taking* are the verbs in these sentences. To be sure, let's try rewriting these sentences and see which words we have to change.

> Jurgen's voice **is** soothing and mellow.
>
> Jurgen's voice **was** soothing and mellow.
>
> Vince **is taking** a course at the college.
>
> Vince **is going to take** a course at the college.

In both sentences we end up having to change some words to change when the event occurred. The word we have to change in the original sentence is the verb.

Exercise S4-1

In the following sentences from "The Sissy" by Tobias Wolff, underline all the verbs. Then label each verb as action or linking.

1. Arthur was testy with me.
2. I liked his acid wit and the wild stories he told and his apparent indifference to what other people thought of him.
3. Arthur had made other such comments.
4. We lay next to each other, gasping strenuously.
5. The other two boys were excited, restless, twitching with the blows they'd imagined striking.

Exercise S4-2

In the following sentences underline all the verbs. Then label each as action or linking. Finally, label each action verb as transitive or intransitive.

1. As soon as Brian's parents left for the party on Saturday night, we set out on the great fishing expedition.
2. Then we headed for the lake, our getaway for the weekend.
3. We felt ecstatic.
4. The first sign of trouble came almost immediately.
5. All of our best friends suddenly seemed distant.

Exercise S4-3

Supply verbs for the blanks in the following paragraph. Label each verb as an action or linking verb.

Last weekend we _____ to go Christmas shopping at a nearby outlet mall.

Setting our clock for 6 a.m., we _____ out of bed and got ready in a flash. We

_____ on the road within an hour. Before we got out of the city limits, Nancy

_____ that she had to go to the bathroom and Bobby _____ hungry.

So we _____ at the first convenience store we saw. While Bobby and Nancy

were inside the store, I _____ steam coming from under the hood of my car.

I _____ it out and _____ water leaking from the radiator. We all

_____ into the car and wisely decided to cancel our trip.

Exercise S4-4

Write sentences using the following words as verbs. Label these verbs action or linking verbs.

1. had been going
2. chuckled
3. remained
4. become
5. whispers

Words That Look Like Verbs But Aren't

Often, you'll find words that look like verbs, but aren't. They seem to be the action of the sentence, but they're not.

    I hope to swim today.

    Carol likes drinking coffee inside on rainy days.

In these sentences, *swim* and *drinking coffee* are not verbs. You can tell they're not because they don't answer the first question properly. What is the subject of the sentence doing? In the first sentence the subject is *I* and *I* is hoping. So, the verb is *hope*. In the second sentence, the subject is Carol and Carol is liking. *Likes*, then, is the verb (*likes* is a linking verb, so it doesn't look as much like an action.)

The second question can help you, too. Verbs give you a sense of when the action occurred. Nouns, when they name an activity, can sound like verbs except they won't clarify when the action is occurring: they won't communicate a sense of time. If you rewrite the sentences to change the time of the sentence, you can see the verb:

I **hope** to swim today.

I **hoped** to swim today.

Carol **likes** drinking coffee inside on rainy days.

Carol **liked** drinking coffee inside on rainy days.

See if you can spot the difference between nouns and verbs in these sentences:

Stating an action (a verb)	Naming an activity (a noun)
Dave jogs every day.	Dave thinks jogging is fun.
Statistics Canada reports on crime, now.	Statistics Canada believes reporting is important.

Exercise S4-5

Find the verbs in the following sentences:

1. I came home from school one day to find fire engines in front of my house, which was the third one from the corner.

2. There was a police car.

3. My mom was holding one hand over her mouth and the dog with her other hand.

4. I couldn't look at the house because I was afraid that I might see one of my family still inside.

5. I just ran to my mom.

6. When she saw me, she put her arm around me.

Exercise S4-6

Take a look at the following paragraph. First, underline the verbs in each sentence. Mark each verb as an action verb or a linking verb.

I had a nice, soft bed in that house. My favourite thing there was a special quilt, something I still have. It belonged to the lady, Mrs. Wilson. She let us all go up in her attic to pick out blankets and sheets and pillows for our beds. The quilt was buried on the bottom. I picked out this quilt, which someone had probably pieced together a long time ago, because it was very soft. When I went to sleep I could put my hands through a worn spot in the lining. It kept my hands warm and made me feel good. If I woke up with a nightmare, I could get a handful of the stuffing and hang on to it. After a bad experience, many children need something like a quilt to comfort them.

Exercise S4-7

Circle the verbs in paragraphs 12 and 13 of Edna Weber's essay (p. 82). Label each verb as an action verb or a linking verb.

How To Identify Verb Phrases

Often verbs work together in groups of words called "verb phrases." Verb phrases may consist of as few as two words or as many as four. One of the words is called the main verb while the other words are called auxiliary or helping verbs. The helping verbs always come first in the phrase. Look at these examples:

We **were excited** about the weekend.

The verb in this example is two words: *were* and *excited*. These two words form the verb of the sentence—a verb phrase.

Check the list of helping/linking verbs on page 102. Note that the verbs in the first three columns—other than the word "be"—can function by themselves as main verbs; they do not necessarily require helpers.

Words That Aren't Part Of The Verb Phrase

Negatives Aren't Part Of The Verb

Words like *not* and *never* are called **negatives**, and they are not part of the verb or verb phrase, even though they appear right in the middle of the verb phrase:

I **am** *not* **going** to the Stampede without my boots.

The word *not* in the previous sentence is not part of the verb. One easy way to tell is to rewrite the sentence changing its tense.

I **did** *not* **go** to the Stampede without my boots.

When the verb phrase changes to the past tense, the word *not* doesn't change with it. That means *not* is not a verb or a part of the verb.

Adverbs Aren't Part Of The Verb

Many of the words that end in –ly are adverbs. Like negatives, adverbs sometimes appear in the middle of a verb phrase, but they're not a part of the verb:

Robert **could** *hardly* **catch** his breath after running the marathon.

The word *hardly* in this sentence is an adverb, so it is not a part of the verb. Again, if we rewrite the sentence and change the tense, the adverb doesn't change, so it isn't a part of the verb:

Robert **will** *hardly* catch his breath after running the marathon.

Question Sentences Sometimes Interrupt The Verb

Sometimes question sentences interrupt the verb phrase with other words. To identify the verb phrase, rewrite the question in statement form. Then it should be easier to isolate the verb phrase. Here's an example:

Will *Robert and Brian* be going fishing?
Robert and Brian will be going fishing.

The question has been rewritten as a statement, so the verb will be easier to locate.

Exercise S4-8

List each noun phrase and prepositional phrase in the first two paragraphs of Edna Weber's Essay "For They Know Not What They Do" (p. 81).

Exercise S4-9

Underline the verb phrases in paragraphs one through four of Ramsey's revised essay on pages 87–88.

Exercise S4-10

Complete the sentences in the following paragraph by making verbal phrases using the information supplied in parentheses.

Sang want _____ (sleep) because he had worked overtime yesterday

afternoon. But one of his roommates was cleaning the house, _____

(vacuum) and _____ (move) furniture around. Tony, Sang's roommate,

wanted everything _____ (look) nice because his parents were coming for a

visit. Tony didn't know what to do about the (batter) couch, _____

_____ (tear) to shreds by their cat Mr. Tigs. _____ (drag) himself out of

bed, Sang found an old bedspread (cover) the couch. _____ (fix) up the

couch was Sang's contribution to house cleaning before he went back to

bed, (dream) _____ of more peaceful days.

Exercise S4-11

Write original sentences using the following phrases.

1. remembered her first day of school
2. is sending out invitations for the party
3. has sunk in the river
4. will attend college and receive a degree
5. was energized by food and sleep

How To Identify Verb Forms

Verbs change their forms to show tense or time. Understanding the principal forms and tenses of verbs will help you communicate more successfully and your writing will become more confident overall.

The Four Verb Forms

Every verb in the English language can appear in four different forms: present, present participle, past, and past participle.

Present	I run.
Present Participle	I am running.
Past	I ran.
Past Participle	I had run.

The Present Or Base Form

The present or base form expresses action that occurs now, in the present: I run. We run. You run. They run. He, she, or it runs.

Here is an example of verbs in their present form:

Dr. Smith firmly *believes* that television programs *misinform* young children about people with dark skin or heavy accents.

The Present Participle Form

The present participle expresses action that continues in both the past and present. To make a past participle verb, simply add *-ing* to the present verb form.

Verb (in present form) + *-ing* = Past Participle
Run + ing = running

The present participle form cannot function alone in a sentence. A present participle must be paired with one or more linking or helping verbs to make the main verb in the sentence: I am running. We were running. You are running. They have been running. He, she, or it is running. (See p. 102 for a list of helping/linking verbs.) The following sentence uses a present participle and a helping or linking verb:

> Dr. Phyllis A. Smith, director of the Institute for Research on Social Problems in Ottawa, Ontario, *has been studying* children and their perceptions about people.

The Past Tense Form

The **past tense** and past participle forms both express action that has happened in the past. Regular verbs form the past tense and past participle forms by adding *-d* or *-ed*: lived, died, learned, moaned. However, irregular verbs form the past and past participles by changing their spellings entirely: run, ran; know, known; see, saw. Of course, past forms of verbs can function as main verbs, as this sentence shows:

> She *found* that children begin to notice differences in skin colour as early as six months old.

The Past Participle Form

Like present participles, past participles require helping verbs, forms of be and have, before they can function as the main verbs of sentences: I *have* run. We *had* run. You *were* known. They *were* seen. He, she, or it *is* known. The following sentence depends on a past participle and a helper as its main verb:

> One white girl *had decided* by the time she was four years old that blacks were "bad."

You can't rely on a rule to help you with irregular verbs: they vary widely between the past and past participle forms. You either have to know each irregular verb, and you probably know several, or you need to keep a reference chart handy so you can look each one up.

Exercise S4-12

Complete the following chart, providing the correct forms for these verbs:

Present	Present Participle	Past	Past Participle
			Sat
		Ate	
Drink			
	Covering		
			Called
Get			
	Becoming		
		Fought	
Drive			
See			

Exercise S4-13

Choose 10 verbs from the essay "For They Know Not What They Do" (p. 81) and make a chart like the one from the previous exercise, identifying the present form, present participle, past tense, and past participle of each verb.

Exercise S4-14

Fill in the blanks with the correct forms of the italicized verbs to make each sentence in the following paragraph complete.

Last summer I _____ (spend) a week with my great-aunt, who lives in the

Bugaboo Mountains in British Colombia. I had _____ (ride) a train for

16 hours, so I _____ (sleep) for 12 hours when I got to her house. I had

_____ (lie) down on an old four-poster bed with a down-filled mattress.

I _____ (dream) about lying in a field of daisies, but I _____ (wake)

up sneezing and chilled. My aunt _____ (make) me some chicken soup,

which I wolfed down as fast as I could get the spoon in my mouth. I hadn't

_____ (eat) since the night before, except for a pop and chips on the

train. Anyway, I _____ (feel) so sick. I just _____ (hang) my head

off the bed and prayed that I would get better. And I did.

Exercise S4-15

Write original sentences using the following forms of these verbs.

1. throw
2. prove
3. burst
4. lead
5. strive

Time And Tense

Verbs relate a sense of time to the reader. We call the general sense of when an action or a state of being occurs the verb's "tense." Writers write a verb in one of six tenses.

The Simple Tenses: Present, Past, And Future

The first three tenses, called the **simple tenses**, denote an action or state of being that occurs in the present, past, or future.

Present:	Inez *works* on her writing assignment every night.
Past:	Inez *worked* on her writing assignment last night.
Future:	Inez *will work* on her writing assignment tomorrow night.

The present tense refers to action that happens now or immediately, while the past tense denotes action that has already occurred. Finally, the future tense expresses action that has not yet been completed.

The Perfect Tenses: Present Perfect, Past Perfect, And Future Perfect

The other tenses are called the **perfect tenses**. They denote action completed by a certain time. The past participle form of the verb—plus certain helping verbs—goes into each of the perfect tenses, as these sentences illustrate:

Present Perfect:	Inez *has worked* on her essay all week.
Past Perfect:	Inez *had worked* on her essay for a week before she turned it in.
Future Perfect:	Tomorrow Inez *will have worked* on her essay for a week.

The present perfect tense refers to action that began in the past but continues or is completed in the present. The past perfect tense indicates action that both began and ended in the past. The future perfect tense expresses action that will be completed at some specific time in the future.

Exercise S4-16

Choose 10 verbs from the essay "For They Know Not What They Do" (p. 81) and complete the following chart. The verb need *is an example.*

Present	Past	Future
Need	Needed	Will need

Present Perfect	Past Perfect	Future Perfect
Has needed	Had needed	Will have needed

Exercise S4-17

List each verb in paragraphs four and five of the first draft of Ramsey's essay (p. 87), and label each one as present, past, or future tense.

Exercise S4-18

Supply a verb in the correct tense to complete each of the following sentences:

My mother and father _____ (encourage, past perfect) me to get involved in our community, but I always _____ (think, past) up an excuse. So this year my friend Carla and I _____ (decide, past) to participate in a local fundraising drive for homeless people. We rarely _____ (take, present) part in such events. But we _____ (feel, past perfect) that we should do something for our community. We just never _____ (take, past) the time. Anyway, we _____ (sign, past) up about a month before the walkathon. Within a week, Carla and I _____ (collect, past perfect) over $200 in pledges. By the day of the event, we _____ (gather, past perfect) almost $750 in pledges. We then _____ (walk, past) the entire six miles with our heads held high.

Exercise S4-19

Write sentences using the following verbs. Then identify each verb's tense.

1. will grow
2. rejected
3. will have sent
4. has notified
5. had applied

 ## COLLABORATIVE WORK

After you revise your explaining essay, exchange papers with a classmate and do the following tasks:

1. Check every sentence for a subject and a predicate. Circle sentences that are missing one or the other.
2. Look at the first paragraph and the last paragraph. Circle every verb and label the verb as a linking verb or an action verb.

REFLECT ON YOUR WRITING PROCESS

When you have completed your own essay, answer these four questions in your journal:

1. What was most difficult about this assignment?
2. What was easiest?
3. What did I learn about explaining by completing this assignment?
4. What did I learn about my own writing process—how I prepared to write, how I wrote the first draft, how I revised it, and how I edited it?

CHAPTER FIVE

Investigating
Reading and Writing for a Reason

The writer is both an eye-witness and an I-witness, the one to whom personal experience happens and the one who makes experience personal for others.

—MARGARET ATWOOD

LEARNING OUTCOMES

This chapter will help you:
- Investigate and report a topic in an essay format;
- Learn to develop several specific paragraph patterns; and,
- Recognize, develop, and punctuate clauses, interjections, and phrases.

Investigation may suggest detectives, secret government agents, or undercover spies. In reality, it is an everyday activity. We want to know who's moving into the house next door, what the weather will be like for the annual picnic, how changes in the educational system will affect us. We may go to the library to find the latest consumer information about a motorbike or computer that we want to buy. We look in the classified ads in the newspaper for jobs or bargains or pets. **Investigating** in writing involves gathering as much information about a person, place, event, or topic as possible. The "five *w*'s and one *h*," as they are known to journalists and other investigative writers, are a handy way of organizing this information. To write an accurate and thorough report, you need to tell your readers all about the *who, what, when, where, why,* and *how* of your topic.

As you gather information, you must be certain that you are addressing *who, what, where,* and *when*. If you do a thorough job, you will also naturally find answers to *why* and *how*. Investigating involves finding these answers and reporting them in such a way that your readers will know not only the facts about an event or circumstance but the underlying details as well. Good investigative writing follows the rule "Show; don't tell." It informs readers not by summarizing but by presenting the facts, details, examples, and quotes related to a specific topic—all the information they need to understand the topic for themselves.

For example, in his well published essay "I'm Not Racist But..." writer Neil Bissoondath investigates the question of racism in Canada. After stating that racism is international and multicultural, he attempts to place the problem in a larger context. Here he does not merely assert that "we seize, as terms of abuse, on whatever is most obvious about the other person," but he provides us with vivid examples of the abusive comments:

> A woman, because of her sex, easily becomes a female dog or an intimate part of her anatomy. A large person might be dubbed "a stupid ox," a small person "a little" whatever. And so a black might become "a nigger," a white "a honky," an Asian "a paki," a Chinese "a chink," an Italian "a wop," a French-Canadian "a frog."

While these phrases are not new to many of us, Bissoondath's reminder provides the evidence we need to agree that this form of insensitivity and abuse exists almost everywhere around us. He gets the reader on-side so that he can continue with his argument.

In many ways, investigating is like recalling. In recalling (see Chapter Two) you ask yourself questions; in investigating, you ask questions of other people. You might find this information through interviews, in books, in magazines, from photographs, and any other such sources. Some of your material may even come from recalling, but your focus is on what you glean from other sources.

LEARNING FROM PUBLISHED WRITERS

The following investigation by a published writer examines through the real-life stories of six women what it is like to be forced to flee one's homeland for sociopolitical reasons. In "Breaking the Barriers: Refugee Women in Canada" written by Helga Kutz-Harder, you will notice how much information the writer was able to collect from her interviews because she asked the basic questions: *Who? What? When? Where? Why? And How?*

Before You Read

Focus Your Attention

Before you read this investigation, take a few moments to respond to the following questions in your notebook.

1. Think of a time when you have found yourself in a situation that was very unfamiliar to you. Why were you there? How did you feel? How easy was it to get out of the situation?

2. In the essay that you are about to read, the writer sketches stories of six refugee women who fled to Canada because life in their homeland was no longer liveable. Have you or someone you know ever felt that it was necessary to leave home and loved ones because the environment was no longer tolerable? Explain, and be as specific as possible. If these are not things you would be willing to talk about, jot down notes but label this section of your writing PRIVATE.

Expand Your Vocabulary

Here are some words that are important to your understanding of the essay. Read the words in context and write a definition for each.

Refugee (paragraph 1)

Defy (paragraph 1)

Flourish (paragraph 1)

Shunned (paragraph 3)

Imposed (paragraph 10)

Helga Kutz-Harder

Breaking the Barriers: Refugee Women in Canada*

The real-life stories collected in Helga Kutz-Harder's reportage often have their source in unspeakable suffering and misery that caused their subjects to flee their homelands and become refugees in Canada.

The socio-political backgrounds of these personal experiences are varied. The Iranian revolution of 1978, led by Ayatollah Khomeini, replaced the Shah's regime with an Islamic government that established a strict Moslem rule. It governed in a way that many people found more repressive than the Shah's reign. From 1979, El Salvador, in Central America, has been the site of relentless battle between the U.S.-supported military government and the leftist popular movement. Thousands of people have been killed or "disappeared"; thousands have sought escape in refugee camps. For years, it has been unable to escape the bloody civil war between the Hutu majority and the Tutsi ruling class. Somalia, an African republic

*From *Pens of Many Colours: A Canadian Reader*, ed. Eva C. Karpinski and Ian Lea. HBJ 1993.

uniting former British and Italian colonies, is subject to both drought and flood, which places this country in the so-called hunger belt. It has received international economic and technical assistance. Sri Lanka, formerly the British colony of Ceylon, has been wracked since its independence in 1948 by the violent religious, linguistic, and ethnic conflict between the majority Sinhalese Buddhists and the minority Tamils who favour an independent Tamil homeland. The politics of violence and terrorism is the island's everyday reality.

The stories of the refugee women I have met in Canada fill me with woe **1** and wonder. The realities of their past sometimes defy my imagination. The courage with which they find their place in a settled society like Canada is awe-inspiring. Many of them have an aura of calm and beauty which masks the turmoil inside when they try to hold in tension, the unbearable memories of the past, the spirit-defying obstacles of everyday life in a cold new country, and the tentative flame of hope which dares to believe that this is the place where their spirits can flourish.

Many of the refugee women are reluctant to talk of their past, sometimes **2** because they are afraid of unleashing emotional despair which they may not be able to control, and sometimes because they need to bury some of the details in order to be accepted by their people here. Breaking the barriers within themselves requires as much courage as breaking the barriers between them and their new society. The stories which I have gathered here are tributes to this courage. They look inward and outward. They give us truth about ourselves, about us, and about the world in which we live together. The women and their stories are a gift to us.

Young Woman From Iran

A young Iranian man started the conversation: "Woman in Iran suffer two **3** times more than men." The young widow accompanying him continued the story. Because her husband wrote down his criticism of the government he was imprisoned. Because she was pregnant with his child, she, too, was imprisoned. When he died, the authorities freed her from prison, but she found herself imprisoned by a society which shunned her because of him. She had no right to study, no right to work, no way to survive and feed a child.

She was bitter about her past: "Women are half of a man, except when **4** they have to go to prison the same as a man." She told me that many women with children fill the prisons, and many women are executed. Many children lose both parents and become the lost children of Iran, because "nobody is allowed to help them."

She arrived at a Canadian airport, carrying a small daughter and "horri- **5** ble memories" of family members' executions, and religious repression, especially of women. Immigration officials treated her well and gave her a hearing only two days later. She came to the meeting tired and worried. She did not know what to do when the official thundered: "Why, why, why don't you go home where you belong? Why are you coming and stealing jobs from Canadians?" In her heart she cried: "I can't go home, I would rather be executed than treated like this. I can't stop crying." She needed to believe that she would be helped, not criticized for why she was where she was.

As a single mother she knew that first of all, she must find work. But before that, she must study French because she was in Montreal. She worried about a lot of things. What could she do with her little girl? How could she manage? How could she live if her baby became sick? She could find work in a factory, but how nice it would be to work at her own profession, even at minimum wage.

She ended her conversation: "Women aren't refugees because of what they have done, but because of what their husbands have done." She bowed her head and, as her lustrous black hair fell over her shoulders, we wept, men and women alike. Will we ever know what keeps her going day after day?

Young Woman From El Salvador

A church heard about her fear of returning to El Salvador, and quickly agreed to sponsor her into Canada. She waited eleven months in Buffalo while the Canadian authorities read through the stacks of paper and signed the right ones before she could finally end her journey. The room they provided was so warm and welcoming, and she sank into some pillows, exhausted. Eventually the young man she had met along the way found her, and became her husband.

Like most new immigrants, their monthly income was minimal, unequal to the expectations she placed on herself as a good wife. In her understanding, that included serving expensive cuts of meat and spending the day at home to protect the timing of the evening meal. Meanwhile, her sponsors ate bean sprouts and granola, and watched her weekly allowance used up in apparently inappropriate grocery bills. They advised when they could, and in time the grocery bills got lower; so did her self-esteem as a wife. She learned how to fit into the Canadian economy, but felt she was betraying her cultural values.

How do any of us know which culture should be imposed on which? Will she eventually be a Canadian Salvadorean woman, or a Salvadorean Canadian woman? Either way, she may feel as if she has failed at being a good woman.

Young Woman From Somalia

She was highly skilled in Somalia: a typist and telex computer operator. But after her husband disappeared (just one of thousands) her life changed, because in Somalia a working woman needs a male sponsor. At first her uncle sponsored her, but he disappeared, too. And so she was fired, with no place to go. "The war in Somalia is an anarchist war. It is a war on women," she

said. Any woman between the ages of eighteen and forty is not safe from being forcibly removed to the army camps to be raped and violated. And that's
only the beginning. If her husband finds out, he kills her for the shame of it
all; if they know that he has found out, they kill him, too; if he goes into
hiding instead, and she won't tell where he is, they kill her.

And so she escaped to Canada, aching because she left a young baby with   **12**
her sister: only a girl with a baby is safe from violation. And so she sacrificed
her baby daughter to save her sister. Most of all she feels so alone because
there are not enough Somalis in Canada to form the kind of community to
which she needs to belong, in order to stand upright in the midst of the pain
and the memory of the flesh and blood she left behind.

Young Tamil Woman From Sri Lanka

As a child she had heard stories of bombings from her mother. Then, one of   **13**
the bombs killed her young husband, and she felt them in her soul when she
realized that her unborn twins would never know their father. She was a
high school teacher, and one extra-violent day her principal warned her to
stay at home. Frozen with fear, three women watched while thugs ran to the
back of the house with torches to burn it down—just because she was a
Tamil. Only wit and the need to survive kept them moving to a temporary
safe haven, a room 6'x10' for fifty people. "I still feel the scars of that burning," she said.

The nurse who helped her wash the twins asked: "When are you going   **14**
home?" She remembers bursting into tears because she had no home to go
to. They kept moving, sleeping with their clothes on and a bit of food
nearby, ready to move when necessary. For three months they stayed in In-
dia, then they found their way to England, where a Canadian church heard
about them and sponsored their move to Canada. They waited eleven more
months before arriving at the welcoming church. One of the first comments
from an unthinking person confused her: "You a refugee? Surely immigrant
is more like it."

The sponsoring church is kind, but the trauma and depression remain.   **15**
Holding her teaching skills in her memory, she wonders why only the men
are easily given studying opportunities here in Canada. She shared some of
her disappointments with us: "The cultural transition lies heavily on the
women. The guilt for having left home is heavy." Beneath the warm smile
and the classic beauty lies a lot of pain.

These refugee women will never forget the land of their birth. Without   **16**
doubt, the scars of past traumas will also never be forgotten. Perhaps they
did not know much about Canada before they arrived here. But now they
know that Canada is their homeland. They know that the peace and safety
they have found in Canada will give them a chance to start a new life. Now
they have an opportunity to develop their potential and contribute their
talents to the land which gave them refuge.

Questions For Critical Thinking

Thinking Critically About Content

1. Why do you think the writer sometimes quotes the exact words of some of the women rather than putting all of the ideas in her own words?

2. Why does she say that the "women and their stories are a gift to us"?

Thinking Critically About Purpose

3. What do you think Kutz-Harder's purpose is in this essay?

4. Why does she focus on women when in fact it is obvious that there is at least one man (see the first line of paragraph three) in the group that she interviews?

Thinking Critically About Audience

5. Who do you think is Kutz-Harder's primary audience for this essay? Why do you think this?

6. Do you think certain types of readers would be more inspired than other readers by this essay? What might they be inspired to do? Explain.

Thinking Critically About Perspective

7. The author brings herself into the essay only in the first and final paragraphs. How objective is she? How do you know?

8. Reread the final two lines of the second paragraph. Why does Kutz-Harder write them? What does she imply by, "the world in which we live together"?

LEARNING FROM YOUR PEERS

Not many of us think about interviewing someone we know as a form of investigation. But friends, neighbours, and acquaintances can be valuable sources of information, historical as well as personal. In response to an investigating assignment that involves interviewing, we are going to follow the writing process of a student named Sharmen Sorsdahl.

Sharmen's Writing Assignment: Investigating

Sharmen's instructor writes a dictionary definition of culture on the blackboard: "the habits, skills, concepts, institutions, expectations, art and instruments, etc., of a particular group of people at a particular time." This leads to a discussion about what it means to belong to a particular culture, and takes some brainstorming to realize what cultures they have in common and to which others they, individually, belong.

The instructor then assigns the topic: she wants students to interview a person who shares a particular culture with them, but a culture in which most of the other students are likely unfamiliar. After the interview, they are to write about the results of the investigation.

Sharmen begins the writing process as outlined in Chapter One: generating ideas, planning, developing, organizing, drafting, revising, and editing.

Generating Ideas

Sharmen's class decides to spend some time together generating possible topics for this essay. They list broad categories of cultures that have been already mentioned and add a few more: religious, sport, academic, party, work, fashion, family, food, medical, political. They then break into smaller groups and choose someone to be group recorder. The recorder writes the broad topic on the top of a sheet of paper and records all topics suggested by members of the group. After 10 minutes, the instructor asks for all topics to be listed on the chalkboard to be shared by the whole class.

They begin their writing assignment by choosing and freewriting on one topic that they find particularly interesting. The instructor hopes that this will help undecided students to choose a specific topic, and help others generate some initial ideas. Sharmen still isn't sure which to choose for her particular essay, although the specific topics listed under fashion and food seem most appealing. While she is freewriting, she comes up with a topic that combines the two. She decides to write about what it is like for her and others to be a part of the "plus-size" culture. Now she has to decide whom she wants to interview. Students are to come to the next class having decided, and with an interview date and time set.

Planning

The next class begins with students planning questions that might guide their interview. They are reminded of the five w's and one h. Each person spends time listing questions to ask, and then the class breaks into small groups so that together they can add more questions to each other's lists. By the end of the class, Sharmen has the following questions ready to ask her best friend Cathy, who also belongs to the plus-size culture:

1. How do you feel about being a part of the plus-size culture?
2. Is body image important to you?
3. When were you aware of being a plus-sizer?
4. How did you get there?
5. What does your family think?
6. What is the most difficult thing about being a part of this culture?
7. What problems have you encountered?
8. How do thin people make you feel?
9. How do thin people respond to you?
10. How would you change if you could?

Cathy agrees to be interviewed. That night, Sharmen meets with her. Sharmen has brought her tape recorder because she worries that she can't write fast enough. She also believes that the recorder will help her stay focused on the interview, and both of them will view the interview as something more serious than a friendly chat. She has also brought a notepad and pen so that she can record other thoughts that she might have as the interview progresses. Cathy, too, takes the interview seriously, and she has come prepared with her own thoughts on the topic.

Developing

Sharmen spends some time listening to the tape and writing out ideas that she thinks might be significant for her essay. As Sharmen looks over her notes, she realizes that her problem will be deciding what to include and what to leave out. Cathy has talked for so long and so passionately that Sharmen will have to choose those details that will create the dominant impression of what Cathy has said. However, because this topic touches on research that has been very much talked about, the biggest problem might be selecting information that readers will still find interesting. Sharmen chooses to focus on Cathy's personal experience and feelings.

Organizing

Sharmen decides that since she is also a part of this culture, her feelings and reasons for interviewing Cathy are an important part of the essay. She will start the essay with these, then move into the results of the interview, and then end with how she feels after she has worked through all that Cathy has said. Here is the draft she wrote.

Sharmen's Essay: First Draft

Main idea: What it is like to belong to the "plus-size" culture.

   Culture, what is my culture? The dictionary defines culture as the ideas or skills of a group of people. Many cultures pertain to me, for example, I belong to the sister culture, the daughter culture, and the student culture. The one culture that I am apart of that strikes out the most in my mind is the "plus size" culture. I don't know what else it could be called, whatever the label, the culture is the same. I know this topic has been beat to death, and people are sick of hearing about this, but this is a topic I have to deal with everyday. Slim people do not understand where I'm coming from. It is not just as easy as losing weight and being done with it. I hate being overweight and have a hard time with it. It is a constant thought in my head.

   I am healthy and for the most part well adjusted and happy. I no longer want to feel like a rhinoceros; I want to join the thin girls. I interviewed my best friend Cathy who also belongs to the "Big Girl" culture. I wanted to see if she had any insights to how I was feeling. I was hoping that she could disprove my feelings. I felt like a big fat article by the time she was done with me though. Unfortunately, she agreed with everything I had to say, she also had some new negative thoughts for me.

   She has struggled with her weight for as long as she can remember. Eating has always been a major part of her life, she grew up with a family who loved to eat, that was how they showed they cared for one another. They would sit around and eat together. Cathy said, "my father wasn't happy until everyone was eating" She never noticed the quantity of food she ate until she got much older and her childhood activities ceased and she gained weight.

   Throughout High School she felt like an ugly duckling. She was not obese, yet she wasn't thin either. Thin was ideal and boys only wanted thin girls, and thin girls are the ones having all the fun. By dealing with these social ideals as well as just being a teenager, Cathy's self-esteem soon plummeted and the onslaught of dieting began.

To this day, Cathy is still in the vicious dieting cycle and she is striving to be someone else. I asked her how she thinks others see her. "Awful and monstrous," she replied. "I know people look at me as unattractive, unsexy and lazy. I get so uptight in public I can't look people in the eyes. I am too embarrassed. I hate running into people I know. I feel like they are looking at me wondering how I could have let myself go." Cathy feels like her extra weight has prevented her from obtaining all she has wanted. She knows she is pretty, but says, "I have always been the girl with the pretty face and that's it."

Society believes it is moving away from the skinny model stereotype, and is becoming more accepting. Unfortunately Cathy says, "if they were to pick up a magazine, it will always feature a skinny model or celebrity." I asked Cathy if she has tried to stop fighting the way she looks and tried to embrace it and I asked if women such as Roseanne or Rosie O'Donell are, or could be role models for this way of thinking. Cathy says, "These women could be role models, but they themselves are trying to achieve skinny bodies. They talk about their weight all the time." She thinks it is impossible for a bigger woman to fully accept who she is. She says, "there would always be that part of them that envy the skinny pretty girls. These are the girls that are happy, confident, and assertive and never look ridiculous."

All my thoughts, feelings, and fears were confirmed by my conversation with Cathy. I had hoped to hear positive and motivative words. We discussed how we would like to see society change their views about big women, and how they treat them. They should be featured more in the movies, on television as well as in magazines and society also does not need to refer to big women as big or plus size. Why can't we just be women, and not referred to as thin or large, but just female and beautiful. Maybe this would help woman to no longer feel the need to be ashamed of themselves like Cathy and I.

Revising

Cathy's passion serves as inspiration for Sharmen's first draft. She is amazed that the words just come tumbling out, sometimes faster than she can write. She knows that revising this essay will take more time than usual because she doesn't pay much attention to how she makes her statements while she is writing; she just wants to get her ideas onto paper. Her general philosophy is "Write now; revise later." So now the time has come to revise.

 ## COLLABORATIVE WORK

PEER GROUP ACTIVITY

After you read the portions of Focus on Paragraphs that your instructor assigns, turn to Sharmen's first draft, and complete the following tasks in small groups.

A. Put an asterisk (*) by any paragraphs that would be more effective if she followed another line of reasoning.

B. Put an X by any paragraph that is not fully developed.

Compare the marks your group recorded with those your instructor will show you. Where do your marks differ from your instructor's? What do you need to review before writing your own essay?

CLASS ACTIVITY

As an entire class, look at the underlined portions of Sharmen's revised draft.

A. Did you identify the revision problems that Sharmen corrected?

B. Do you think her changes are good ones? Discuss her changes.

Editing

Now that Sharmen has expanded her paragraphs to more accurately represent her individual thoughts and logical reasoning, she needs to turn her attention to some aspects of the sentences before handing in her essay.

COLLABORATIVE WORK

PEER GROUP ACTIVITY

After you read the portions of Focus on Sentences that your instructor assigns, turn to Sharmen's first draft and complete the following tasks in small groups:

A. Circle all the phrases and underline the clauses in each sentence. Mark dependent clauses with a *D* and independent clauses with an *I* (see p. 123).

B. Read the essay aloud to listen for variety of sentence construction. Make sure you pause appropriately at the punctuation marks. How does the essay sound? Mark where you would make changes.

Compare your answers with another peer group. Where do your answers differ from theirs? What do you need to review before writing your own essay?

CLASS ACTIVITY

As an entire class, look at the portions of Sharmen's revised draft to see how she changed each sentence.

A. Did you identify the editing problems that Sharmen corrected?

B. Do you think her changes are good ones? Discuss her changes.

Sharmen's Revised Essay ....

Cultures

Culture: what is my culture? The dictionary defines culture as the ideas ~~or skills~~ , expectations, habits and skills of a group of people. With this definition, we can see ourselves as belonging to many cultures at any one time. ~~Many cultures pertain to me, for~~ For example, I belong to the sister culture, the daughter culture, and the student culture. Each of these comes with certain expectations and ideas. The one culture that I am ~~apart~~ a part of that ~~strikes~~ stands out most ~~in my mind~~ for me is the "plus size" culture. I don't know what else it could be called~~,~~ ; whatever the label, the culture is the same. I know this topic <u>of body image</u> has been ~~beat~~ beaten to death, and people are sick of hearing about ~~this~~ it, but ~~this is a topic~~ I have to deal with ~~everyday~~ this topic every day.

Slim people do not understand where I'm coming from. <u>For those of us who are "plus size", being slim</u> ~~It~~ is not as easy as losing weight and being done with it. I hate being overweight and have a hard time with it. ~~It is a constant thought in my head.~~ <u>I am constantly aware of my size, although</u> I am healthy and for the most part well adjusted and happy. <u>My problem is that</u> I no longer want to feel like a rhinoceros; I want to join the thin girls. I interviewed my best friend Cathy who also belongs to the "Big Girl" culture. I wanted to see if she had any insights to how I was feeling. I was hoping that she could disprove my feelings. <u>However,</u> I felt like a big fat article by the time she was done with me ~~though~~. ~~Unfortunately, she agreed~~ <u>Not only did she agree</u> with everything I had to say, she also had some new negative thoughts for me.

She has struggled with her weight for as long as she can remember. Eating has always been a major part of her life~~,~~ <u>as</u> she grew up with a family who loved to eat~~, that~~ <u>. Eating</u> was how they showed they cared for one another. They would sit around and ~~eat~~ <u>chow down</u> together. Cathy said, "my father wasn't happy until everyone was eating." She never noticed the quantity of food she ate until she got much older and her childhood activities ceased and she gained weight.

Throughout High School she felt like an ugly duckling. She was not obese, yet she wasn't thin either. <u>She just didn't look the same in the short skirts and mid-riff tops. She was embarrassed about showing off her belly-button.</u> Thin was ideal and boys only wanted thin girls, and thin girls ~~are~~ <u>were</u> the ones having all the fun. <u>Thin,</u>

skinny, scrawny were the good words. By dealing with these social ideals as well as just being a teenager, Cathy's self-esteem soon plummeted and the onslaught of dieting began.

To this day, Cathy is still in the vicious dieting cycle and she is striving to be someone ~~else~~ that she sees in magazines. I asked her how she thinks others see her. "Awful and monstrous," she replied. "I know people look at me as unattractive, unsexy and lazy. I get so uptight in public I can't look people in the eyes. I am too embarrassed. I hate running into people I know. I feel like they are looking at me wondering how I could have let myself go." Cathy feels like her extra weight has prevented her from obtaining all she has wanted, things like a great job and tons of friends. She knows she is pretty, but says, "I have always been the girl with the pretty face and that's it."

Society believes it is moving away from the skinny model stereotype, and is becoming more accepting. Unfortunately Cathy says, "if they were to pick up a magazine, it will always feature a skinny model or celebrity." I asked Cathy if she has tried to stop fighting the way she looks and tried to embrace it and I asked if women such as Roseanne or Rosie O'Donell are, or could be role models for this way of thinking. Cathy says, "These women could be role models, but they themselves are trying to achieve skinny bodies. They talk about their weight all the time." She thinks it is impossible for a bigger woman to fully accept who she is. She says, "there would always be that part of them that envy the skinny pretty girls. These are the girls that are happy, confident, and assertive and never look ridiculous."

~~All my thoughts, feelings, and fears were confirmed by my conversation with Cathy.~~ I had hoped to hear positive and motivative words, but my conversation with Cathy confirmed my thoughts.

feelings and fears. ~~We discussed how we would like to see society change their views about big women, and how they treat them. They should be~~ Society might be changing its view of women, but it is changing it awfully slowly. If Cathy is not happy with the way that she looks, and I am not happy, and neither of us really is obese, then maybe other women feel this way too. Maybe most women are not happy with the bodies that they have, and the ideal is simply an ideal that most people can't reach. Perhaps if big women were featured more in the movies, in magazines and on television, society might change its view. ~~on television as well as in magazines and society also does not need to refer to big women as big or plus size. Why can't we just be women, and not referred to as thin or large, but just female and beautiful.~~ Maybe then we would just be women, female and beautiful, and not big, or plus size. Maybe ~~this would help woman to~~ then women would no longer feel the need to be ashamed of themselves like Cathy and I.

PRACTISE OUTLINING

As a class, spend time thinking, planning, developing, and organizing a potential investigating essay.

1. Spend five minutes brainstorming a list of names of people or places that are currently in the news.

2. Choose five for the subject of a potential essay. Discuss what makes one idea better than another. Choose the best one.

3. Decide on the audience and the purpose.

4. Draw a web to answer *who, what, when, why, where,* and *how* for this particular topic.

5. Develop the ideas to give a sense of what a person might potentially write.

6. Organize the ideas so they appear in the best order for the best effect.

Could you write this essay? What would be the main topics for each paragraph?

WRITING YOUR OWN INVESTIGATING ESSAY

So far, you have seen a professional writer and a student at work investigating people they felt worth writing about. As you read the published essay and followed the writing process of the student from first to final draft, you likely absorbed ideas and ways of giving those ideas a form of their own. The reading and writing activities have prepared you to write your own essay investigating a person or topic that is meaningful to you.

What Have You Discovered?

Before you begin writing, review what is necessary to write a good investigating essay.

- Gather as much information as possible about a person, place, or topic.

- Answer the questions *who, what, when, why, where,* and *how.*

- Show as well as tell your readers–give concrete details and examples to support your statements.

- Organize your ideas.

- Learn as much as possible about your readers.

- Decide on a perspective toward your subject.

- Revise for sentence variety.

- Edit for grammar, usage, and sentence structure.

Your Writing Topic

Choose one of the following topics for your investigating essay.

1. Choose a person, preferably someone older than you (perhaps a grandparent), or someone from another country. Interview that person about her or his educational experiences. Pose questions to determine whether the educational conditions and opportunities that existed were different from the ones you experienced. Did your subject have the opportunity to attend school for as long as she or he wanted? Was education important to your subject? Does your subject have any advice to give about the value of education?

2. Interview a friend, neighbour, or relative whose life was affected by war or political problems, and write about how that person's life was changed by those events. Find out what the person thought was most difficult about the experience and what she or he is most thankful for now.

3. Interview someone who accomplished an extremely challenging task—someone who built a house with very little assistance; someone who learned to walk or

read again after being disabled in an accident; someone who has completed a marathon run or another test of physical endurance. Then write about that person's unique feeling of accomplishment. How does this accomplishment differ from other accomplishments? Would the person work again to achieve this or a similar goal?

4. Think about culture in the way that Sharmen does in her essay. Interview someone who shares one of the cultures to which you belong. Write an essay that investigates some aspects of belonging to this particular culture.

5. Create your own investigating topic and write an essay in response to it. You might like to check this one with your instructor.

When you have selected one of these writing topics, you may choose to begin your writing process in the same way Sharmen did. Remember, though, as you write your own investigating essay, that you will develop your own personal writing ritual. If you don't know how to begin, however, follow the ways that have been successful for others.

Developing Paragraphs

Checklist For Developing Paragraphs

✓ Is each paragraph fully developed?
✓ Are the details in each paragraph organized into a specific pattern?
✓ Does the specific paragraph pattern best serve the information in the paragraph?

Urban planners, important members of the teams that develop or renew cities, look for the most logical ways to meet citizens' needs. Then they create the spaces, streets, and buildings that are appropriate for the many different people and activities of a given city. You may find that developing paragraphs is a bit like the procedure urban planners follow. For example, if your readers need to understand an unfamiliar word, you might build a paragraph that defines that word for them. If you want to bring to mind a special place, you might write a descriptive paragraph.

Kinds Of Paragraphs

One way of developing paragraphs is to use specific patterns that capture the way you think about different issues and topics. For instance, if you want to communicate the atmosphere of a wonderful restaurant, you might use a description that appeals to your readers' senses. Or if your investigating essay deals with a topic unfamiliar to your audience, you might compare your topic to something they are already familiar with. The following methods are widely used for developing paragraphs logically. Each represents a different way of thinking about a topic. Sometimes you will use several of these methods in a single paragraph; other times you will use one method for an entire paragraph.

Definition

When you explain the meaning of a term for your audience, you are **defining**. For example, Sharmen opens her essay with a dictionary definition of culture before presenting to her readers one of the cultures to which she and a friend belong. However, as she begins to revise her essay, she realizes that she does not make it entirely clear why she considers "plus size" a culture. She needs to expand on this before she moves on.

First Draft: Culture, what is my culture. The dictionary defines culture as the ideas or skills of a group of people. Many cultures pertain to me, for example, I belong to the sister culture, the daughter culture, and the student culture.

Revision: Culture: what is my culture? The dictionary defines culture as the ideas, expectations, habits and skills of a group of people. With this definition, we can see ourselves as belonging to many cultures at any one time. For example, I belong to the sister culture, the daughter culture, and the student culture. Each of these comes with certain expectations and ideas.

Now Sharmen's audience will more fully understand what she means when she begins to talk about "plus size" as a culture.

Description

A **description** draws a verbal picture for your audience of a place, object, person, group, or situation. Kutz-Harder provides several strong examples of description in her essay. Note how these examples create a vivid picture of the people she interviews and a strong sense of their stories.

"She bowed her head and, as her lustrous black hair fell over her shoulders, we wept, men and women alike."

"The room they provided was so warm and welcoming, and she sank into some pillows, exhausted."

"Frozen with fear, three women watched while thugs ran to the back of the house with torches to burn it down—just because she was a Tamil. Only wit and the need to survive kept them moving to a temporary safe haven, a room 6' × 10' for fifty people."

Sharmen decided to expand paragraph four of her essay to include more description:

First Draft: Throughout High School she felt like an ugly duckling. She was not obese, yet she wasn't thin either. Thin was ideal and boys only wanted thin girls, and thin girls are the ones having all the fun. By dealing with these social ideals as well as just being a teenager, Cathy's self-esteem soon plummeted and the onslaught of dieting began.

Revision: Throughout High School she felt like an ugly duckling. She was not obese, yet she wasn't thin either. She just didn't look the same in the short skirts and mid-riff tops. She was embarrassed about showing off her belly-button. Thin was ideal and boys only wanted thin girls, and thin girls were the ones having all the fun. Thin, skinny, scrawny were the good words. By dealing with these social ideals as well as just being a teenager, Cathy's self-esteem soon plummeted and the onslaught of dieting began.

Thanks to Sharmen's description, her audience can better visualize the way that both she and Cathy felt others saw them.

Classification

Another way of developing an idea is by **classifying** or grouping similar items in a paragraph. For instance, people can be grouped by similar occupations, hobbies, regions where they live, political beliefs, and so on. In the example on the opening pages of this chapter, Neil Bissoondath classifies some examples of insensitive and abusive comments:

A woman, because of her sex, easily becomes a female dog or an intimate part of her anatomy. A large person might be dubbed "a stupid ox," a small person "a little" whatever. And so a black might become "a nigger," a white "a honky," an Asian "a paki," a Chinese "a chink," an Italian "a wop," a French-Canadian "a frog."

Sharmen might have focused in on paragraph four and revised it as a classification paragraph:

First Draft: Throughout High School she felt like an ugly duckling. She was not obese, yet she wasn't thin either. Thin was ideal and boys only wanted thin girls, and thin girls are the ones having all the fun. By dealing with these social ideals as well as just being a teenager, Cathy's self-esteem soon plummeted and the onslaught of dieting began.

Revision: Throughout High School she felt like an ugly duckling. She was not obese, yet she wasn't thin either. Thin girls were the popular girls, the pretty girls, the athletes. Thin girls were the happy ones, the funny ones, the confident ones. Thin was ideal and boys only wanted thin girls, and thin girls are the ones having all the fun. Thin girls were the ideal girls, and Cathy wasn't ideal. Cathy's self-esteem soon plummeted and the onslaught of dieting began.

Cause-Effect

Writers often need to explain causes that lead to a particular effect or an effect that comes from a particular cause. Explaining is an important tool. The papers that you will need to write for your other courses in college—history and science, for example—often draw on this ability. Sharmen uses **cause-effect** reasoning in the third paragraph of her essay.

> Revision: **She has struggled with her weight for as long as she can remember.** Eating has always been a major part of her life. She grew up with a family who loved to eat; that was how they showed they cared for one another. They would sit around and eat together. Cathy said, "my father wasn't happy until everyone was eating" She never noticed the quantity of food she ate until she got much older and her childhood activities ceased and she gained weight.

Sharmen begins with the effect, the fact that the cause, overeating, has created a weight problem for Cathy. Then she outlines what Cathy sees as the root causes of the problem. The revisions in this paragraph were simply a matter of correcting the sentence structure.

Comparison-Contrast

When you point out similarities, you use **comparisons** to develop your ideas. When you emphasize differences, you use **contrasts**. This skill will prove to be especially useful in other courses such as literature or political science. Sharmen draws on the comparison-contrast technique in two of her paragraphs:

> Paragraph four: Throughout High School she felt like an ugly duckling. She was not obese, yet she wasn't thin either. Thin girls were the popular girls, the pretty girls, the athletes. Thin girls were the happy ones, the funny ones, the confident ones. Thin was ideal and boys only wanted thin girls, and thin girls are the ones having all the fun. Thin girls were the ideal girls, and Cathy wasn't ideal.

> Paragraph six: Society believes it is moving away from the skinny model stereotype, and is becoming more accepting. Unfortunately Cathy says, "if they were to pick up a magazine, it will always feature a skinny model or celebrity."

In paragraph four, Sharmen contrasts Cathy's perception of herself with what she perceives to be society's ideal. In paragraph six, she contrasts society's perception with the reality as shown in popular magazines.

Analysis

To **analyze** an idea, you must break it into its basic parts, then show the relationships between those parts. Analysis is a major component of many types of essays, and is a useful skill to learn for any field that requires inquiry and investigation. Sharmen uses analysis in much of her essay because she is investigating a particular topic. She decided to revise her final paragraph to emphasize her analyzing skills.

First Draft: All my thoughts, feelings, and fears were confirmed by my conversation with Cathy. I had hoped to hear positive and motivative words. We discussed how we would like to see society change their views about big women, and how they treat them. They should be featured more in the movies, on television as well as in magazines and society also does not need to refer to big women as big or plus size. Why can't we just be women, and not referred to as thin or large, but just female and beautiful. Maybe this would help woman to no longer feel the need to be ashamed of themselves like Cathy and I.

Revision: I had hoped to hear positive and motivative words, but my conversation with Cathy confirmed my thoughts, feelings and fears. Society might be changing its view of women, but it is changing it awfully slowly. If Cathy is not happy with the way that she looks, and I am not happy, and neither of us really is obese, then maybe other women feel this way too. Maybe most women are not happy with the bodies that they have, and the ideal is simply an ideal that most people can't reach. Perhaps if big women were featured more in movies, in magazines and on television, society might change its view. Maybe then we would just be women, female and beautiful, and not big, or plus size. Maybe then women would no longer feel the need to be ashamed of themselves like Cathy and I.

In this revision, Sharmen examines her own feelings alongside those that she has gathered from her friend Cathy, and analyzes why they both feel this way.

Exercise P5-1

Find paragraphs in Sharmen's first draft that could be developed further using at least three of the methods of paragraph development that we have looked at in this section. Jot down your suggestions.

Exercise P5-2

Reread paragraph two of Sharmen's first draft. Rewrite it using one of the methods of development you have learned in this chapter. Compare your version to one of your classmate's who has rewritten it using a different method.

Exercise P5-3

Using the methods of paragraph development that you have studied in this chapter, write additional sentences that give supporting details for each of the topic sentences below. Discuss which ones lend themselves to particular types of paragraph development.

1. Many people do not understand exactly what the mass media are.
2. Most people have a sense of right and wrong.
3. Wages control a firm's cost of doing business.
4. My down jacket is a useful item of apparel.
5. A library is like a gold mine in many ways.
6. Rock and country are both popular types of music at my school.
7. The study methods that work for me might not be the right ones for you.
8. Every one of us has the potential for improving his or her daily life.
9. Strong paragraphs can be logically developed in several ways.
10. Who needs big business in North America?

Exercise P5-4

Develop the following paragraph using at least one of the methods of development you have reviewed in this section.

Basically, details are building blocks that you combine to construct a paragraph. The following techniques can help you develop your topic sentences with details that provide information in several ways.

Supporting Details

Urban planners need to ensure that the city facilities they develop for different activities are adequate. For example, a baseball park that seats only 10,000 people would need to be expanded in Vancouver, but an opera house of the same size would work admirably in that city. Like these planners, you need to build not only the right kind of support into your paragraphs but also enough details to develop your main ideas adequately. Often you will need to furnish different types of support within a single paragraph; the amount of support may also vary, but one guideline remains constant: *specific details are the building blocks of well-developed paragraphs*. Some ideas may need a great many details; others will not. If you cram too many details into one paragraph, you may confuse your readers rather than clarify your thoughts. On the other hand, using too few details leaves your essay weak and unclear.

Examples

Giving examples of what you are writing about is an effective way to make sure your ideas are clear to your audience. **Examples** support your ideas by making them specific, interesting, and memorable. In the opening paragraph of her essay, Sharmen uses examples to support her topic sentence.

> Culture: what is my culture? The dictionary defines culture as the ideas, expectations, habits and skills of a group of people. With this definition, we can see ourselves as belonging to many cultures at any one time. For example, I belong to the sister culture, the daughter culture, and the student culture.

Sharmen's readers are given a sense of what types of cultures a single individual might belong to.

Facts And Numbers

Providing your audience with **facts and numbers** about your topic is another way to develop your paragraphs. Sharmen might have included some facts and numbers so that her readers would understand the scope of the problem. She might have researched and made reference to how many women are caught up in "the vicious dieting cycle" and included it in paragraph five.

First Draft: To this day, Cathy is still in the vicious dieting cycle and she is striving to be someone else.

Revision: To this day, like <u>XXX</u> of women in Canada, Cathy is still in the vicious dieting cycle, striving to be someone else, someone with a picture-perfect body.

The numbers from the research support her argument, and help her readers see why Cathy's problem is also one that affects many women.

Exercise P5-5

Find three places in Sharmen's first draft where she might add examples, facts, or numbers to further develop her topic.

Exercise P5-6

For each of the following topic sentences, write examples, facts, or numbers that further develop the idea.

1. Crowded classrooms make learning difficult in some subjects that are part of my school's core curriculum.

2. For example, in my biology lab, we are often unable to have hands-on experiences with certain experiments.

3. We are the most disadvantaged because of the low teacher-to-student ratio.

4. Limiting class size seems to be the only answer.

5. In some subjects, however, large numbers of students in the same class are not as much of a problem.

Exercise P5-7

Rewrite the following paragraph using examples, facts, and numbers to develop the topic.

> Children who watch television are exposed daily to some of the highest-pressure advertising in mass-media. They hear about toys, candy, and new kinds of gum until they essentially become salespeople to their parents for the children's market in North America.

COLLABORATIVE WORK

PEER GROUP ACTIVITY

After writing a draft of your own investigating essay, exchange papers with a classmate and do the following tasks:

A. List the different ways paragraphs can be developed. Then, in the margins of your classmate's essay, suggest alternative ways to develop specific paragraphs.

B. Put a check mark by each paragraph that needs more examples, facts, or numbers.

Then, return the paper to its writer and use the information in this section to revise your draft.

CLASS ACTIVITY

Choose one paragraph from the essay you are writing that clearly shows a particular pattern of development. Pin a copy to your class bulletin board. Once other members of the class have done the same, choose one from the board to see if you can identify that paragraph's pattern. Offer revision suggestions if needed.

Clauses, Interjections, And Phrases

Checklist For Recognizing And Developing Clauses, Interjections, And Phrases

✓ Does each clause contain a subject and a verb?
✓ Does each sentence contain at least one independent clause?
✓ Is each independent clause joined to an independent clause with an appropriate conjunction?
✓ Are sentences containing multiple clauses punctuated correctly?
✓ Do your interjections simply provide an emotional pause in the sentence?
✓ Are all sentences containing interjections punctuated correctly?
✓ Does each phrase work as a single unit as part of a larger sentence? Remember, phrases do not contain a subject and verb and so do not stand alone.
✓ Does each phrase modify something else in the sentence?

Clauses

In Chapter Two we learned to identify subjects and predicates. We also said that a sentence must contain both of these in order to be a complete sentence. A group of words that contains these two essential elements, both a subject and a predicate, is called a **clause**. There are two main types of clauses.

Independent Clauses

An **independent** clause can stand alone as a sentence because it contains a subject and a predicate and expresses a complete idea. The subject includes the noun or pronoun (or group of words that functions as a noun or pronoun) and other words that give more details about the subject. The predicate includes the main verb and all the words that tell us something about the verb.

When an independent clause stands alone as a sentence, it is called a simple sentence. Read these examples from the essays in this chapter. Both are examples of simple sentences:

Kutz-Harder:	The women and their stories are a gift to us.
	Compound subject Predicate
Sharmen:	Thin, skinny, scrawny were the good words.
	Subject Predicate

Dependent Clauses

Like an independent clause, a **dependent clause** contains a subject and a predicate. However, the words that introduce a dependent clause make its meaning dependent on the rest of the sentence. These words are called subordinating conjunctions and show that the clause is dependent on the independent clause for its meaning. A dependent clause is not a complete thought and, therefore, cannot be a sentence on its own. The following examples come from the chapter essays.

Kutz-Harder: *Because her husband wrote down his criticism of the government*, he was imprisoned.

(because is the subordinating conjunction introducing the dependent clause)

Sharmen: My father wasn't happy *until everyone was eating.*

(until, another subordinating conjunction, introduces the dependent clause)

Each of these examples contains two sets of subjects and verbs; therefore there are two clauses in each sentence. To be a complete sentence, at least one clause must be an independent clause. What makes the clause dependent is the presence of the subordinating conjunction. *Because* and *when* make the clause dependent. In these particular sentences, the only thing that makes the clause dependent is the subordinating conjunction, the word that introduces the clause. Without the conjunction, the clause would be independent.

Note that the dependent clause can appear either before or after the independent clause. If it does appear before the independent clause, it needs a comma after the dependent clause to tell the reader to pause briefly before reading the main clause. If the independent clause appears first, however, no comma is needed.

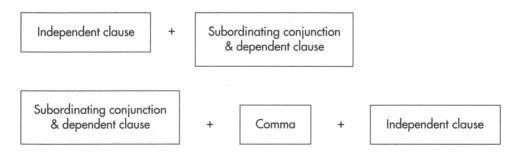

Some dependent clauses are a bit tricky to identify. Read the following example:

My father is one who believes *that this works.*

That is a subordinating conjunction introducing the dependent clause *that this works*. *My father is one* is the independent clause. We know that *believes* is a verb, so we suspect that it is a part of a clause. The problem, then, is identifying the subject and the conjunction.

Who is a special type of pronoun that can be used to introduce a dependent clause. Here it introduces the dependent clause and connects it to the independent clause. The independent clause serves as the subject of the dependent clause. We'll look at this in greater detail in Chapter Seven.

Note that sentences can contain more than one dependent clause but must always have at least one independent clause. In the next two chapters, you will learn how to use combining words, called **conjunctions**, to combine clauses and form more complicated sentences.

Exercise S5-1

Label all of the dependent and independent clauses in the following sentences.

1. If I had the money, I would buy that piano.
2. It rained steadily for an entire week.
3. As I said before, you cannot go to the Edmonton Exhibition.
4. The cougars didn't make any noise as they walked along the riverbank.
5. This play was written by a Canadian who lived in the 1930s.

Exercise S5-2

Write sentences that include dependent clauses beginning with the following words.

1. Which
2. Although
3. Wherever
4. Whose
5. While

Interjections

Interjections exist to express strong feeling or sudden emotion. *The word interjection* comes from Latin words meaning *to throw between*. Unlike other parts of speech, interjections have no grammatical relation to other parts of the sentence. They are simply thrown between, acting as an emotional pause for the reader. An interjection can be almost any word that breaks up the flow of the sentence.

Some common interjections include the following: *Ah, aha, alas, eh, goodness, gracious, hallelujah, help, hey, mmm, oh, ouch, shucks, well, whew, wow, yeah, yippee.* Curse words also fall into this category. Note that some of the interjections are not actually words, but we can represent the sounds they express:

Whew! It's hot!

Mmmm! These are marvelous muffins.

Though, *therefore*, and *however* can sometimes work as interjections:

I have been wrong before; this, **though**, is the right choice.

I have, **therefore**, made up my mind.

You do know, **however**, that I won't go home.

The degree of emotion expressed is indicated by punctuation. Interjections expressing mild feeling are set off by commas; interjections indicating strong emotion are followed by an exclamation mark. Note how to punctuate an interjection.

Exercise S5-3

Draw a box around the following interjections. Then read each sentence aloud with the appropriate emotion and pauses at punctuation.

1. Good Heavens! I never thought I'd see you two together.
2. Hallelujah! The hockey season is over!
3. She, too, is camping at Dinosaur Provincial Park.
4. You have, however, created a masterpiece.
5. You know what you're doing, eh?
6. Alas, I knew him well.

Exercise S5-4

Write a sentence for each of the following interjections.

1. However
2. Yeah
3. Help
4. Bah humbug
5. Well
6. Also

Phrases

After reviewing how interjections can function as parts of speech, you will find that forming, using, and understanding phrases is much the same. When you put several words together, you form a **phrase**, as long as the words are related and do not include a subject and a verb.

After dinner, I saw the cookbook with the red cover.

After dinner and *with the red cover* are phrases that tell us when the cookbook was seen and what the colour of the book's cover was. They tell us something more about the main thought, the seeing of the cookbook.

Phrases are groups of words that tell us more about something in the sentence. The words in a phrase work together within a sentence and function as a single unit. They are added like interjections but work as modifiers. When we talk about modifiers, we mean something that changes, limits, or adds to the sentence in some way.

Notice how the phrases in the following sentence make the content more interesting:

Outside it was dark with only a fraction of light from a single star high above the horizon.

We walked under the Northern Lights of Whitehorse to find the snowy owl.

The independent clause in the first example is *it was dark*. All of the other bits of the sentence tell us more about this darkness. We can say that they modify the independent clause, it was dark; telling us more about some aspects of this darkness:

where it was dark (inside)

how dark it was (with only a fraction of light)

where the light was coming from (a single star)

where the window was (high above the horizon)

The independent clause of the second example is *we walked*. Again, the phrases modify the independent clause:

where did we walk (under the Northern Lights)

what northern lights (of Whitehorse)

why did we walk (to find the snowy owl)

The phrases give us more information about what is going on in the sentence without adding subjects and verbs.

There are various types of phrases, and each of them is classified by the part of speech that it modifies. But all of them are made up of groups of words that act as single units. These units allow us to add more information to specific words in the sentence. Like interjections, they can appear in almost any part of the sentence. The best position for them, however, is close to the word or words they modify.

Prepositional Phrases

The simplest phrases to identify are **prepositional phrases**. Prepositional phrases begin with **prepositions**. Prepositions, like conjunctions, are connecting words. While conjunctions join clauses, prepositions join phrases to the parts of the sentence that they modify. A preposition always connects a noun, a pronoun, or a word group working as a noun to another word in the sentence. The preposition plus the connected noun, pronoun, or word group is the prepositional phrase. Here are some common prepositions. We use many of them, and often use many of them in the same sentence.

Common Prepositions					
about	at	concerning	inside	on top of	toward
above	because of	despite	in spite of	out	under
according to	before	down	instead of	out of	underneath
across	behind	during	into	outside	
after	below	except	like	over	up
against	beneath	except for	near	past	upon with
among	between	from	of	regarding	within

Prepositional phrases are modifiers, and they usually function as adjectives or as adverbs.

As an **adjective**: My son is the boy *in the green overalls*.

The phrase describes the noun, boy.

As an **adverb**: Our dog, Pepper, hides his toys *under the carpet*.

The phrase describes the verb, hides.

Exercise S5-5

Circle each prepositional phrase in the following paragraph. Indicate if it functions as an adjective or an adverb, and draw an arrow to the word or word group that it modifies.

Example:

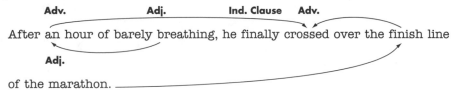

After an hour and over the finish line modify the verb, crossed. Of barely breathing modifies after an hour, and of the marathon modifies finish line.

The man in blue coveralls ran from the woman on the bicycle. He sprinted into Millrise Close, through a walkway, and down a back alley. At the alley, the woman fell from her bicycle. She landed in a puddle, and looked up with tears in her eyes. After wiping her tears, and wiping the mud from her eyes, she searched up and down the alley, but during her distraction, she lost sight of the man. She got up, turned around, mounted her bicycle, and went back through the opening in Millrise Close.

Exercise S5-6

Combine the sentences in each of the following, making one of the clauses into one or two prepositional phrases. You will have to add and delete some words to have the sentence make sense.

Example: They went for a hike. The trail wound up a hill through a forest.
They went for a hike on a trail winding up a hill through a forest.

1. Everyone attended the party. It was given by Joan's parents.
2. I bought all of the groceries. Mom paid for the tomatoes and eggs.
3. The doctor used all of the sample medications. She had no choice.
4. The lashing rain continued. The hail pounded the house.
5. We were told to answer all of the questions. We were taken to the police station. A park warden arrested us.

 COLLABORATIVE WORK

After you revise your own investigating essay, exchange papers with a classmate and do the following tasks:

A. Put an X by any sentence that does not contain an independent clause.

B. Underline any sentence that could be expanded by way of modifying phrases.

C. Use an arrow to mark any sentences that might be combined using prepositional phrases.

Then return the paper to its writer and use the information in this section to edit your draft.

Researching

But it is part of the business of the writer—to examine
attitudes, to go beneath the surface, to tap the source.

—JAMES BALDWIN

LEARNING OUTCOMES

This chapter will help you:
- Understand and write a research essay;
- Understand and include other sources in your essays effectively; and,
- Recognize and use compound sentences.

When you research something, you look for what other people have said on your subject. You may research for a couple of reasons. Sometimes, people do research because they want to learn about a subject. Imagine that someone gave you $500 and you wanted to buy a stereo. What kind of stereo should you buy for $500? Which features do you need? Which is the best brand name? When you understand enough, you can purchase a stereo with confidence—knowing you made the best choice. Research is what helps you understand a subject, and will give you confidence to talk about it. You'll often write an essay on a topic that you don't know much about. Instead of pretending you know something about the subject, you consult books written by experts, or figures and statistics someone else has put together.

Sometimes people do research to find people who agree with their point of view who can help them sound more knowledgeable. Imagine that in discussion with a friend you suggest a certain movie star was born in Manitoba. Your friend gets upset with you and insists that it can't be possible. Your friend just won't trust you enough to believe you. So, you rummage through your backpack and find a copy of a magazine with an article on the movie star. You flip to the page and point it out to your friend. Your friend reads what you're pointing to and then says, "Oh, I guess you were right." Research helps you sound like you know what you're talking about, and it makes it harder for other people to disagree with you. When you include expert opinions or research that agrees with what you're saying, it's like you're forming a group of people who agree with you. Sometimes people do research to find out what people who don't agree with them are saying. When they discover what these people have to say, they can write an essay to attack these points of view.

Whatever your reason is for including research, you need to learn how to take someone else's information and include it in your own essay. The experts' words may come from sources such as books, lectures, illustrations, personal interviews, newspapers, maps, or the Internet. Sometimes you'll want to quote the experts' words exactly; sometimes you'll reword what the experts say; and sometimes you'll restate the experts' words in your own way. Finally, you'll want to let your reader know who the experts are and where you found their words.

There are specific techniques for including experts' words in your essays and for informing your reader about where you borrowed the words from. This chapter focuses on including experts' words in your essay.

LEARNING FROM PUBLISHED WRITERS

The professional essay is an example of using research to make its main point with more force. The research elements of this essay convince you that the author has investigated the issue and knows what he's talking about.

Before You Read

Focus Your Attention

Before you read the following essay, take a few moments to respond to the following questions in your journal:

1. What does the flag, the Canadian flag, mean to you?

2. If you were allowed to pick a new symbol to represent Canada and Canadians, what would it be? Why would you choose it?

Expand Your Vocabulary

In order to understand the story properly, you need to understand everything about it. Here are some words you may not know. Spend some time and read the sentences around the word and see if you can figure out what it means without using a dictionary.

Symbol (paragraph 1)

Custom (paragraph 1)

Distinction (paragraph 1)

Significance (paragraph 2)

Paragons (paragraph 4)

Bill Bunn

A Few Reasons To Redesign The Flag

The subject of our country's flag, until a few years ago, was a sensitive sub-   **1**
ject, one not to be talked about in polite company. Canada, a patchwork of
nationalities and politics, couldn't agree on a symbol to represent it, so the
very search for a symbol became a 100-year-old national custom:

> The seemingly endless quest for the national flag quickly became an al-
> most formalized ritual through which the nation agonized over its emo-
> tional identity. The … ironic concern was … how Canadians would han-
> dle the deprivation, if their favourite controversy was ever actually settled.
> (fraser.cc/FlagsCan/Nation/ CanFlag.html#n85, August 30, 1999)

No one could agree on a symbol adequate enough to represent us all. Yet, as
the Canadian government was adopting the Maple Leaf as the Canadian flag,
February 15, 1965, senate speaker Maurice Bourget stated that the flag "represents all the citizens of Canada without distinction of race, language, belief or
opinion": one leaf fits all.

Not many Canadians I know understand how the leaf represents them.   **2**
The cliché likeness between Canadians and leaves is one I heard recently
restated by a friend: there are eleven points, he said. One point for each
province and territory: one leaf with eleven points (I was taught the same
thing in school.) He was stumped when I reminded him about Nunavut.
Nunavut, the new territory, ruins the whole traditional maple metaphor.
Now we have nine provinces and three territories, which means we've
overloaded the eleven-pointed leaf. Even the Federal Government
admits that "there is no special significance to the eleven points
(www.pch.gc.ca/ceremonial-symb/english/emb_flag_qa.html, August 30, 1999).
Perhaps the federal government, in the interests of nationalism, could hire a
team of geneticists to tinker with the maple's DNA to get a 12-point leaf.
The new mutant leaf could replace the old one on the flag.

A leaf doesn't seem very respectable. Many flags carry symbols of power   **3**
and strength: inspirational ideas. The Americans have a flag you can respect: the stars and stripes. They have one star, one burning ball of gas for
each of the 50 states. Each bit of gas is as important as the other gas. I'm
certain you'd never have the American government declaring that the
burning balls had "no special significance."

Another friend told me that she thought the leaf was appropriate because   **4**
we're a peace-loving country. How is a leaf peaceful, exactly? I asked. She

seemed unsure. Here's my guess: we think peaceful thoughts of leaves because leaves don't do anything. The number of deaths around the world attributed to leaves, maple leaves in particular, are extremely low. Leaves aren't predatorial paragons, nor are they known for their nimbleness of thought. This time of year, leaves just hang around. In the fall, the leaves lie around. This does explain the way many Canadians live, but it's not what you want on a flag. Besides, it puts us in conflict with our other national symbol: the beaver. Are we busy as beavers or lazy as leaves?

Maybe we could borrow the old Soviet flag. The hammer and sickle had kind of an aggressive feel to them. Would you mess with a country that had a hammer and a sickle as its symbol? That's like honking your horn at someone driving a vehicle with a Harley-Davidson sticker on it. You just don't do it. Besides, the hammer and sickle told the truth about life: life is work. Now that they're into capitalism, I'd bet they'd sell their old flag for a song.   **5**

Another friend expressed a similar idea: the leaf reflects the Canadian attitude. Canadians, he said, are as gentle as leaves. Maple leaves, like most leaves, are mild-mannered and polite. The tree uses the leaves to get what it needs to support itself. And, when the tree thinks the usefulness of the leaves is over, it just downsizes. Millions of leaves are suddenly out of work, lying in the grass waiting for someone to help. Then, people rake them up, load them into bags, and throw them away. This may be an accurate picture of Canadian life, but it isn't particularly inspiring: "Hey! Look at me. I'm Canadian. I'm that thing you hate to rake every fall."   **6**

Perhaps the best solution is to just have colours on the flag—like France. Forget the leaf and just go with the red, white, and red. That'd take the fight out of the issue. I'm certain everyone could find some meaning in either red or white. I'd take the red, thank you. It's the colour of blood, love, anger, and 50-dollar bills. Some might prefer white, though: it's the colour of snow, purity, cleanliness, bathroom tile, and paper used to make 50-dollar bills.   **7**

No, the old maple leaf isn't good enough any more. If we're going to keep the maple leaf, we should update it at least. We need more tooth, more muscle, more fire. How about a flaming leaf? What about a leaf with vicious incisors? Or a muscular leaf with rippling abdominals? What about a leaf sporting a registered hand gun? If nothing else, we could add crossbones under the maple leaf so we'd look like piratey leaves. I'm not convinced any of these ideas are the right ones to go on the flag, but one thing I am sure of: I have no idea how a leaf might represent the good things of the country. What I do understand about leaves doesn't seem worth a one-hour special on CBC, let alone the flag. We need to redesign the flag. This time, we'll choose a new national symbol, one that truly wears well on the fabric of Canada.   **8**

? QUESTIONS FOR CRITICAL THINKING

THINKING CRITICALLY ABOUT CONTENT

1. How does the Maple Leaf represent you?
2. Do you agree with the author's views? Why?

THINKING CRITICALLY ABOUT PURPOSE

3. How do you think the writer hopes the reader will react to this essay?
4. What is the point of this reaction?

THINKING CRITICALLY ABOUT AUDIENCE

5. Who do you think the writer wrote his essay for? Why?
6. How would this essay change if it was meant to convince the government to reverse the decision to adopt the maple leaf as the flag?

THINKING CRITICALLY ABOUT PERSPECTIVE

7. How would you feel about this essay if the author was American or English?
8. How does the author feel about the Canadian flag?

LEARNING FROM YOUR PEERS

The writing assignment in this chapter is slightly different from the writing tasks you have studied so far. Instead of drawing on your own experiences to write your essay, you must research and include information from someone else. Researching skills will help you whenever you have to include the main points of someone else's research or writing. To watch the process of researching in action, we are going to follow the writing process of a student named Ezra Long as he writes his essay.

Ezra's Writing Assignment: Write a Research (Restating) Essay

Ezra's instructor assigned the following essay assignment to the class:

Write an essay on something you feel strongly about. To support your opinions, restate information from at least three different sources.

Ezra took the assignment and headed home to begin working through his own writing process.

Thinking

Ezra came home from his afternoon classes frustrated. His last class of the day was English and the instructor assigned a research essay. He didn't have a topic. His English assignment added a little frustration, but the main source of his frustration came from a computer class earlier that day. In that class, the teacher talked about how important technology was becoming. Ezra was frustrated because he disliked technology and resented that it was a required component of his career. Though he didn't want to use technology, it seemed that to perform well in his career he would have to work well with it. Ezra tried to focus on his English essay but his mind kept going back to his computer class. So, instead of starting his essay, he sat at his desk, pen in hand, paper waiting for his words, brooding over his computer class and the black cloud that seemed to be hanging over his future. His frustration was growing as he realized he hadn't been able to do a thing on his essay.

After Ezra sat for a little while longer, he realized he felt very strongly about the topic of technology and the importance it played in everyone's life. The more he thought about it, the more excited he became. He wasn't sure exactly what he wanted to write about, so he decided to browse for ideas. He threw on his coat and headed to the best place he could think of: the library. He searched the library catalogue for technology and there were over 1,000 items listed. As he stared at the list, he noticed that several of the books were old. Ezra knew enough about technology to know that if a book was three years old, it was probably out of date. So, he narrowed his search to include books from 1997 to the present. The list dropped down to 100 books. Then he began to look through the entries for titles that caught his eye and helped him narrow his topic. He found a book called *No More Teachers, No More Books*. The title sounded interesting, so he took down the call number. He found another book entitled *Turning Away From Technology*. The title sounded like it matched his own feelings on the subject, so he jotted down the number for that book, too. The Canadian government had a pamphlet listed in the catalogue called "Minding Our Future: A Report on Federal Science and Technology 1997." He was interested in finding out how the Canadian government felt about technology.

Ezra left the card catalogue and found all the books he had listed. Then, he took a look through each book to see if he was interested. He glanced through the table of contents looking for chapters or sections that appealed to him. When he found something interesting in the table of contents, he would flip to the appropriate page and scan the writing to see if he was still interested. Three out of the four books seemed like good candidates, but Ezra still didn't have a clear idea of what he wanted to write about.

He took the books to a table in the library and spread out his writing and research supplies. He pulled out his pen and paper and began to write. First he wrote his own feelings. Then, he mingled his feelings with ideas he got from his books. Whenever he wrote something down from a book, he wrote the name of the book beside it. Here is some of what he wrote:

> I'm tired of always hearing about how great technology is. It isn't as great as all the hype I hear everyday.

> If the Internet is so great, why do I enjoy watching TV more?

> I think it's a bunch of sales hype. I heard that it actually adds extra work to most offices. More people play more often, and when the junk breaks down, the whole office ends up sitting around.

He scanned the pamphlet from the federal government called "Minding our Future: A Report on Federal Science and Technology 1997." Here's what he wrote.

> The government seems pretty excited about technology. They think it's the key to the future for everyone.

These two sentences restated what Ezra read.

Then, Ezra picked up the book entitled *No More Teachers, No More Books: The Commercialization of Canada's Schools*. As he scanned through a few sections of the book, he realized the book was criticizing technology. He turned to a chapter called "Selling Education" and scanned it. He liked the parts he read a lot, so he decided to read the chapter in more detail. After he read the first part of the chapter, his frustration had transformed into excitement. Here's what he wrote:

> Artifacts have politics. A computer isn't just a computer. It changes the way we do things and some of those changes aren't very good. This woman thinks technology is wrecking things !!!! Excellent stuff.

Ezra realized that there were other people who felt the same way about technology, which made him feel better. Finally, Ezra flipped through his third book called *Turning Away From Technology: A New Vision for the 21st Century*. He found an essay called "In Defence of the Living Earth" in the book's foreword. Here are his notes on this book:

> These guys are quite a bit more radical than the others. They explain about the Luddites, people like me who hated what technology was doing to their lives, yet they did believe technology was OK in its place—properly used. I should find out more about Luddites.

After he'd spent time reading, Ezra began to doodle on the page. He let his mind sift through all he'd read and processed it.

He wrote a few other thoughts that had entered his mind after all of his reading:

> Technology doesn't change the basics. We still need to eat sleep and stuff.

> Science and technology seem more important to many people than being a decent human being.

> Why does everything have to focus on being productive?

> Isn't technology supposed to help us work less?

Ezra signed out all three sources and took them home. Late that night, as he was making a pot of President's Choice Macaroni and Cheese, Ezra realized that two of his sources had to do with employment and technology. As he contemplated how he felt about using a computer on the job, he realized he wanted to show that computers weren't the greatest thing in the world for everyone in the workplace. He thought about what he had to say about computers in the workplace and realized he needed to get more information to back up his case. He wanted to be able to quote some statistics. Statistics, he thought, would be hard to argue against.

The next day he returned to the library to look for statistics on how technology affects employment and productivity. He arrived at the library later than he'd planned to, but he found an article published in *The Globe and Mail* on April 14, 1997. Before he could look it up, the library closed and Ezra had to head home for the evening.

He decided to look up information on the Internet. He found a news release from the Government of Canada with an explanation of why the government felt technology was important. He also looked up "Luddite" in an online encyclopedia.

Armed with all of this information, he sat down to work.

Planning And Developing

The statistics he found demonstrated that technology had not increased productivity in the workplace at all. So Ezra decided to add the statistics to his piece. He thought about the ideas on his list.

~~I'm tired of always hearing about how great technology is. It isn't as great as all the hype I hear everyday.~~ (No one cares if I'm tired of technology.)

~~If the internet is so great, why do I enjoy watching TV more?~~ (This is off topic.)

~~I think it's a bunch of sales hype.~~ (I don't think I can prove this point.) I heard that it actually adds extra work to most offices. More people play more often, and when the junk breaks down, the whole office ends up sitting around. (I need stats to prove this point.)

The government seems pretty excited about technology. They think it's the key to the future for everyone. (The pamphlet and Internet news release support this point.)

Artifacts have politics. A computer isn't just a computer. It changes the way we do things and some of those changes aren't very good. This woman thinks technology is wrecking things !!!! Excellent stuff. (The reader just needs to understand this point; I don't need to prove anything here.)

These guys are quite a bit more radical than the others. They explain about the Luddites—people like me who hated what technology was doing to their lives, yet they did believe technology was OK in its place—properly used. I should find out more about Luddites. (This is a historical thing. I need to show that I understand these people—this might be a good way to begin the essay.)

(I don't think this relates to the other stuff either.)

Science and technology seems more important to many people than being a decent human being. Why does everything have to focus on being productive?

Isn't technology supposed to help us work less?

Ezra spends some time thinking about the order of things he wants to talk about. He also considers each of his list items to see if there are any that aren't on topic. Now Ezra is ready to expand his points.

Drafting

Ezra's Essay: First Draft ....

Possible titles:

Why I am a Luddite

In Defence of the Luddites

A small group of men bask in the light of a weaving machine on fire. They're not trying to save the machine, they are enjoying watching it burn. They are happy because for a moment, they have beaten back the effects of technology. This is revenge. Their employer had a choice between paying labourers or buying a machine. The employer chose the machine.

Many people look down on the Luddites because they feel the Luddites hated technology. But the Luddites didn't hate technology. The Luddites did not want to go back to a primitive form of existence (*Turning Away From Technology*, page vii). And, they weren't frightened of technological change. They were angry at the social consequences of the devices that ruined their lives. And so, they took their anger out on machines, not people. Only one person was ever killed by a Luddite (*Turning Away From Technology*, page viii)

And there are good reasons for the Luddites' anger against technology. As Langdon Winner concluded, "things have intrinsic political consequences" (*No More Teachers*, page 234). Technological devices have built-in consequences for the members of society. Here is an example of the technological consequences of a tomato harvester:

The development of the mechanical tomato-harvester was not a political statement, but its introduction dramatically shifted power relations nonetheless. Because the harvester decreased the need for field workers, Mexican labourers lost their jobs. The profits of Anglo farmers increased, but only until they too lost their livelihood to big agribusiness. While the inventors of the harvesting machine harboured [no]...racist or mega-capitalist biases..., their motives were irrelevant. ... [Technologies] have their own politics. (*No More Teachers*, page 235)

The social consequences were a part of the new technology of the tomato harvester. And, so it is with all other technologies. The computer, the cellular phone, and our favourite technological devices have the same sorts of social effects, too.

At the heart of the Luddites' complaints is the most disturbing aspect of most of our technologies. They burned the machine to mark one of the most dehumanizing moments of the Industrial Revolution: humans were of less value than machines. The social consequences of a particular technology almost always mean that somehow, somewhere someone has to choose to employ a human instead of a machine. In that moment, that person decides that a lump of silicon or a piece of metal is of more value than a human life. This person's decisions are made on the basis of productivity and profit, which is the prime standard of our modern world. But in the process they elevate the life of a technology above the life of a human, transforming the social consequences of a technology from possibility to reality. It is this aspect of technology that made a person an ardent luddite: our technology is better than we are.

If this is disturbing, what is more disturbing is the way governments, the Canadian government in particular, push and encourage technology into every possible sector of Canadian life, while barely acknowledging the social consequences of their policies. A news release from the Canadian government demonstrates the government's commitment to technology. The government's "emphasis on technology is not a new one. It reflects the government's recog-nition of the fact that technology is key to innovation in all sectors of our economy, increasing productivity, which, in turn, results in growth and the creation of jobs" (news release from the Web, page 1). There are several interesting points to notice about this statement. First, the government's commitment is to technology, not to humans. Technology is key—humans are not. The machine is more important to the Canadian government than its people. Secondly, the piece almost entirely ignores the layoffs and ruined lives that most often result when a technology is employed instead of a human. The quote does suggest that once the technology is in place, that growth will occur and jobs will be created. But where are these jobs created? They are created to serve and maintain the machines that have replaced them. And there are fewer employees needed to do much more work.

The government reports the same kind of trends in Canada. A government document reports that from 1980 to 1994 800,000 jobs were created in technology related fields for those with "advanced post-secondary education." During the same period, there was a loss of 1.4 million jobs for those with a "high school education or less." The employee math seems fairly clear. Canada lost a total of 600,000 jobs as technology strolled into town. There are fewer jobs and those who hold them need more training. The trend, according to some experts, is that few workers are required to do much more than ever before. Ted Goldsmith suggests that the technology based, global economy may function with only "20 percent of the world's labor force." (*Turning Away From Technology*, page 143). Who is going to lose out? The same people who are losing out in Canada at the moment—the uneducated, the poor, those in sectors being taken over by technology. Goldsmith suggests that "600 million Indian peasants fall into this category, and possibly a billion Chinese peasants." (*Turning Away From Technology*, page 143). Like the Luddites, these people will become irrelevant to the new economy.

The Canadian Government's urge to technological innovation, in the light of what the technology could mean and has already done to the job market, seems like more of an encouragement to learn and deal with technology before anyone else does so we're not the country with the large population of redundant workers.

The issues the Luddites faced, and the issues we face with our technology are much the same. Corporations choose technologies to emphasize productivity and profit over the valuing of a human life. And machines replace people's jobs every day, hacking human lives into financial pieces. Governments encourage and support that choice. These machines are probably the greatest threat to the livelihood of more people world wide than anyone can possibly imagine. Don't our technologies, our machines, deserve hatred? Shouldn't they be despised? And wouldn't a responsible, caring person be helping the world by lighting the match to destroy these machines, before they destroy us?

Revising

Ezra was pretty happy with the first draft of his essay. He saw a few problems but he left the draft alone for a while to think for a bit about what he wrote. He was fairly sure his point was clear and that the research he used supported his points well. Now he wanted to smooth out the rough edges of his essay, and find support for a couple of points.

Ezra spent time reviewing the Focus on Sentences: Combining Sentences section in this chapter. He wanted to join sentences together well so his essay would effectively and elegantly make his point.

His instructor told the class to concentrate on finding words that say exactly what they need to say, to include them by quoting, and to let the reader know that the essay is using another person's words.

Ezra read the Focus on Paragraphs section and did all the assigned exercises. Returning to his draft, he worked through the checklist carefully, found every time he used another person's words, and checked the technique for how to include those words to make sure each technique was working well. Then he checked his own words around his experts' words to make sure his words flowed smoothly into the experts'.

 ## COLLABORATIVE WORK

PEER GROUP ACTIVITY

After you read the portions of the Focus on Paragraphs section your instructor assigns, turn to Ezra's first draft (p. 155) and complete the following tasks in small groups:

A. Put a star near every location where Ezra used another person's words.

B. Check to see if Ezra included the experts' words using one of the three techniques explained in the Focus on Paragraphs section. Underline any places where Ezra needs to do some work.

C. Read the rest of Ezra's paper. Suggest any improvements he should make.

Compare the marks your group made with those your instructor will show you. Where do your marks differ from your instructor's? What do you need to review before writing your own essay?

CLASS ACTIVITY

As an entire class, look at the underlined portions of Ezra's revised draft (this page) to see how he changed some of his sentences and how he wrote up his sources.

A. Did you identify the revision problems that Ezra corrected?

B. Do you think his changes are good ones? Discuss his changes.

Ezra's Revised Essay

Why I am a Luddite

A small group of men bask in the light of a weaving machine on fire. They're not trying to save the machine, they are enjoying watching it burn. They are happy because for a moment, they have beaten back the effects of technology. This is revenge. Their employer had a choice between paying labourers or buying a <u>machine: machine.</u> <s>The</s><u>the</u> employer chose the machine.

Many people look down on the Luddites because they feel the Luddites hated technology. But <s>the Luddites didn't hate technology.</s><u>they didn't</u>. The Luddites did not want to go back to a primitive form of existence (*Turning Away From Technology*, page vii). And, they weren't frightened of technological change. <s>They</s><u>But, they</u> were angry at the social consequences of <s>the devices that</s><u>technology. Technology</u> ruined their <s>lives.</s><u>livelihood.</u> And so, they took their anger out on <s>machines, not people. Only one person was ever killed by a Luddite (Turning away from Technology, page viii)</s><u>those machines.</u>

<s>And there are good reasons for the Luddite's anger against technology. As Langdon Winner concluded, "things</s><u>The Luddites were reacting to something our century has awakened to: technology had a</u>

deep impact on how people live. Langdon Winner puts it this way: "things [technologies] have intrinsic political consequences" (*No More Teachers*, page 234). Technological devices have a built-in ~~consequences for the members of society.~~societal impact. Here is an example of the technological consequences of a tomato harvester:

> The development of the mechanical tomato-harvester was not a political statement, but its introduction dramatically shifted power relations nonetheless. Because the harvester decreased the need for field workers, Mexican labourers lost their jobs. The profits of Anglo farmers increased, but only until they too lost their livelihood to big agribusiness. While the inventors of the harvesting machine harboured [no]…racist or mega-capitalist biases…, their motives were irrelevant. [Technologies] have their own politics. (*No More Teachers*, page 235)

The social consequences were a part of the new technology of the tomato harvester. ~~And, so~~So it is with all other technologies. The computer, the cellular phone, and our favourite technological devices have the same sorts of social side effects, too.

At the heart of the Luddite's ~~complaints is~~complaint lies the most disturbing aspect of ~~most of our technologies. They burned the machine to mark~~technology, one of the most dehumanizing moments of the Industrial Revolution: humans were of less value than machines. The social consequences of a particular technology almost always mean that somehow, somewhere someone ~~has to~~will choose to employ a ~~human~~machine instead of a ~~machine.~~human. In that moment, that person decides that a lump of silicon or a piece of metal, the bottom line profit, is of more value than a human life. ~~This person's decisions are made on the basis of productivity and profit, which is the prime standard of our modern world. But in the process they elevate the life of a technology above the life of a human, transforming the social consequences of a technology from~~And, in the process, the plastic sheen of a technology surpasses human life. ~~possibility to reality. It is this aspect of technology that made a person an ardent luddite: our technology is better than we are.~~

If this is disturbing, what is more disturbing is the way governments, the Canadian government in particular, push and encourage technology into every possible sector of Canadian life, while barely acknowledging the social consequences of their policies. A news release from the Canadian government demonstrates the government's commitment to technology. The government's "emphasis on technology is not a new one. It reflects the government's recognition of the fact that technology is key to innovation in all sectors of our economy, increasing productivity, which, in turn, results in growth and the creation of jobs" (news release from the Web, page 1). There are several interesting points to notice about this statement. First, the government's commitment is to technology, not to humans. Technology is key—humans are not. The machine is more important to the Canadian government than its people. Secondly, the piece almost entirely ignores the layoffs and ruined lives that most often result when a technology is employed instead of a human. The quote does suggest that once the technology is in place, that growth will occur and jobs will be created. But where are these jobs created? They are created to serve and maintain the machines that have replaced them. And there are fewer employees needed to do much more work.

The government reports the same kind of trends in ~~Canada. A government document reports that~~Canada: from 1980 to 1994, 800,000 jobs were created in technology related fields for those with "advanced post-secondary education." During the same period, there was a loss of 1.4 million jobs for those with a "high school education or less." The employee math seems fairly clear. Canada lost a total of 600,000 jobs as technology strolled into town. There are fewer jobs and those who hold them need more training. The trend, according to some experts, is that few workers are required to do much more than ever before. Ted Goldsmith suggests that the ~~technology-based,~~technology-based, global economy may function with only "20 percent of the world's labor force." (*Turning Away From Technology*, page 143). <u>Only 20 percent of the world will have a job.</u> Who is going to lose out? The same people who are losing out in Canada at the moment—the uneducated, the poor, those in sectors being taken over by technology. <u>Who will be unemployed globally?</u> Goldsmith suggests that "600 million Indian peasants fall into this category, and possibly a billion Chinese peasants." (*Turning Away From Technology*, page 143). Like the Luddites, these people will become irrelevant to the new economy.

~~The Canadain Government's urge to technological innovation, in the light of what the technology could mean and has already done to the job market, seems like more of a encouragement to learn and deal with technology before anyone else does so we're not the country with the large population of redundant workers.~~

The issues the Luddites faced, and the issues we face with our technology are much the same. Corporations choose technologies to emphasize productivity and profit ~~over the valuing of a~~<u>through</u> <u>technology over</u> human life. And machines replace people's jobs every day, hacking human lives into financial pieces. Governments encourage and support that choice. These machines are probably the greatest threat to the livelihood of more people ~~world wide~~<u>world-wide</u> than anyone can possibly imagine. ~~Don't our technologies, our machines, deserve hatred?~~<u>In the light of the destruction our technologies cause,</u> <u>shouldn't we hate technology?</u> Shouldn't they be despised? And wouldn't a responsible, caring person be helping the world by lighting the match to destroy these machines, before they destroy us?

PRACTISE OUTLINING

Spend time as a class thinking, planning, developing, and organizing a potential researching essay.

1. Spend about 10 minutes brainstorming potential topics.

2. Once three or four have been suggested, choose one or two for the subject of a potential essay. What makes one idea better than another idea? What are we looking for?

3. Decide on the audience and the purpose.

4. Brainstorm this memory's possible significance to the audience. Have someone write ideas on the overhead or blackboard.

5. What research would you look for to support your points? Where would you get it from?

6. Organize the ideas so they appear in the best order for the best effect.

Could you write this essay? How long would it take you to finish this essay?

WRITING YOUR OWN RESEARCH ESSAY

So far, you have read several small sections featuring professional writers, and watched a student use the professional essays to help build his own essay. As you read the published essay and followed the writing process of another student from first to final draft, you absorbed ideas and ways of giving those ideas a form of their own. These reading and writing activities have prepared you to write your own research essay.

What Have You Discovered?

Before you begin your own research essay, let's review what you have learned in this chapter so far:

- When you research, you're looking for what other people have said about your topic.

- When you use another person's words in your essay you make it easier for your reader to believe what you say. Your essay becomes more powerful.

- When you use another person's words, you can show your reader that you understand the material you've used.

- There are three main ways to include another person's thoughts in your own essay: you can restate a person's words in your own words; you can reword a person's words; or, you can quote the person's words directly.

- To present your research effectively, you need to organize your ideas.

- To help you shape your essay, you should learn as much as possible about your readers.

- Before you write a draft, you should understand the original author's point of view toward the subject.

- After you write a draft, you should revise your essay for meaning and organization.

- After you revise your essay, you should edit its grammar, usage, and sentence structure.

Your Writing Topic

Find a topic that interests you and talk to your instructor to get his or her opinion about it. Then, go to the library and find a newspaper or magazine article and a book that talks about your subject. If you can't find a newspaper or magazine article, that probably means you need to switch topics. Find a computer and surf the Internet on your topic. Print the pages and take down the details of your visit. When you have selected one of these topics, you may begin your writing process in the same way Ezra did. (You may find his experience helpful in giving you ideas.) This time your purpose is to write your own research essay. If some tasks occur out of order, that adjustment is probably part of your personal writing ritual. Follow your instincts, and let them mold your own writing process. But make sure you've worked through all the stages to your final draft. Write your essay and use three sources to help you make your point. If one of your sources isn't going to help you, go and look for another source of the same kind.

Turn in your revised draft to your instructor.

Some Final Thoughts

When you have completed your own essay, answer these four questions in your journal:

1. What was most difficult about this assignment?
2. What was easiest?
3. What did I learn about researching by completing this assignment?
4. What did I learn about my own writing process—how I prepared to write, how I wrote the first draft, how I revised, and how I edited?

Including Other People's Words In Your Essay

Checklist For Including Other People's Words

✓ Are you quoting, rewording, or paraphrasing your sources?

✓ If you're quoting, do you

✓   Put the other person's words in quotation marks?

✓   Introduce the quote properly?

✓   Indent quotes that take more than four lines in your paper?

✓   Edit the quote—add or remove words—to make the quote say what it needs to say clearly?

✓ Do you introduce your paraphrased sources properly?

✓ Do you introduce your fragment quotes properly?

There is an art to including other people's words in your essays. This section will provide you with techniques that can help you get started. There are three ways to include a person's words in your essay: you can reword the person's words in your own words; you can rearrange some of the person's own words; or, you can quote the person's words exactly. Each technique has its own effect. You need to choose the technique for a good reason. In each case there are some specific techniques you can use to make sure the other person's words are well integrated into your essay.

How To Quote Other People's Words

When you take the exact words someone has written or spoken and you use them in your essay, you are quoting their words. You'll want to use a direct quote if the quote is well worded, it makes your point better than your own words, or if you need to have someone else deliver the point.

Whenever you include someone else's words in your essay, you need to use your own words to introduce the quote. You want to use your own words to guide your reader into the other person's words. There are two main techniques. If your quote begins with a partial sentence—a sentence fragment—then you'll use the first technique. If your quote begins with a whole sentence, or is a single whole sentence, you'll want to use the second technique.

Quoting A Sentence Fragment

If the words you wanted to quote aren't a complete sentence, then introduce the quote with a phrase that completes the quoted sentence fragment. Let's say that you want to use a quote out of this paragraph:

There has never been a movement that simply and unthinkingly hated machines and set about destroying them. There has never been a movement that called all technology evil and demanded its repeal in favor of reverting to fingernails and incisors. There has never been a movement that suggested that we live in caves and do without running water. The original Luddites were not such people. The Neo-Luddites who have produced this book are not such people. The Ur-Luddites of the English Industrial Revolution were angry weavers who had been "downsized" out of their jobs by factory owners who ousted them in favor of power looms and knitting frames. The weavers, the first victims of technological unemployment, with no union to speak for them and no welfare benefits to draw upon, understandably found this unfair. They appealed for justice, first to the owners, then to Parliament. Their petitions, regarded as illiterate and presumptuous, went unanswered. Only then did they go underground and resort to guerrilla tactics.

Suppose you want to include this sentence in your essay:

The Ur-Luddites of the English Industrial Revolution were angry weavers who had been "downsized" out of their jobs by factory owners who ousted them in favor of power looms and knitting frames.

Now, you don't want to use the first part of the sentence because your readers won't know what you're talking about. And you don't want to bring in power looms and knitting frames because you don't want to talk about either object. You just want to include the idea that the Luddites were "'downsized' out of their jobs by factory owners." You want to quote a fragment of the sentence.

All quotes need an introduction, and this one is no exception. You can introduce the quote by using one of three techniques: summarizing what the quote is about, announcing who the words belong to, or announcing who the words belong to and where they came from. Our quote comes from a piece written by Theodore Roszak titled "In Defense of the Living Earth." It's the foreword of a book titled *Turning Away From Technology*. Be sure to make your introduction flow right into the quoted words. Here's the same quote introduced three different ways:

As Theodore Roszak noted, Luddites "had been 'downsized' out of their jobs by factory owners." (The introduction attributes the quote to the author of the words.)

In the foreword of a book entitled *Turning Away From Technology*, Theodore Roszak suggests that the Luddites "had been 'downsized' out of their jobs by factory owners." (The introduction attributes the quote to the author and the source.)

The first people to lose their jobs because of technology were the Luddites who "had been 'downsized' out of their jobs by factory owners." (The introduction summarizes what the quote says.)

Make sure the introduction and the quote form a whole sentence. Put quotation marks around all the quoted words.

Just a little advice about introducing quotes: make sure to vary the introductions to your quotes. If you introduce all your quotes with one technique, you're likely to bore your reader.

What To Do If The Quote Is Longer Than Four Lines In Your Essay

If the quote you're using takes up more than four lines of your essay, then you need to make the quote into its own paragraph and indent the paragraph on both sides. You still introduce the quote using the same techniques outlined above. The only difference is that in the longer version of the quote, because you indent it, you can remove the quotation marks from the beginning and end of the quote. Here's an example of a longer version of our original quote:

> As Theodore Roszak noted, the Luddites
>
> > had been "downsized" out of their jobs by factory owners who ousted them in favor of power looms and knitting frames. The weavers, the first victims of technological unemployment, with no union to speak for them and no welfare benefits to draw upon, understandably found this unfair. They appealed for justice, first to the owners, then to Parliament. Their petitions, regarded as illiterate and presumptuous, went unanswered. Only then did they go underground and resort to guerrilla tactics.

Notice that the introduction still flows right into the quote, forming a complete sentence. There is no punctuation between the introduction and the quote because the introduction and the first phrase of the quote form a complete sentence. Notice, too, there are no quotation marks around the quote. When the words are indented and separated from the main paragraph, your reader will realize that you are quoting someone else's words, so the quotation marks aren't necessary. Finally, any of the three introduction techniques could introduce this quote.

Quoting Whole Sentences

If the quote isn't a sentence fragment, then you're quoting a whole sentence. To introduce a whole-sentence quote, you must use a complete sentence. Let's say that you want to use a quote out of this paragraph:

> There has never been a movement that simply and unthinkingly hated machines and set about destroying them. There has never been a movement that called all technology evil and demanded its repeal in favor of reverting to fingernails and incisors. There has never been a movement

that suggested that we live in caves and do without running water. The original Luddites were not such people. The Neo-Luddites who have produced this book are not such people. The Ur-Luddites of the English Industrial Revolution were angry weavers who had been "downsized" out of their jobs by factory owners who ousted them in favor of power looms and knitting frames. The weavers, the first victims of technological unemployment, with no union to speak for them and no welfare benefits to draw upon, understandably found this unfair. They appealed for justice, first to the owners, then to Parliament. Their petitions, regarded as illiterate and presumptuous, went unanswered. Only then did they go underground and resort to guerrilla tactics.

Let's say you want to include this sentence in your essay:

> There has never been a movement that simply and unthinkingly hated machines and set about destroying them.

The quote is a whole sentence, and it needs an introduction. You must introduce the quote using one of the three introduction techniques described in quoting sentence fragments. You can introduce the quote by summarizing what the quote is about, announcing who the words belong to, or announcing who the words belong to and where they came from. As mentioned earlier, this quote comes from a piece written by Theodore Roszak titled "In Defense of the Living Earth." It's the foreword of a book titled *Turning Away From Technology*. However, this time, instead of making the introduction and the quote form a complete sentence, the introduction must be a sentence by itself. Here is the same quote introduced three different ways:

> Theodore Roszak once wrote these words: "there has never been a movement that simply and unthinkingly hated machines and set about destroying them." (This introduction attributes the quote to the author.)

> Theodore Roszak, in the foreword of a book entitled *Turning Away From Technology*, has this to say about anti-technology movements: "there has never been a movement that simply and unthinkingly hated machines and set about destroying them." (This introduction attributes the quote's author and source.)

> Theodore Roszak denies that anti-technology groups simply hate technology: "there has never been a movement that simply and unthinkingly hated machines and set about destroying them." (This introduction attributes the quote to the author and summarizes the quote's content.)

Notice that the introduction for each example is a full sentence. Notice that the first word of the quote, even though it was capitalized in the source, is now lower case. Notice, too, that the introduction is followed by a colon. Use a colon whenever you use a full sentence to introduce your quote (see p. 181).

How To Remove Words From A Quote

Sometimes you might want to cut some words from the middle of a quote. You need to use special punctuation to show that you removed them. The special punctuation is called an ellipsis. Let's say this is the original quote:

> The Ur-Luddites of the English Industrial Revolution were angry weavers who had been "downsized" out of their jobs by factory owners who ousted them in favor of power looms and knitting frames. The weavers, the first victims of technological unemployment, with no union to speak for them and no welfare benefits to draw upon, understandably found this unfair. They appealed for justice, first to the owners, then to Parliament. Their petitions, regarded as illiterate and presumptuous, went unanswered. Only then did they go underground and resort to guerrilla tactics.

And let's say you want to remove some of the words in the middle of this quote. First, remove the unwanted words. Make sure that the quote still makes sense after you've removed the words. Then, where you removed the words, place three periods in a row. Add an extra period if the words following the words you removed begin a new sentence. The three periods in a row, or ellipsis, tell your reader that you removed some words from the quote. Here's how it works:

> The Ur-Luddites of the English Industrial Revolution were angry weavers who had been "downsized" out of their jobs by factory owners who ousted them in favor of power looms and knitting frames....They appealed for justice, first to the owners, then to Parliament....Only then did they go underground and resort to guerrilla tactics.

We've shortened the quote considerably, yet it still makes sense. As long as it clearly supports what you're saying in your essay, then removing words helps.

How To Add Words To A Quote After Removing Some

Occasionally a quote might use a word that could confuse your readers, or the words used in the quote don't fit with the terminology of your paper. In this kind of situation you'll want to add words to your quote to help the quote support your essay in a stronger way. Here's the original quote:

> The Ur-Luddites of the English Industrial Revolution were angry weavers who had been "downsized" out of their jobs by factory owners who ousted them in favor of power looms and knitting frames. The weavers, the first victims of technological unemployment, with no union to speak for them and no welfare benefits to draw upon, understandably found this unfair. They appealed for justice, first to the owners, then to Parliament. Their petitions, regarded as illiterate and presumptuous, went unanswered. Only then did they go underground and resort to guerrilla tactics.

First, you'll want to remove the confusing words and replace them with an ellipsis, like this:

> The … were angry weavers who had been "downsized" out of their jobs by factory owners who ousted them in favor of power looms and knitting frames. The weavers, the first victims of technological unemployment, with no union to speak for them and no welfare benefits to draw upon, understandably found this unfair. They appealed for justice, first to the owners, then to …. Their … went unanswered. Only then did they go underground and resort to guerrilla tactics.

Then, add the terms you want to use in square brackets within the quote, like this:

> The … [Luddites] were angry weavers who had been "downsized" out of their jobs by factory owners who ousted them in favor of power looms and knitting frames. The weavers, the first victims of technological un-employment, with no union to speak for them and no welfare benefits to draw upon, understandably found this unfair. They appealed for justice, first to the owners, then to the …[government]. Their …[complaints] went unanswered. Only then did they go underground and resort to guer-rilla tactics.

When your reader encounters words in square brackets, he or she will realize that these are words you added to the original quote. You probably won't want to add too many words to your quote, otherwise your reader will suspect that you're trying to force your source to say something it doesn't say. Be careful that the words you add clarify what you want to say and don't change the meaning of the original quote.

How To Paraphrase Other People's Words

When you paraphrase a source, you rewrite what is being said in your own words and you don't attribute the information directly as you rewrite. The reader knows that you paraphrased your information when he or she sees that you documented what you wrote. This technique interrupts your own writing the least because you don't have to try and fit someone else's words into your essay. You rewrite their words with your own. The other reason this technique might make a good choice is if the person who authored the words and the way the quote is worded aren't important to your essay.

Paraphrasing means that you put the other person's ideas in your own words. You don't have to mention who wrote the words, or where the words came from. Your reader will know that you rewrote someone else's ideas when they see that you docu-mented the idea. Here's the original quote:

> The Ur-Luddites of the English Industrial Revolution were angry weavers who had been "downsized" out of their jobs by factory owners who ousted them in favor of power looms and knitting frames. The weavers, the first

victims of technological unemployment, with no union to speak for them and no welfare benefits to draw upon, understandably found this unfair.

And here's an example of paraphrasing:

> The Luddites were disgruntled employees who were laid off after factory owners purchased the latest technology. These employees lives' were unjustly ruined and they didn't even have the advantages we have in our system: welfare benefits, or a union to help them cope.

The words are completely different, but the ideas are the same. The paraphrase has roughly the same number of words as the original.

This is a dangerous technique because if a person forgets to document the source, there is nothing in the writing to indicate the ideas were someone else's. This is known as plagiarizing. Plagiarizing is using someone else's words or ideas in an essay without giving credit. Whenever you use someone else's words or ideas, be careful to quote carefully and document properly!

How To Reword Other People's Words

Sometimes you want to mention what a source says but you don't want to quote the source directly. This is probably a time when you want to reword the quote just slightly. You tend to do this kind of rewording often in your conversations. Say, for example, you meet some friends at a coffee shop. Someone asks you if another friend is going to stop by the shop. You might say something like this: "Jim said that he was coming." You don't use your friend's exact words, but the meaning is the same. You can use the same technique when you want to include a source, when a direct quote would be too long and the reader only needs the general gist of the quote. Rewording emphasizes who the words belong to, and what was said. So if who authored the words and the general gist of what they say is important, this technique works well. This technique is particularly useful when the quote talks about a few things that aren't related to your topic. When you reword the quote, you can remove some of the distracting material and focus on one aspect of what's being said.

When you reword another person's words, you want to give a general summary of what they said and give them credit for saying it. Most of the time, with this kind of quotation, you have to use the word "that" to reword the quote properly. Let's say you want to reword this quote:

> The Ur-Luddites of the English Industrial Revolution were angry weavers who had been "downsized" out of their jobs by factory owners who ousted them in favor of power looms and knitting frames. The weavers, the first victims of technological unemployment, with no union to speak for them and no welfare benefits to draw upon, understandably found this unfair.

The author's name is Theodore Roszak, so we could reword this quote like this:

> Theodore Roszak said that the Luddites were actually the first workers to lose their jobs because of technology.

Notice that some of what Roszak said in the original quote was lost in the rewording. That's all right as long as what remains is true to what the original source said and helps you make your point.

Exercise P6-1

Spend some time completing the following exercise. Make sure you understand each technique.

1. Go to the library and find one six- to ten-sentence quote.
2. Return to the class and spend time introducing a quote fragment and a whole sentence quote.
3. Try working with the four lines quoting technique.
4. Try rewording and paraphrasing your quote.

 ## COLLABORATIVE WORK

After you revise your essay, exchange papers with a classmate, and do the following tasks:

A. Find any quotes, paraphrases, and rewordings used in the essay.
B. Check every quote to make sure it's been introduced and the introduction connects properly to the quote.
C. Does the essay vary the introductory techniques?
D. Should any of the quotes be turned into a paraphrasing or rewording? Should any of the paraphrases or rewordings be quoted instead?

Then return the paper to your classmate. When you receive your essay, use the information in this section to edit your draft.

Building Compound Sentences

Checklist For Building Compound Sentences

✓ Are both sentences in the compound sentence complete sentences?
✓ Have the sentences been joined correctly using one of the three techniques to build a compound sentence?
✓ Does the combined sentence (the compound sentence) communicate meaning precisely?

What Is A Compound Sentence?

Those who have read many essays tend to think that longer sentences are more elegant and the mark of more sophisticated writing. There are three kinds of sentences that will help you achieve this goal: compound sentences, complex sentences, and compound-complex sentences.

The compound sentence combines two or more independent clauses (simple sentences). There are three simple techniques to help you understand how to build compound sentences: the FANBOYS technique, the semicolon technique, and the colon technique.

Joining two independent sentences together is easy enough to do, but the most important thing to remember is that when you join sentences together, you alter the meaning of both sentences. Aim to join sentences together to better communicate your meaning.

Notice how the meaning changes when we use different words to join two sentences. Here are our two sentences:

Sentence 1:   They're not trying to save the machine.

Sentence 2:   They are enjoying watching it burn.

Let's put these two sentences together in a few different ways:

Combination 1: They're not trying to save the machine, so they are enjoying watching it burn.

This sentence suggests that the people watching the machine burn are enjoying the fire because they don't have to try to put it out. The sentence changes meaning, however, if we change the word we use to join the two sentences:

Combination 2: They're not trying to save the machine, for they are enjoying watching it burn.

This sentence suggests that people around the burning machine aren't putting out the fire because they're enjoying it. Here's another change:

Combination 3: They're not trying to save the machine, yet they are enjoying watching it burn.

In this sentence, the people watching the fire are enjoying the blaze even though they're not helping to put it out.

The meaning changes every time we change the way we join the sentences. Which of these three combinations is right? All three combinations are combined correctly, so they're right in the grammatical sense. The important question, then, is which combination says what you're trying to say most accurately? Our examples come from Ezra's essay. Which of the three sentences best reflect what he's is trying to say? I think we'd have to agree that Combination 2 works best.

The FANBOYS Technique

One way to combine sentences is to use a coordinating conjunction. There are seven of them, and you'll remember all seven of them if you remember the word "FANBOYS." Here's what each letter stands for:

F = for
A = and
N = nor
B = but
O = or
Y = yet
S = so

These are all of the coordinating conjunctions.

When you have two sentences, or independent clauses, you can join them together with one of the FANBOYS using this formula:

F
A
N
B
O
Y
S

Independent clause **,**   Independent clause **.**

Let's say you have two independent clauses and you want to combine them using a conjunction:

Sentence 1:   I like my computer.

Sentence 2:   It helps me write.

According to our formula, we can join them this way:

Combination 1: I like my computer **, and** it helps me write **.**

Try it yourself.

Exercise S6-1

Join the following sentences together with a coordinating conjunction. Obviously, you can't choose a conjunction based on the best meaning. Just put the sentences together correctly.

1. The government cut social programs heavily.

    The children of welfare recipients suffered the most.

2. Air travel with Zeppelins was popular until the Hindenburg disaster.

    The airplane ruled the sky afterwards.

3. Men and women's thought processes operate differently.

    Quite often men and women fail to understand one another.

4. I've learned to enjoy jazz.

    It took me a while to learn to love it.

5. Our culture is obsessed with cleanliness.

    Many homes operate as though they were sterile environments.

A Variation On The FANBOYS Technique

Instead of using one of the FANBOYS by itself, try using a FANBOY with an extra word or two at the beginning of the first independent clause. Here is an example of this technique:

> Either the cow can talk, or Bob has lost his mind.

You'll recognize "or" as one of the FANBOYS. The extra word is the word "either." A few of the FANBOYS can take an extra word or words in this kind of pattern. Besides the famous either/or combination from the previous example, you can add "neither" to "nor" and "not only" to "but." Here's the formula:

Either / Neither / Not only	Independent clause	**,**	or / nor / but (also)	Independent clause	**.**

Here are two sentences we can join with this technique:

Sentence 1:   I like my computer.

Sentence 2:   It helps me write.

And, when we join them, here's what we get:

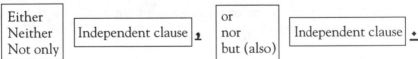

Either I like my computer , or it helps me write.

The sentence doesn't make much sense, but it is correct. You can see it's not too difficult.

Exercise S6-2

Try this technique on the next few sentences:

1. The government cut social programs heavily.

   The children of welfare recipients suffered the most.
2. Air travel with Zeppelins was popular until the Hindenburg disaster.

   The airplane ruled the sky afterwards.
3. Men and women's thought processes operate differently.

   Quite often men and women fail to understand one another.
4. I've learned to enjoy jazz.

   It took me a while to learn to love it.
5. Our culture is obsessed with cleanliness.

   Many homes operate as though they were sterile environments.

The Semicolon Technique

The second way to join two independent clauses is with a semicolon. A semicolon is different than a period. It is a weak version of the period. It's too weak to end a sentence the way a period does. It always has to be followed by a sentence ending in a period.

Punctuation means something just as words do. The semicolon means the same as the word *and*. It's an elegant piece of punctuation, but be careful not to overuse it. One semicolon every paragraph is enough in most situations.

Here is the formula for how to use it:

> Independent clause **;** Independent clause **.**

Let's try to combine these two sentences with the semicolon technique:

Sentence 1:   I like my computer.

Sentence 2:   It helps me write.

If we combined them, they would look like this:

> I like my computer **;** it helps me write **.**

Exercise S6-3

Try the semicolon technique on these sentences:

1. The government cut social programs heavily.

   The children of welfare recipients suffered the most.

2. Air travel with Zeppelins was popular until the Hindenburg disaster.

   The airplane ruled the sky afterwards.

3. Men and women's thought processes operate differently.

   Quite often men and women fail to understand one another.

4. I've learned to enjoy jazz.

   It took me a while to learn to love it.

5. Our culture is obsessed with cleanliness.

   Many homes operate as though they were sterile environments.

A Variation On The Semicolon Technique

We can add one complication to the technique we just learned. We can use a semi-colon and an extra word to change the relationship of the independent clauses. The words we use with the semicolon are formal. We call them conjunctive adverbs. Here are several of them:

Accordingly	However	Otherwise
Consequently	Likewise	Then
Furthermore	Moreover	Therefore
Hence	Nevertheless	Thus

Here is the formula for using conjunctive adverbs with a semicolon:

| Independent clause | ; | **conjunctive adverb** , | independent clause | . |

Let's combine these two sentences:

Sentence 1: I like my computer.

Sentence 2: It helps me write.

The two sentences form one compound sentence that should look something like this:

I like my computer **; therefore,** it helps me write **.**

As with some of the other techniques, you don't want to use this one too often—aim for variety in your sentences.

Exercise S6-4

Try joining the following sentences together using this technique:

1. The government cut social programs heavily.

   The children of welfare recipients suffered the most.

2. Air travel with Zeppelins was popular until the Hindenburg disaster.

   The airplane ruled the sky afterwards.

3. Men and women's thought processes operate differently.

   Quite often men and women fail to understand one another.

4. I've learned to enjoy jazz.

   It took me a while to learn to love it.

5. Our culture is obsessed with cleanliness.

   Many homes operate as though they were sterile environments.

The Colon Technique

The third technique for joining two independent clauses is the colon technique. Using the colon isn't much different than using a semicolon, except the colon has a different meaning. The colon is roughly equivalent to the mathematical equal sign. When you use it, it means that the sentence before the colon is equal in meaning to the sentence after the colon.

The house was falling apart: there were no doors or windows left in place.

The first sentence is equal to the second part of the sentence—both sentences are saying the same thing in different words. Most of the time, the first sentence will make a general observation and the second sentence gives some specific detail. The important thing to remember is that the meaning of the sentences has to be equal. If the meaning is not equal, then the colon has been used incorrectly.

Coffee has been blamed for many ailments: the trees are in full bloom.

This example uses the colon properly in the grammatical sense. But the relationship between the two sentences is not equal, so the colon isn't being used properly. Here's the formula for using the colon:

| Independent clause | : | Independent clause | . |

Here are our two demonstration sentences:

Sentence 1:   I like my computer.

Sentence 2:   It helps me write.

Let's join our two sentences to see how this works:

I like my computer : it helps me write .

You do not need to capitalize the first letter of the second sentence. Colons can easily be overused the way semicolons can. One colon per paragraph is plenty in most situations.

Exercise S6-5

Give the technique a try with these sentences:

1. The government cut social programs heavily.

   The children of welfare recipients suffered the most.

2. Air travel with Zeppelins was popular until the Hindenburg disaster.

   The airplane ruled the sky afterwards.

3. Men and women's thought processes operate differently.

   Quite often men and women fail to understand one another.

4. I've learned to enjoy jazz.

   It took me a while to learn to love it.

5. Our culture is obsessed with cleanliness.

   Many homes operate as though they were sterile environments.

 COLLABORATIVE WORK

After writing a draft of your own research essay, exchange papers with a classmate and do the following tasks:

A. Underline every semicolon, colon, or use of FANBOYS in the essay.

B. For any sentences you've underlined, highlight the subject and predicate for each sentence—there should be two subjects and predicates because there are two sentences in a compound sentence. Make a note of sentences that are missing one or more subject or predicate—these sentences are not compound sentences.

C. Underline each compound sentence completely.

D. For each compound sentence, identify the technique used to join the two sentences together.

E. Mark any compound sentence that isn't combined correctly.

F. If you cannot find any compound sentences, suggest several places where one would work well.

Then return the paper to your classmate. When you receive your own essay, use the information written on your paper to edit your draft.

Other Uses For The Colon

As we've seen, the colon can be used to join two independent clauses. But the colon has other uses, too: you can use it to help introduce a list, introduce a quote, or emphasize a few words.

Introducing A List

Colons are often used to introduce a list. Here's an example:

> Here are the things I need to buy at the grocery store: tape, gum, salad dressing, Kleenex, and bleach.

In this example, the sentence before the colon introduces the list in quite an obvious way. Here's another list where the introduction is a little less obvious:

> Most of the pets I've owned have died on me: the hamster, the dog, the salamander, the flounder, and the pigeon.

In some ways, the colon in the list has the same meaning as it did when it brought two sentences together. The colon is like an equal sign, and the first sentence gives a general summary of the items in the list. So the colon still means the same as it did when it joined two sentences together. Here's the formula for introducing lists with a colon:

| Independent clause | **:** | list item | **,** | list item | **, and** | list item | **.** |

Let's use it to try and bring this sentence and this list together.

| **Sentence** | I use my computer for many different tasks. |
| **List:** | Writing, budgeting, surfing, and faxing. |

Here's what it could look like:

I use my computer for many different tasks **:** writing **,** budgeting **,** surfing **, and** faxing **.**

Exercise S6-6

Try this technique on these examples:

1. Most provinces struggle with the same problems.
   Social programs, balanced budgets, and deficits.
2. Several food additives are harmful in large quantities.
   Monosodium glutamate, salt, nitrates, several kinds of food dyes.
3. Several inventions have altered the way humankind thinks.
   The printing press, the radio, TV, and now the Internet.
4. The blues have contributed to a wide range of other musical heritages.
   Country and western, jazz, folk, and, of course, rock.
5. Many revolutionaries were driven to other places.
   Morocco, Tanzania, England, and Greece.

Introducing A Quote

Writers often use the colon to introduce a quote (see the Focus on Paragraphs section in this chapter). The colon's meaning hasn't changed for this technique either: what goes before the colon and what comes after are equal in their meaning. In this case, put an independent clause before the colon. It should be an independent clause that introduces the quotation in a general way. Here's an example:

> Frank's words criticize the Canadian people: "the government is not responsible for everyone's life."

Make sure you put an independent clause before the colon. The quote should be an independent clause, too. Here's the formula:

Here's our introductory sentence and sentence quote:

Sentence: We can summarize Jill's attitude toward computers with her own words.

Quote: "I can't live without my computer."

Let's combine them:

> We can summarize Jill's attitude toward computers with her own words: "I can't live without my computer."

You'll be using colons to introduce quotes in the next section so we'll save the exercises for then.

Emphasizing A Few Words

You can also use a colon to emphasize a few words. Here's an example:

> I changed to please one person: my aunt.

In this example, *one person* is emphasized. The words after the colon repeat part of what is expressed in the sentence before the colon and often adds a little to the idea. *One person* was mentioned in the first sentence, and that person was identified in the words after the colon: *my aunt.*

The colon still means the same thing as it did in all the other techniques. It's like a weak equal sign. What comes before the colon should equal what comes afterward.

This technique also works well if you introduce something without mentioning it in the first sentence, then use the words after the colon to identify it. Usually, it's best to pick the last main noun mentioned in the first sentence as the one to expand on after the colon. Here's an example:

> Simon likes to run a <u>marathon</u> every year: the Boston Marathon.

What comes after the colon is not a complete sentence: it's a piece of a sentence, a sentence fragment. Sentence fragments are only allowed in a few specific places. This is one of them. Here is the formula:

| Independent clause | :| noun or noun phrase | . |

Let's try it on this test sentence:

Sentence :   Jasmine started her own company.

Detail :   a cosmetics firm

Here's what we get:

Jasmine started her own company: a cosmetics firm.

We have now emphasized and added detail to the words "a cosmetics firm."

Exercise S6-7

Try this technique on the following sentences. The exercise presents two sentences. Reduce the second sentence to a noun or a noun phrase (you may want to paraphrase the second sentence with a different word):

1. Marx's writing introduced a radical idea.
   He encouraged revolution.
2. After the Bre-X scandal, several financial institutions were damaged.
   They were hurt severely.
3. Giving birth is never easy, but it is a joy.
   It is a deep joy.
4. A dog is a human's best friend.
   The dog is a friend until it dies.
5. Therapy helps many Canadians recover from difficulties.
   Often, they never need help again.

Reading Aloud

Each punctuation mark means something different, and it sounds different when you read each out loud, too. A period is a full pause. The colon is slightly less of a pause, and the semicolon is a smaller pause yet. They are not the same punctuation, and they must be "read" differently.

Exercise S6-8

Read the following paragraph out loud to a partner two or three times. Start slowly and emphasize each pause until you get a "feel" for how to read each punctuation mark. Have your partner read the paragraph back to you two or three times, as well. Try and read the punctuation properly so your partner can hear a difference:

It's never easy to own a pet; however, people often feel that a pet would be a fun thing to have, so they go out and buy one before they know what they're getting into. I would want to stop them before they buy and ask them an important question: do you know what you're doing? I would put on my priest's collar: a huge collar. When they came to pay for the animal, I would marry them. Marriage is what owning a pet is all about: it's the same kind of commitment. People want their pets until they become too much work; then, they dump or neglect them. This is not what pet ownership is about: it's for better or for worse, until death separates the pet and owner.

Other Uses Of The Semicolon

The semicolon is not as versatile as the colon, but you can do one other thing with a semicolon—punctuate a list. The semicolon is used to separate items in a list that use other punctuation or list items that are self-contained sentences. The list is introduced by a full sentence and ends with a colon as we learned in the previous section. Here's an example:

> Here's what everyone wants for Christmas: Dave needs a ski suit; Lynn needs some new clothes; Judith wants a comfy chair; and I want a new guitar.

Here's an example with punctuation in each list item:

> Here are the people on our new committee: Dave, president of the company; Susan, one of the shareholders; Frank, the founder of the group; and, Lola, the head engineer.

It's fairly easy to use. Here's the formula:

> Independent clause : List item **;** list item **;** list item **.**

Here's a sentence and a list:

Sentence:	Each western province has it's own flower.
List:	British Columbia, the dogwood.
	Alberta, the wild rose.
	Saskatchewan, the Western red lily.

We notice that there is punctuation in each list item, so we cannot use commas to separate these list items. This is a job for the semicolon. Here's the combined sentence:

> Each western province has its own flower: British Columbia, the dogwood; Alberta, the wild rose; and Saskatchewan, the Western red lily.

Exercise S6-9

Write a complete sentence to introduce the list in each numbered item and punctuate each list item properly:

1. The only tools you need to build a garage

   Skill saw—to cut sheathing and studs

   Hammer—to nail everything together

   Level—to straighten everything up

   Square—to draw straight lines

   Tape measure—to measure everything

   Pencil—to mark the wood and record measurements

2. My father gave me several pieces of advice when I went back to school

   Don't party too much until graduation

   Get the best marks you can

   Apply for all the scholarships you are eligible for

   Eat well

 ## COLLABORATIVE WORK

After you revise your researching essay, exchange papers with a classmate and do the following tasks:

A. Find any semicolons or colons used outside of compound sentences.

B. Check every colon and semicolon. Make sure each mark is properly used and makes good sense.

C. If you cannot find any colons or semicolons, suggest several places where one or the other would work well.

Then return the paper to your classmate. When you receive your essay, use the information in this section to edit your draft.

CHAPTER SEVEN

Analyzing

I don't know if other writers have that strange place in their
heads, but I seem to have always had it: the part which takes
notes, which observes even the most private and personal
parts of my own life and makes comment, the part which
looks and listens at other people and analyzes words,
interprets gestures, makes note of silences. . .

—ANNE CAMERON ("THE OPERATIVE PRINCIPLE IS TRUST" IN
LANGUAGE IN HER EYE: WRITING AND GENDER.)

LEARNING OUTCOMES

This chapter will help you:
- Understand and write an essay about a topic you have analyzed;
- Recognize and develop complex sentences; and,
- Link paragraphs with unifying devices.

Perhaps the word *analyzing* reminds you of the experiments scientists perform in
their laboratories. In fact, we all engage in the process of analyzing without even re-
alizing it. Think about the last time you watched a sporting event, listened to a political debate, or read a newspaper or a magazine article. You probably didn't simply
watch or listen or read; you analyzed. When you watch a basketball game, you evaluate the players' movements so that you can better understand their strategy. The
same thing happens when you listen to a speech or read an article. You analyze what
you are hearing or reading by looking for underlying reasons, influencing factors, and
possible outcomes. In other words, you break a topic into parts to look at them from
all angles so that you can understand the topic as fully as possible.

In much the same way, when you write an **analyzing** essay, your purpose is to present
information about a subject in such a way that your reader—and you—will gain either
a new understanding or a far more complete picture than you had before. When you
make an analysis, you are not simply describing something to your reader; you are not

trying to persuade your reader to do something; you are not explaining something; you are not giving your opinion; and you are not necessarily offering a solution to a problem. Instead, you are helping your reader obtain a complete understanding of a topic by using a combination of these tasks to explain unique relationships between ideas.

In a book titled *Return of the Answer Lady*, Marg Meikle analyzes the tradition of making New Year's resolutions, and makes comparisons of their origins to what is commonly practised now:

> No one knows exactly when New Year's resolutions began, but our modern ritual (read: big bash) to welcome in the New Year certainly has its roots in ancient times. Our resolutions started as ancient purifications and confessing of sins at end-of-the-year festivals. Ancient peoples did wild things, all in aid of constructing order out of the chaos of their lives. They would beat drums and shout to scare off demons and indulge in alcoholic excess to create the chaos that would soon be banished. There were fights, too, but people saw them as ceremonial battles between the old year and the new. Definitely the same idea we have now. You can put out of your mind what has passed. You no longer have any control over the past, but the new year—it's a whole new period of life; it's a time of promise; the world is your oyster. And you can make all of these solemn vows about what you will do with your life and start afresh.

This passage does more than simply describe the rituals associated with New Year's; it examines the origins and makes comparisons to today's "big bash." She then furthers her analysis by focusing on the idea of order-out-of-chaos, and suggesting that this is the origin of the current practice of making resolutions that have to do with "getting organized" and cutting out the excess in our lives. She uses examples, comparison-contrast, explanation, and cause-effect reasoning to help her develop her analysis.

LEARNING FROM PUBLISHED WRITERS

The essay "A Way of Life" comes from the book *Men of the Saddle* written by Andy Russell who is considered by many to be the true voice of the Canadian cowboy. Here, Russell analyzes some aspects of the life of the contemporary cowboy, and compares these to the old ways.

Before You Read

Focus Your Attention

Before you read this analysis essay, take a few moments to respond to the following questions. Jot down the answers in your notebook.

1. Try to recall a discussion you have had recently with other students, with your

friends, or members of your family in which you considered a problem, concern, or an issue. At the end of the discussion, did you understand the topic more thoroughly than at the beginning? What happened to increase your understanding?

2. In the essay you are about to read, the writer analyzes changes to the way of life of the traditional Canadian cowboy. He suggests that not all of the changes are necessarily advantages. Think about your projected career, and list the changes that have taken place over the years. Are some changes more advantageous than others?

Expand Your Vocabulary

Find each of the listed words in the following essay. Read them in context and jot down a definition of each. Compare your definitions with those that you find in a dictionary.

Chinook (paragraph 11)

Preponderance (paragraph 12)

Virulent (paragraph 19)

Forebears (paragraph 23)

Vagaries (paragraph 27)

Andy Russell

A Way of Life*

There have been changes. No longer does the cowboy or his boss spend the long hours in the saddle covering hundreds of miles of open range. Nor is the cow business quite so much of a poker game with the weather. It is a rare thing now for cattle to be caught starving in a killing winter storm. The ranchers know how much feed it takes to winter a cow and they work hard to keep enough on hand with some surplus to take care of the unexpected.   1

But the weather hasn't changed; it is as unpredictable as ever with winter colds and blizzards just as fierce. Where teams of horses hitched to bobsleds and basket racks were once the only way of spreading hay, now tractors and four-wheel-drive trucks are the transport on almost every ranch. Where it once took a man all day to feed 200 head of cows, it can now be done in two   2

*From *True North: Canadian Essays For Composition*, 1999, p. 98–ff. Reprinted with permission of Pearson Education Canada.

or three hours. But still, some ranchers keep a team in reserve for times when wheels are bogged by snow conditions.

Hay is no longer stacked loose in big stacks for it is too slow to handle; it is now baled, which makes feeding much easier and quicker. Thus, every animal gets its quota of feed per day with guesswork pretty much eliminated. **3**

There are still a few of us around, however, who remember the old ways in the hard, cold days of winter. When I was growing up on a small cow and horse ranch at the foot of the mountains in southwest Alberta, there was a time when I came to know what it was like to work long hours in the bone-chilling cold. It was mid-January when a blizzard hit the country dropping two feet of snow. Then it cleared and the temperatures dropped to forty below zero. My father came down with flu and was flat on his back in bed. So it was up to me to see that the cattle were fed. I was thirteen years old. **4**

Up well before daylight, I threw hay and oats into the manger in front of our big team and then wrestled the heavy harness onto them. Leaving them to feed, I went to the house where mother had a hot breakfast ready. Then I hitched up and drove to a stack on the other side of the ranch, picking up on the way an old cowboy who lived in a tiny log cabin with his wife and daughter. He was a tough, stringy old Irishman, by the name of Phil Lucas, with a crippled hand. Together we forked loose hay onto the rack and spread it for the cattle, while sundogs glittered coldly in the steely sky. Then we loaded the rack again. **5**

That work filled the morning. After lunch we fed the cattle being kept close to the buildings, then I took Phil home. By the time the team was fed, watered and put in the barn for the night, the woodbox filled and the other chores done, the stars were out. At night I did more than sleep, I passed out. It seemed as though I had just closed my eyes when the alarm clock would cut loose. Sometimes I slept through its clamor and then mother would come to shake me awake. **6**

The days were a blur of unending cold, tired muscles, creaking hooves and sleigh runners, and the steamy smell of horses. One night the thermometer dropped to fifty-two below, but it didn't seem to be much colder when I went out next morning. **7**

On the way to the haystack old Phil told me, "Your nose is freezing. You'd better thaw it out with your hand." I took a look at him to see that his beaky nose was white as bone. "Yours is froze solid," I told him. He felt it gingerly and cussed, "Damn if it ain't! Hard enough to peck holes in a board!" **8**

I couldn't help laughing and he looked hard at me with sharp blue eyes past the hand that was holding his nose, in a way that shut me up. Then he chuckled and remarked, "We can still laugh anyway. Things could be worse." **9**

Like almost every body in the country, I had aspirations to become a cowboy, but this part of it I could do without. There seemed to be no end to the cold. Dad was up and around again, but too weak to do very much. I couldn't remember what it was like not to be tired.

Then one evening just as we were finishing supper, the house suddenly cracked. Dad went to the door and looked out. "It's a chinook!" he ex- **10** claimed. "It feels warm as summer!" Next morning it was forty above and water was dripping from the eaves. The temperature had risen about eighty degrees in fourteen hours. In three days the hills were bare on the south slopes and the stock was lazing about enjoying the warmth. The wind continued to blow soft and warm, and apart from a few short snow storms the back of the winter had been broken.

Winter weather in wintertime is one thing, but when cold and snow hold **11** on stubbornly into spring and the calving season, the life of a cowman can be tough. In the old days on the open range the cows were pretty much alone when it came to calving. If one got into trouble and was lucky enough to be spotted in time, she got help, but much more often she was on her own. It was a stark matter of survival of the fittest. Consequently, genetics had arranged that they didn't have trouble nearly as often as the more pampered cattle of today. Vets were few and far between and such things as caesarean operations were unknown. It is amazing what a cow can stand and even more impressive how newborn calves manage to survive, though there is a preponderance of bobbed tails and cropped ears from being frozen in a bad spring.

I remember a miserable night twenty odd years ago, when our phone rang **12** at midnight and a neighbor was on the line. One of his heifers was in trouble calving and would I give him a hand? I put on some warm clothes and tied on my snowshoes, for the roads were blocked by drifts. When I arrived at his place, it was to find him out among his cattle with his Land Rover. The heifer had a calf stuck in her pelvic opening with its front feet showing, and she was so spooky that he couldn't get her into the barn. A good-looking, strong Aberdeen Angus, she was in no mood to be pushed around. While I watched she lay down and heaved on the calf, but it was being just as stubborn as the mother and didn't budge.

I got a lariat and a short piece of sashcord, then sat on the hood of the **13** vehicle, while my friend eased it up to the heifer. She jumped up and started to move off, but I got a loop over her head and snubbed her to the bumper of the truck.

Closer examination showed the calf's head was where it should be, so I **14** looped the sash cord over its feet like short hobbles and pulled. Seeming to realize that I wanted to help, the heifer lay down. Sitting down and bracing my feet against her rump, I timed my pulls with her heaves and in a few moments the calf was out in the snow. I picked it up and put it on some dry straw, then turned its mother loose. While we watched, she went to it and began to lick it vigorously and before long it was up on wobbly legs and busy sucking a bellyful of warm milk.

Even there in the dark with snow spitting on the wind there was some- **15** thing wonderful about it—an inert, wet, little thing suddenly blossoming into life and responding to its mother's care. The tired lines of my friend's face softened and smoothed out as he watched. "He'll make it now," he said. "Let's go have a drink. I got a bottle of Old Stump Blower for times like this."

Sometimes a birth can be a lot more complicated when a calf is coming backwards or has its head or a front leg bent back. Then it is hard work being a midwife—working with an arm buried in the cow's uterus against her straining muscles as one tries to rearrange the calf so it can get out of the gate of her pelvis. It is always messy and difficult, but heart-warming when it works out right. It is miserably discouraging when it doesn't. **16**

In these times of high expense and low returns in the cow business, the ranchers work hard at all hours if the day and night to save every calf they can. Family teams work in shifts, so the cows have someone watching them closely almost every hour of the day and night, particularly in bad weather. There are vets on call to help with complicated cases. The survival of the fittest is not the rule any more. **17**

After a miserably cold, wet spring, it is particularly pleasant to ride out at last across green meadows, warm under the sun, among contented cows with new calves at their heels. Their old winter hair is slipping; they are "slicking up" and there is lots of milk for the calves. Sometimes this promotes scours, which can be a virulent intestinal infection that will kill calves. So even then the owner is watchful. **18**

With the coming of warm weather, there are miles and miles of fences to repair and branding to be done. As always, the ranchers help each other with the branding. Now the cattle are worked in corrals, but the methods haven't changed much. A roper still heels the calves and drags them to the fire. There teams of wrestlers throw them and hold them down for dehorning, branding, castrating of the bulls, vaccination and ear tagging. Some outfits heat the irons with propane gas, but many still use a willow-wood fire. **19**

The modern cowboy always has a vaccine syringe close at hand to administer an injection of antibiotics in case of infection and to immunize the cattle against such diseases as blackleg, brucellosis and redwater. Now practically every herd is treated against redwater twice a year. In the fall the cattle are chemically treated to discourage the warble fly. **20**

When the branding is done, the cattle are put on summer pasture, sometimes on big fenced leases on the prairie or far up various mountain valleys. Salt is scattered and the bulls turned loose—generally one to every thirty or forty cows. While artificial insemination is being practiced by some ranchers, it is by no means universal, for it is a time-consuming and expensive process, not altogether practical in rough, brushy country. **21**

On the bigger summer pastures cowboys are hired to ride among the cattle keeping an eye on fences and watching for rustlers, disease and predators. As in the early days, it is a lonely life, although now pick-up trucks and CB radios give the men advantages of communication and transportation such as their forebears never dreamed about. Many of the cowcamps even have telephones. **22**

Meanwhile, back on the ranches hay is irrigated, and when ready it is cut, baled and stacked for winter feed. It is a time of long hours and hard work there too. **23**

By the time the aspen leaves are turning gold, the cattle are rounded up,   **24**
various herds cut out and then trailed or trucked back to wintering pastures.
It is market time, when yearlings or calves are shipped out to feedlots or sold
by auction at various sales centres to feeders who route them in the same
direction.

With the return of winter, the whole cycle begins another revolution.   **25**

Some of the changes from the old ways have been immense. But ranching people are still as enterprising and adventurous as ever. They are at once
innately conservative and yet the greatest gamblers upon earth—anyone
who stakes his future against the vagaries of weather and markets has to be a
gambler to the marrow of his bones. Ranching is a business that brings bank
account riches to very few people; it is a way of life. It is a challenge to make
the best use of the good earth without abusing it. It is an art in its dealing
with animals, where one must mix a strong back with a wise head and a
warm heart. It involves many things, from training a skittish colt to the
careful study of bloodlines, from welding a broken piece of machinery to the
intricate plaiting of a hackamore from thin strips of rawhide.

Above all, ranchers have to be practical. Their spirit has not changed   **26**
even though the vast, open ocean of grass has gone forever. It is good to
pause once in a while to contemplate how much we owe those oldtimers who
blazed the trails and showed the way. They worked hard and played hard and
through their sacrifices made it easier for their great-grandchildren.

 ## Questions For Critical Thinking

Thinking Critically About Content

1. What changes in the cowboy's way of life does Andy Russell analyze?
2. Russell says that ranchers are "innately conservative and yet the greatest gamblers on earth." Where in the essay does he support this statement?

Thinking Critically About Purpose

3. What is the author's purpose in writing this essay?
4. Russell uses many personal episodes. What makes this an essay of analysis rather
   than a story?

Thinking Critically About Audience

5. What group of readers would find this essay most interesting? Why?
6. How much cowboy knowledge does Russell expect his readers to have? How do
   you know?

THINKING CRITICALLY ABOUT PERSPECTIVE

7. How does the author feel about the changes to the cowboy's way of life? How do you know?

8. What specific incidents suggest that Russell romanticizes the old ways?

LEARNING FROM YOUR PEERS

Analyzing helps us to understand why something happened and what the effects of the event are on our lives. When you write an analysis, you should make these connections very clear, both for yourself and for your readers. Learning to write analytically is a skill that will be useful to you in many areas of life. In other college classes, you may be asked to analyze a scientific process, a political or historical event, or a piece of literature. The skills you use to write essays of this type are basically the same: take the event apart, and put it together again in a way that makes sense to you. Watching another writer's analysis take shape can be an informative experience. To help you learn how to approach writing assignments requiring analysis, we are going to follow the writing process of a student named Matthew Machias.

Matthew's Writing Assignment: Analyzing

This is the topic Matthew's instructor assigned:

Some events in our lives do not seem important at the time they are happening, but when we look back on them later, we understand that they were actually turning points in our attitude toward the world. Think of an important event in your life that caused you to change your attitude toward life, and analyze the change.

Matthew goes through the process as outlined in Chapter One: generating ideas, planning, developing, organizing, drafting, revising, and editing.

Generating Ideas

In response to the assignment, Matthew begins to freewrite. He was a cross-country runner in high school and he knows that the discipline of practice made him stretch his physical and emotional limits, but he does not think that he can analyze those changes in himself. He knows that he has learned to run in any weather, that his body yearns for that daily exercise, but he can hardly remember a time when he felt any different. Then Matthew thinks about his attitude toward studying. He can see that his self-discipline has paid off, but again, he has always been the type of student who does homework right after dinner.

Matthew keeps on writing and thinking. He starts listing all the major events in his life over the past three years:

First job

First car

High school graduation

Starting college

Sitting on a jury

Taking a trip without family

Suddenly he realizes that the experience of being on a jury really changed his perspective about justice, about drunk driving, about being held accountable for one's actions.

Planning

Matthew begins writing notes about his experiences on the jury. He can almost feel his palms sweating in anxiety as he recalls the moment when he realized that he held the fate of another human being in his hands. Matthew starts listing the feelings he connects with each stage of the jury deliberation:

Anxiety

Self-doubt

Anger

Empathy

Sympathy

Questioning

Acceptance

Then he decides to focus his analysis on the changes that occurred throughout the whole process of deliberation. He wants to look at how others in the group influenced his thinking, and he wants to capture the difficulty of coming to some agreement within the group. He feels that this assignment has greater complexity than the other writing assignments so far this term; he decides to carefully record all that he thinks about the topic so that he has complete notes of anything that might be useful to him later.

Developing

Matthew starts a list with two columns. In the first column, he copies down his list of feelings. In the other column, he writes down the ideas he associates with the feelings he listed. His list looks like this:

Feelings	Events
Anxiety	My heart was pounding and my hands were sweating.
Self-doubt	Could I vote to send this man to jail?
Anger	He had gone out and driven recklessly while drunk, even though his licence was suspended.
Empathy	I could picture him at a party having a few brews.
Sympathy	He should be going to college, studying, or flipping burgers.
Questioning	Would I trust my life to him? Did he betray his friend?
Acceptance	We all voted that he was guilty.

Matthew looks over his list and knows that many ideas are there, but he also knows that he still has to go into detail about his experience. The list helps him discover how he felt during the first hour or so of jury deliberation, but he knows that he has not told the whole story. He writes down several more notes to himself, focusing on the facts that led to changes in his own thinking. Here are his notes:

The facts:

The guy killed his best friend because of his drinking.

He had a history of drunk driving.

He had been to "drunk school."

His licence was suspended.

He drove anyway.

He should have known better.

We had to decide whether it was murder or manslaughter. Accident or intentional? I was the only one who could not bring myself to pronounce him a murderer.

I changed my mind:

I couldn't feel sorry for the guy.

He knew what he was doing.

His friend had paid the price for the driver's drinking.

After Matthew spends some more time thinking about his feelings and changed attitudes, he is ready to organize the material.

Organizing

Now Matthew has an abundance of feelings, facts, and opinions to work with. But he also needs to put this material into some kind of order that will be meaningful and interesting to his readers. So far, he has simply let one item lead into another as he followed his basic instincts for putting his paper in order. Now he decides to let "the big question" be his main focus.

The big question: Could I vote to send this man to jail?

His guilt was certain—but what was he guilty of? Was it an accident or was it intentional?

We had to decide whether it was murder or manslaughter. I was the only one who could not bring myself to pronounce him a murderer.

The facts:

The guy killed his best friend because of his drinking.

He had a history of drunk driving.

He had been to "drunk school."

His licence was suspended.

He drove anyway.

He should have known better.

Other influences:

It's hard to sort out the consequences of things like this—was his friend foolish for getting in the truck with him? He must have known about the driver's previous hassles with the law.

"Granny"—the oldest woman on the jury—asked me how I would feel if the person killed had been my best friend. She reminded me of the driver's past convictions. She said he knew very well what happened to him when he drank—he knew the consequences, and no previous punishment had changed his behaviour.

My conclusions:

I knew everyone else was right.

I couldn't feel sorry for the guy.

He knew what he was doing.

His friend had paid the price for the driver's drinking.

So what changed?

This experience has made me less likely to say, "Lock 'em up and throw away the key." Seeing real people with real problems is not like seeing someone on television or in the movies. When I saw the human side of a drunk driver, it was hard to condemn his actions.

Matthew is now ready to write his first draft. He definitely has enough material to work with, and he is bursting with the emotions connected with the event.

Drafting

After adding even more detail and thinking further about the process of changing his attitude, Matthew wrote his first draft.

Matthew's Essay: First Draft ....

Main Idea: Analyzing a drunk driver case was more difficult than I thought it would be.

The trial was almost over. The jury still had to deliberate. I was on the jury, and the most difficult part of the trial was ahead of me. Try to understand. Determining someone else's future was the toughest thing I'd ever done.

As the jury walked out of the jury box, my heart was pounding. I looked at the defendant out of the corner of my eye. Looking sad and alone, the man sat next to his attorney. The defendant was pretty good-looking and seemed well-mannered. Could I vote to send Allen Wayne Grant, Jr. to jail for five or ten years? What would happen to the defendant? I didn't know.

We had finished listening to both sides present evidence, examine witnesses, and summarize their arguments. We had looked at photographs of the terrible automobile accident, shots of the wreckage, close-ups of Grant's best friend, even photos of him being taken away. We heard that Grant had been driving while intoxicated on Highway 281 at 2 a.m. after a party. Yes, his blood alcohol level was .11, well over the legal limit. He had been convicted of drunk driving on previous occasions during 1994/95, and he had completed a special program in mid-May to educate drunk drivers. Grant had gone out and driven 130 km per hour while drunk, even though his licence was suspended. "Why did he do it?" I wondered.

As the jury walked to the room where the jurors were supposed to decide the defendant's fate, I could not help thinking how much the defendant looked like all my friends. I could picture this man at a party having a few brew, joking with my friends, flirting. The defendant did not seem like an evil person. He did not seem like a murderer. Yet I asked myself who would want to get into a car with him. Would I trust my life to him? The answer was "No way." Still, I did not want to decide how he should spend the next years of his life. He should be going to college, studying and flipping burgers to support his good times.

We finally were sitting around the jury table. Then an old man volunteered to be the jury foreman. He was a retired physician, Dr. Samuel Anderson. "Great!" I thought. "We're already agreeing." It seemed like everyone just wanted this process to be over and done. We decided to take a vote and decide if the defendant was guilty or innocent of murdering his friend. He looked like a really nice guy. However, we all voted that he was guilty.

Then the difficult discussions came out. What exactly was he guilty of doing? Did Grant mean to kill his friend? Was he negligent? We had to decide whether he had taken his friend's life by accident or intentionally. We looked at the photographs again. We reviewed the evidence.

As we went through that process, I thought about all the parties I have been to where people drank, listening to CDs, danced, and having fun. I have seen people leaving parties after they have been drinking; I've seen them head for their cars. I have even tried to stop a few of them from time to time. I have had a few drinks at those parties myself. Sometimes I am a designated driver. At those times I never drink. No way! Anyway, if Grant's friend got in the car with him that night, surely he knew what's Grant's history was maybe he thought he knew Grant better than he really did. So was the friend partly to blame for his own death? We were not allowed to hear any testimony about his friend's drinking habits or driving history therefore I could not answer that question. Besides, we were supposed to make our decision on the basis of the facts before us.

We took another vote. There were eleven votes for second-degree murder meaning that he had intentionally killed his friend. Of course, I admitted voting for manslaughter. Everyone looked at me and asked me my reasons.

Calmly I explained that I did not think that Grant meant to kill his best friend. There was a soft-spoken grandmotherly woman there. She had a friend who was a member of MADD. "Matthew, how would you feel if the person killed was a close friend of yours?" she asked. She reminded me that the defendant had been convicted of drunk driving on earlier occasions. She asked me gosh, I wanted to scream and get everything over if I would want to drive on the same road as that man when he was drunk. Then two other people middle-aged businessmen reminded me that the man knew the consequences of his actions. He knew that he was driving without a licence and he knew that his past record was not a good one. Did he learn anything? He should of been riding with a friend, not driving.

In my heart, I knew they were right. Even though the twenty-two year old defendant looked like a nice person, he was guilty I still wanted to shake his hand and wish him well. His best friend's family would have to live with the image of that horrible, heartbreaking accident for many years. They would never see their loved one again. He was only 23. My responsibility was to the law and to society. Even good people make mistakes of judgment however when mistakes are made over and over, they become a pattern. Grant knew what he was doing when he drove to the party that night, and he knew what he was doing when he took that first drink. He did not know that his actions would lead to his best friend's death his friend trusted him to drive him home, that was the last decision he was ever able to make. We held the vote again, which was unanimous for second degree murder.

After we filed back into the jury box, the foreman read the jury's verdict. I knew that the group's judgment was the right one. I still felt sorry for the defendant. I told myself as I walked out of the room that I never wanted to be on another jury again. I was always the person who said, "Lock up those criminals and throw away the key." This experience made me realize that is easy to say. You didn't have to look closely at the person and the situation involved.

Revising

After Matthew wrote his first draft, he felt he had learned many new things about himself and about the responsibility of judging other people's actions. In fact, he felt that writing this essay moved him closer to understanding this particular event in his life, as well as the process of analysis itself.

Now it is time to revise his work. The instructor tells the class to focus the revision process on a few specific, related items that involve the unity and logic of the paragraphs in their essays.

Matthew reviews the Focus on Paragraphs section of this chapter and does the exercises his instructor assigns. Although some of the guidelines sound mechanical, he realizes that he can improve his essay as a whole. He sets out to remedy the problems one by one.

 ## COLLABORATIVE WORK

PEER GROUP ACTIVITY

After you read the portions of Focus on Paragraphs that your instructor assigns, turn to Matthew's first draft and complete the following tasks in small groups:

A. Underline any sentences that do not develop logically from the previous sentence.

B. Put a caret (^) where your group thinks transitions between sentences are missing.

Compare the marks your group makes to those your instructor shows you. Where do they differ? What do you need to review before writing your own essay?

CLASS ACTIVITY

As an entire class, look at the underlined portions of Matthew's revised draft to see what changes he makes.

A. Did you identify the **revision** problems that Matthew corrected?

B. Do you think his changes are good ones? Discuss his changes.

Editing

Now that the sentences in each of Matthew's paragraphs are unified and logical, he needs to do some further editing before handing in his essay. His instructor talks about sentence patterns and how to add interest to the essay by combining shorter ideas and varying sentence structure. She directs students to the Focus on Sentences section. Matthew focuses on these, and also pays close attention to the rules for punctuation.

 ## COLLABORATIVE WORK

PEER GROUP ACTIVITY

After you read the portions of Focus on Sentences that your instructor assigns, turn to Matthew's first draft and complete the following tasks in small groups:

A. Choose a paragraph in Matthew's essay. Look at each sentence carefully. Identify which are simple, which are compound, and which are complex.

B. Rewrite Matthew's paragraph. Try combining clauses differently than he has done, i.e., make simple sentences compound or make compound ones complex. Determine which ones read better.

C. Look at Matthew's essay. Mark the sentences that you think should be combined.

D. Circle any other editing problems in Matthew's draft.

CLASS ACTIVITY

As an entire class, look at the underlined portions of Matthew's revised draft to see what changes he made.

A. Does he combine the sentences that you suggest?

B. Did you identify the **editing** problems that Matthew corrected?

C. Do you think his changes are good ones?

Matthew's Revised Essay ....

A Matter of Life and Death

The trial was ~~almost~~ <u>finally</u> over~~.~~ <u>, but</u> ~~T~~the jury still had to deliberate. <u>Since</u> I was on the jury, ~~and~~ the most difficult part of the trial was ahead of me. Try to understand. Determining someone's future was the toughest thing I'd ever done.

As ~~the jury~~ we walked out of the jury box, my heart was pounding. I looked at the ~~defendant~~ man on trial out of the corner of my eye. Looking sad and alone, the ~~man~~ defendant sat next to his attorney. The ~~defendant~~ fellow was ~~pretty good-looking~~ fairly handsome and seemed well-mannered. Could I vote to send Allen Wayne Grant, Jr., to jail for five or ten years? What would happen to ~~the defendant~~ him? I didn't know.

~~Finally, w~~We had finished listening to both sides present evidence, examine witnesses, and summarize their arguments. Early in the trial, ~~w~~We had looked at photographs of the terrible automobile accident, shots of the wreckage, close-ups of Grant's best friend, even photos of ~~him~~ the body being taken away. Next, ~~w~~We heard that Grant had been driving while intoxicated on Highway 281 at 2 a.m. after a party. Yes, his blood alcohol level was .11, well over the legal limit. After ~~h~~He had been convicted of drunk driving on ~~previous~~ other occasions during 1994/95, ~~and~~ he had completed a special program in mid-May to educate drunk drivers. Still, Grant had gone out and driven 130 kph while drunk, even though his licence was suspended. "Why did he do it?" I wondered.

As the jury walked to the room where ~~the jurors~~ we were supposed to decide the defendant's fate, I could not help thinking how much ~~the defendant~~ he looked like all my friends. I could picture ~~this man~~ him at a party having a few brew, joking with my friends, flirting. ~~The defendant~~ He did not seem like an evil person. He did not seem like a murderer. Yet I asked myself ~~who~~ whether I would want to get into a car with him. Would I trust my life to him? The answer was "No way." Still, I did not want to decide how he should spend the next years of his life. He should be going to college, studying and flipping burgers to support his good times.

We decided to take a vote and decide if the defendant was guilty or innocent of murdering his friend. He looked like a really nice guy.

However, we all voted that he was guilty. ~~When~~ <u>When</u> ~~W~~<u>w</u>e finally were sitting around the jury table~~. Then~~<u>,</u> an old man volunteered to be the jury foreman. He was a retired physician, Dr. Samuel Anderson. "Great!" I thought. "We're already agreeing." It seemed like everyone just wanted this process to be over and done. We decided to take a vote ~~and~~ <u>to</u> decide if the defendant<u>, who looked like a really nice guy,</u> was guilty or innocent of murdering his friend. ~~He looked like a really nice guy. However, we~~ <u>We</u> all voted that he was guilty.

Then the difficult discussions came out<u>:</u> What exactly was he guilty of doing? Did Grant mean to kill his friend? Was he negligent? We had to decide whether he had taken his friend's life ~~by accident or intentionally~~ <u>accidentally or intentionally</u>. We looked at the photographs again. We reviewed the evidence.

As we went through that process, I thought about all the parties I have been to where people ~~drank~~ <u>were drinking</u>, listening to CDs, ~~danced~~ <u>dancing</u>, and having fun. I have seen people leaving parties after they have been drinking. I've seen them head for their cars. I have even tried to stop a few of them from time to time. I have had a few drinks at those parties myself~~. Sometimes I am a designated driver. At those times I never drink.~~<u>,</u> <u>but I never drank when I was the designated driver.</u> No way! Anyway, if Grant's friend got in the car with him that night, surely he knew what Grant's history was<u>.</u> <u>(M</u>~~m~~aybe he thought he knew Grant better than he really did.<u>)</u> So was the friend partly to blame for his own death? We were not allowed to hear any testimony about his friend's drinking habits or driving history<u>;</u> therefore<u>,</u> I could not answer that question. Besides, we were supposed to make our decision on the basis of the facts before us.

We took another vote. ~~There were~~ <u>E</u>~~e~~leven ~~votes~~ <u>voted</u> for second degree murder<u>,</u> meaning that he had intentionally killed his friend. Of course, I admitted voting for manslaughter~~.~~<u>, meaning that he had</u>

accidentally killed his friend. Everyone looked at me and asked me my reasons.

Calmly, I explained that I did not think that Grant meant to kill his best friend. There was a soft-spoken grandmotherly woman there. ~~She~~ who had a friend who was a member of MADD. "Matthew, how would you feel if the person killed was a close friend of yours?" she asked. She reminded me that the defendant had been convicted of drunk driving on earlier occasions. She asked me—gosh, I wanted to scream and get everything over—if I would want to drive on the same road as that man when he was drunk. Then two other people, middle-aged businessmen, reminded me that the man knew the consequences of his actions. He knew that he was driving without a license, and he knew that his past record was not a good one. ~~Did he learn~~ If he had learned anything? ~~He should~~ , he would ~~of~~ have been riding with a friend, not driving.

In my heart, I knew they were right. Even though the ~~twenty-two~~ 22 year old defendant looked like a nice person, he was guilty. (I still wanted to shake his hand and wish him well.) His best friend's family would have to live with the image of that horrible, heartbreaking accident for many years. They would never see their loved one again. He was only 23. My responsibility was to the law and to society. Even good people make mistakes of judgment; however, when mistakes are made over and over, they become a pattern. Grant knew what he was doing when he drove to the party that night, and he knew what he was doing when he took that first drink. He did not know that his actions would lead to his best friend's death. ~~H~~his friend trusted him to drive him home~~,~~ ; that was the last decision he was ever able to make. We held the vote again, which was unanimous for second degree murder.

After we filed back into the jury box, the foreman read the jury's verdict. I knew that the group's judgment was the right one~~.~~ , even

<u>though</u> I still felt sorry for the defendant. I told myself as I walked out of the room that I never wanted to be on another jury again. I was always the person who said, "Lock up those criminals and throw away the key." This experience made me realize that <u>it</u> is ~~easy~~ easier to say. ~~You~~ <u>that when you</u> do not have to look closely at the person and the situation involved.

COLLABORATIVE WORK

CLASS ACTIVITY

As a class, spend time thinking, planning, developing, and organizing a potential analyzing essay.

1. Spend five minutes brainstorming some issues that have recently been in the news.
2. Choose five for the subject of a potential analyzing essay. Discuss what makes one better than another.
3. For each of the five, list several points worth analyzing.
4. Determine an audience and purpose.
5. Add three details to each point to give a sense of what a person might potentially write.
6. Organize the details so that they appear in the best order for the best effect.

Could you write this essay? What would the topic sentences be for each paragraph?

WRITING YOUR OWN ANALYZING ESSAY

So far, you have seen a professional writer and a fellow student at work trying to analyze ideas, impressions, experiences, and information. As you read the published essay and followed the writing process of another student from first to final draft, you absorbed not only ideas but ways of giving those ideas a form of their own. These reading and writing activities have prepared you to write your own analysis of a topic that is meaningful to you.

What Have You Discovered?

Before you begin your own writing task, let's review what you have learned about analysis:

- Analyzing involves evaluating a subject.

- Analyzing enables you to better understand the world.

- Analyzing involves describing, persuading, explaining, giving your opinion, and offering a solution to a problem.

- To present your analysis effectively, organize your ideas.

- To help you shape your essay, learn as much as possible about your readers.

- Before you write a draft, decide on a point of view toward your subject.

- After you write a draft, revise your essay for meaning and organization.

- As you revise your essay, edit its grammar, usage, and sentence structure.

Your Writing Topic

Choose one of the following topics for your analyzing essay:

1. In the professional essay that you read at the beginning of this chapter, the writer, Andy Russell, analyzes the changes that have taken place in the way of life for the Canadian cowboy. Choose another profession or trade that has significance for you, and analyze the changes over the years.

2. Write an essay about an important event that changed your attitude toward an authority figure (a parent, a religious leader, a teacher, a club sponsor, a supervisor, or boss), and analyze the change.

3. Write about an event (a personal event or one in the media) that has significance for you, and talk about how that event has changed your outlook.

4. Write about an event that is currently in the news and analyze its significance to you or your community.

5. Create your own analyzing essay (with the assistance of your instructor), and write a response to it.

After you have chosen one of these topics, you may find it useful to begin writing in the same way that Matthew did. If, in writing your own analysis essay, some tasks occur out of order, that adjustment is likely your own writing ritual. Follow your instincts and let them mold your own writing process. Be sure you've worked through all of the tasks to your final draft.

Writing Unified Paragraphs

Checklist For Writing Unified Paragraphs

✓ Do your paragraphs contain effective unifying devices?
✓ Do all pronouns refer directly to a noun in the preceding sentence?
✓ Do transitional words or phrases guide the reader through your ideas?
✓ Do synonyms emphasize related ideas?
✓ Do you use parallel form to show a relationship among ideas?
✓ Do you use repetition of key words and phrases to emphasize related ideas?

A ship's captain about to embark on a long journey always charts a course at the outset. An important part of making this chart involves identifying and focusing on the best course from the point of departure to the destination. Similarly, for your readers to follow your thoughts in an essay, you need to chart the best course between your sentences and between your paragraphs. These include the use of pronouns, transitional words and expressions, synonyms, parallelism, and repetition. Using these strategies will allow you to produce unified paragraphs that cohere, or hold together, both within the paragraphs and with the paragraphs around them.

Unifying Devices

Pronoun Reference

Many writers link sentences in a paragraph by using a **pronoun** to refer to a noun in the preceding sentence. By using pronouns that refer to nouns or other pronouns in a sentence or a paragraph, you help your readers follow the course you have charted through the ideas of the essay. For example, in the following paragraph from "A Way of Life," the author uses pronouns to hold the paragraph together.

> **I** remember a miserable night twenty odd years ago, when **our** phone rang at midnight and a neighbor was on the line. **One** of **his** heifers was in trouble calving and would **I** give him a hand? **I** put on **some** warm clothes and tied on **my** snowshoes, for the roads were blocked by drifts. When **I** arrived at **his** place, **it** was to find **him** out among **his** cattle with **his** Land Rover. The heifer had a calf stuck in **her** pelvic opening with **its** front feet showing, and **she** was so spooky that **he** couldn't get **her** into the barn. A good-looking, strong Aberdeen Angus, **she** was in no mood to be pushed around. While **I** watched **she** lay down and heaved on the calf, but **it** was being just as stubborn as the mother and didn't budge.

The pronouns in this passage serve two purposes: they link the ideas in the paragraph and they prevent needless repetition of nouns. Notice that it is absolutely clear in this paragraph which noun each pronoun replaces.

As Matthew Machias looked back over his essay analyzing his reactions as a juror, he decided that using pronouns in paragraph four would help him connect his thoughts.

First Draft: As the jury walked to the room where the jurors were supposed to decide the defendant's fate, I could not help thinking how much the defendant looked like all my friends. I could picture this man at a party having a few brew, joking with my friends, flirting. The defendant did not seem like an evil person. He did not seem like a murderer.

Revision: As the jury walked to the room where ~~the jurors~~ **we** were supposed to decide the defendant's fate, I could not help thinking how much ~~the defendant~~ **he** looked like all my friends. I could picture ~~this man~~ **him** at a party having a few brew, joking with my friends, flirting. ~~The defendant~~ **He** did not seem like an evil person. He did not seem like a murderer.

Transitions

Words, phrases, and clauses that guide readers through your ideas are often referred to as **transitions**. Transitions can help establish time, space or distance, contrasts, examples, additions, order, or conclusions. Here is a list of some transitions that might be useful to you:

Time: now, then, meanwhile, before, afterward, first, second, thus far, soon, next, immediately, eventually, currently, in the future.

Space: nearby, farther, on the other side, down, above, below, adjacent to, parallel.

Comparison: similarly, likewise, in like manner, in the same way, in comparison.

Contrast: but, yet, still, however, despite this, although, on the other hand, nevertheless, nonetheless, in contrast, on the contrary, at the same time.

Example: for example, in fact, for instance, thus, specifically, namely.

Addition: in addition, also, besides, furthermore, even, too, moreover, and, further.

F
O
C
U
S

O
N

P
A
R
A
G
R
A
P
H
S

Conclusion:	since, thus, therefore, finally, lastly, in conclusion, in short, to summarize.
Result:	therefore, thus, consequently, so, accordingly, as a result, hence.

Transitions help your reader fit the pieces of your essay together in the way you intend because they explain the relationships between your ideas. In the following example from "A Way of Life," transitions guide the reader through the complexities of the comparisons.

> **With** the coming of warm weather, there are miles and miles of fences to repair and branding to be done. **As always,** the ranchers help each other with the branding. **Now** the cattle are worked in corrals, **but** the methods haven't changed much. A roper **still** heels the calves and drags them to the fire. **There** teams of wrestlers throw them and hold them down for dehorning, branding, castrating of the bulls, vaccination and ear tagging. Some outfits heat the irons with propane gas, **but** many **still** use a willow-wood fire.

All the boldfaced transitions in this paragraph serve to show the relationship between the author's ideas and, in turn, move the readers as smoothly as possible through the sentences. The result is a clear, readable, unified paragraph.

As Matthew continued revising his essay to create unified paragraphs that would link his ideas, he added transitional words, phrases, and clauses to explain the process of a trial more clearly for his audience.

First Draft:	We had finished listening to both sides present evidence, examine witnesses, and summarize their arguments. We had looked at photographs of the terrible automobile accident, shots of the wreckage, close-ups of Grant's best friend, even photos of him being taken away. We heard that Grant had been driving while intoxicated on Highway 281 at 2 a.m. after a party. Yes, his blood alcohol level was .11, well over the legal limit. He had been convicted of drunk driving on previous occasions during 1994/95, and he had completed a special program in mid-May to educate drunk drivers. Grant had gone out and driven over 120 km per hour while drunk, even though his licence was suspended. "Why did he do it?" I wondered.
Revision:	**Finally,** w~~W~~e had finished listening to both sides present evidence, examine witnesses, and summarize their arguments. **Early in the trial,** w~~W~~e had looked at photographs of the terrible ~~automobile accident, shots of the~~ wreckage, close-ups of Grant's best friend, even photos of ~~him~~ **the body** being taken away. **Next,** w~~W~~e heard that Grant had been driving while intoxicated on Highway 281 at 2 a.m.

FOCUS ON PARAGRAPHS

after a party. Yes, his blood alcohol level was .11, well over the legal limit. **After** h~~He~~ had been convicted of drunk driving on ~~previous~~ **other** occasions during 1994/95, ~~and~~ he had completed a special program in mid-May to educate drunk drivers. **Still,** Grant had gone out and driven over 120 km per hour while drunk, even though his licence was suspended. "Why did he do it?" I wondered.

Synonyms

Sometimes the repetition of key words can become so monotonous that it detracts from an essay. In this case a writer may use **synonyms**, words that share a meaning or are closely related in meaning, to emphasize an idea. In the opening paragraph of his essay, Russell uses synonyms to emphasize some of the changes to the cowboy's life.

There have been changes. **No longer** does the cowboy or his boss spend the long hours in the saddle covering hundreds of miles of open range. **Nor** is the cow business quite so much of a poker game with the weather. **It is a rare thing** now for cattle to be caught starving in a killing winter storm. The ranchers know how much feed it takes to winter a cow and they work hard to keep enough on hand with some surplus to take care of the unexpected.

The phrases *no longer, nor,* and *it is a rare thing* all help to emphasize the changes that have taken place.

Matthew decides that synonyms would break up the monotony of the following paragraph from his essay:

First Draft: As the jury walked out of the jury box, my heart was pounding. I looked at the defendant out of the corner of my eye. Looking sad and alone, the man sat next to his attorney. The defendant was pretty good-looking and seemed well-mannered. Could I vote to send Allen Wayne Grant, Jr. to jail for five or ten years? What would happen to the defendant? I didn't know.

Revision: As ~~the jury~~ **we** walked out of the jury box, my heart was pounding. I looked at the ~~defendant~~ **man on trial** out of the corner of my eye. Looking sad and alone, the ~~man~~ **defendant** sat next to his attorney. The ~~defendant~~ **fellow** was ~~pretty good-looking~~ **fairly handsome** and seemed well-mannered. Could I vote to send Allen Wayne Grant, Jr. to jail for five or ten years? What would happen to ~~the defendant~~ **him**? I didn't know.

Matthew's revision is easier to read and is more interesting than his first draft.

Parallelism

Writers often write key words and phrases in **parallel form**—a series of words, phrases, and clauses that have the same grammatical structure—to show their relationship to one another and to unify sentences and paragraphs. In the following example from "A Way of life," Russell relies heavily on parallel structure to provide emphasis to his ideas.

> **Ranching is** a business that brings bank account riches to very few people; **it is** a way of life. **It is** a challenge to make the best use of the good earth without abusing it. **It is** an art in its dealing with animals, where one must mix **a strong back** with **a wise head** and **a warm heart**. It involves many things, **from training a skittish colt to the careful study of bloodlines, from welding a broken piece of machinery to the intricate plaiting of a hackamore** from thin strips of rawhide.

In the first three sentences of this example, Russell begins to create a definition for ranching. Notice the repetition of the verb *is*. In the third sentence, he uses a pattern of article, adjective, and noun to list what personal characteristics are necessary to become a rancher. And, in the final sentence, he uses adverbs to introduce the gerund phrases. Note that the parallel structure not only helps to unify the sentences, but also provides a certain rhythm to the paragraph.

Matthew found two places where he could improve his essay by using parallel structure. In paragraph seven, Matthew revised the following sentence:

First Draft: As we went through that process, I thought about all the parties I have been to where people drank, listening to CDs, danced, and having fun.

Revision: As we went through that process, I thought about all the parties I have been to where people ~~drank~~ **were drinking, listening** to CDs, ~~danced~~ **dancing,** and **having** fun.

This example focuses its parallel structure on present participles (*-ing* verb forms). The structure shows us that we are reading a list of equivalent terms.

Next, Matthew revised another sentence to be parallel.

First Draft: We had to decide whether he had taken his friend's life by accident or intentionally.

Revision: We had to decide whether he had taken his friend's life ~~by accident or intentionally~~ **accidentally or intentionally.**

Both of these examples are clearer and easier to read in parallel form.

Repetition

Repeating key words and phrases not only helps your sentences and paragraphs cohere but also emphasizes important ideas. For example, notice how the repetition of the words *gamblers* and *gambler* emphasizes the very nature of what it is to be a rancher.

> Some of the changes from the old ways have been immense. But ranching people are still as enterprising and adventurous as ever. They are at once innately conservative and yet the greatest **gamblers** upon earth—anyone who stakes his future against the vagaries of weather and markets has to be a **gambler** to the marrow of his bones.

Russell's use of repetition helps to set up his definition of what it is, fundamentally, to be a rancher.

As Matthew looked back over his first draft and his first revision, he saw that he could clarify the relationship between his ideas and emphasize the difficulties in his job by repeating some key words in paragraph eight.

First Draft: We took another vote. There were 11 votes for second degree murder, meaning that he had intentionally killed his friend. Of course, I admitted voting for manslaughter.

Revision: We took another **vote.** ~~There were~~ **E**eleven ~~votes~~ **voted** for second degree murder, **meaning that he had intentionally killed his friend.** Of course, I admitted **voting** for manslaughter**, meaning that he had accidentally killed his friend.**

Here Matthew uses the technique of repetition (*vote, voted, voting* and *meaning, meaning*) as well as parallel structure (*meaning that he had . . . meaning that he had . . .*) to make the ideas in this paragraph clear and to show how they are related.

Exercise P7-1

Choose a couple of paragraphs from Russell's "A Way of Life." Underline and identify the pronoun references, transitions, synonyms, parallelism, or repetition that connect Russell's ideas logically and emphasize his important ideas.

Exercise P7-2

Read paragraph four of Matthew's first draft and suggest some unifying devices that might strengthen it.

Exercise P7-3

Rewrite the following sets of sentences using pronoun references, transitions, synonyms, parallelism, and repetition to make the sentences coherent. You might want to combine some of the sentences.

1. Dennis is slightly overweight. Dennis is aware of his condition. Dennis ate some cheesecake.

2. You think the world has many good qualities and it couldn't be better. You have a realistic attitude toward the government. You might want to be a political scientist.

3. I feel sure that the people of Quebec want a forceful leader who will stick by decisions. This person will accept the consequences of his actions.

4. Many people have good reasons for earning a college degree. One good reason is a better life. Another is to gain respect.

5. I think dogs make better pets than cats. Dogs are loyal. Cats are sneaky. Some people might not agree.

Exercise P7-4

Rewrite the following paragraph supplying logical transitions in the blanks. Use pronouns, transitional words or phrases, synonyms, parallelism, and repetition.

Health is important for each of us in reaching our goals. _____ , a sick

person does not function as well as usual; _____ , some people will learn

to function at a higher level than _____ or _____ did before

becoming ill. _____ , we are all capable of learning to function with

varying degrees of health.

Exercise P7-5

Working with a partner, write a paragraph and leave out the cohesive devices. Use Exercise P7-4 as a model. Exchange paragraphs with another group to have them fill in your blanks.

 COLLABORATIVE WORK

After writing a draft of your own analyzing essay, exchange papers with a classmate and do the following tasks:

A. Mark with a caret (^) places where you feel cohesive devices are needed, either within a sentence or paragraph, or between sentences or paragraphs.

B. In the margin beside each mark, suggest a type of cohesive device or specific words, phrases, or clauses to use.

Then return the paper to its writer and use the information in this section to revise your draft.

Building Complex Sentences

Checklist For Building Complex Sentences

✓ Is at least one of the clauses independent?
✓ Have you made into a dependent clause those details that are subordinate to the main idea?
✓ Have the dependent clauses been joined correctly using subordinating conjunctions?
✓ Do the combined clauses communicate precisely what you mean?

What Is A Complex Sentence?

Because we want to add sophistication to our writing, and keep our readers from getting bored, we want to use a variety of sentence types in our writing. We have already examined how to build simple and compound sentences. The difference between these types of sentences and a **complex sentence** is simply the type of clauses used. The complex sentence combines an independent clause with one or more dependent clauses.

Quick Review Of Clauses

In Chapter Two you learned about simple sentences. A simple sentence contains a subject and a verb—one independent clause. It stands alone, meaning it makes sense by itself.

Independent clause

Example: Loya ate jellybeans.

In Chapter Five you learned how to identify phrases and clauses, and how to tell the difference between a dependent and independent clause.

Phrase   **Independent Clause**

Example: Forever and a day, **Loya ate jellybeans**.

Phrase   **Independent Clause**   **Dependent Clause**

Example: Forever and a day, **Loya ate jellybeans** because she could.

In Chapter Six you learned about joining two or more independent clauses to form a compound sentence. The word or words that join them are called conjunctions.

Conjunctions *conjoin*, which means *to associate* or *connect*, but conjunctions also tell us something about the *relationship* between the items they are joining. In com-

F
O
C
U
S

O
N

S
E
N
T
E
N
C
E
S

pound sentences, each clause has equal value, equal importance in meaning. The clauses are joined by coordinating conjunctions. They are called coordinating because *coordinate* means of the same value or rank. It is important to remember that the coordinating conjunctions, the FANBOYS, join the clauses but are not considered part of either clause.

	Independent clause	C. Conj.	Independent clause
Example:	Loya ate jellybeans,	and	Loya loved jellybeans.

If the clauses that you wish to join are not equal in value, you will want to use a type of joining called *subordination*.

Subordination

Subordination helps readers distinguish between the most important ideas in the sentence and the details that simply tell us more about the main ideas. The main ideas are expressed in the independent clause, and the details that tell us more about the main ideas are expressed as a dependent clause or in a series of dependent clauses.

Unlike independent clauses, **dependent clauses** cannot stand alone as complete sentences. Dependent clauses contain subjects and verbs, but certain words that begin dependent clauses make them subordinate to the independent clause. They are dependent on the independent clauses for meaning.

Example: Loya ate jellybeans **because she could**.

In this example, *because she could* is the dependent clause. It depends on the independent clause, *Loya ate jellybeans*, for its meaning. The main idea of the sentence is expressed in the independent clause. The dependent clause tells us more about the main information, so it is not the most important idea in the sentence. Therefore, we give it a subordinate position. This is why it is sometimes called a **subordinate** clause. A dependent or subordinate clause must be connected to an independent clause to become meaningful and complete.

Consider the dependent clause in the above example: *because she could*. You and I know this clause is not complete. It leaves us wondering "because she could what?" To make sense, the dependent clause needs to be combined with an independent clause, in this case, *Loya ate jellybeans*.

Writing dependent clauses and connecting them to independent clauses is a simple process. First, you must decide what to make subordinate, or secondary. Then you need to find the best word to connect the subordinate or dependent clause to the main clause. You can use either **subordinating conjunctions** or **relative pronouns**.

Subordinating Conjunctions

The subordinating conjunction joins two complete thoughts by making one thought dependent upon the other. We make it dependent by adding a subordinating conjunction. What results is a *subordinate* or *dependent* clause, a group of words that has a subject and verb, but that, because of the subordinating conjunction, cannot stand by itself as a complete sentence. The subordinating conjunction not only makes the clause dependent but also connects the dependent clause to the independent clause, which can stand by itself.

> **Example:**   I am hungry.
>
>   I hear the ice cream truck.

This example provides two independent thoughts. To make the second idea dependent on the first, we combine them using subordination. We add a subordinating conjunction to the beginning of the clause that we wish to subordinate.

>   I am hungry because I hear the ice cream truck.

The word *because* is the subordinating conjunction. *Because* makes the clause dependent on the main clause. The addition of the subordinating conjunction makes the independent clause into a dependent/subordinate clause. *Because I hear the ice cream truck* does not make sense on its own. It depends on the independent clause for meaning.

Complex Sentences

When we use dependent clauses, we begin to build sentences with a more complex structure; we call these sentences complex sentences. A **complex sentence** consists of one independent clause and one or more dependent clauses.

Dependent clauses do not always have to follow the independent clause. We could also begin this sentence with the dependent clause, and the sentence would still make sense.

> **Example:**   Because I hear the ice cream truck, I am hungry.

If you do begin the sentence with the dependent clause, it is necessary to separate the dependent clause from the independent clause with a comma:

> | Dependent clause**,** | independent clause |

Do not use a comma if the independent clause comes first:

> | Independent clause | dependent clause |

You may have been told that you can't start sentences with *because*. You can't, if the sentence is a simple sentence. However, since *because* is a subordinating conjunction, as long as its clause is subordinate to an independent clause, you can use it freely.

Read both examples aloud. The dependent clause still shows the same relationship, that *because I hear the ice cream truck* is subordinate to the rest, but the emphasis changes. Switching the clauses around can also add variety to your sentences. And remember, when you begin a sentence with a dependent clause, you must put a comma after the clause to separate it from the independent clause. If the dependent clause follows, the comma is not necessary because the conjunction suggests the separation between the clauses.

Because is not the only subordinating conjunction. There are many. Each one adds a different meaning and suggests a different relationship to the clause that it subordinates.

Common Subordinating Conjunctions			
After	Even though	Before	Whenever
Although	How	Except	Where
As	If	Because	Wherever
As if	In order that	That	Whether
As long as	Since	Though	While
As soon as	So	Unless	Provided
As though	So that	Until	Provided that

Exercise S7-1

Experiment with the use of various subordinate conjunctions. How does the meaning in the sentence change when you join the following two clauses with each of the common subordinating conjunctions?
I am hungry.
I hear the ice cream truck.

Exercise S7-2

Join the following clauses to form complex sentences. Make sure you choose a subordinating conjunction that shows an appropriate relationship between the clauses. Try a couple of variations for each.

A. She chews pink bubblegum.

   She sticks it under her chair.

B. Judy asked about the Prime Minister.

   She knew something about him.

   He lived near the river.

C. The wolves live in Jasper.

   Jasper is a protected area.

   It is a National Park.

D. I ate fish for dinner.

Cats followed me everywhere.

E. Jim likes to run.

He is not running in tomorrow's race.

He doesn't like competing.

Exercise S7-3

Fill in the blanks with conjunctions that logically complete the following sentences. Tell whether you used a coordinating or a subordinating conjunction and explain why.

1. _____ I am tired, I will watch TV, _____ I will study some more.

2. He said _____ he will love and cherish her _____the end of time.

3. _____ you take a nap, I am going to pay my bills.

4. Juanita will work at the restaurant _____ she can.

5. We won't make reservations _____ more people decide to go.

Implied Conjunctions

Sometimes we are easily able to locate clauses in a sentence, but the conjunction joining the clauses does not seem to be present. In this case, we say that it is **implied**, or understood. We understand that, grammatically, the sentence contains the conjunction, but for the sake of brevity in speech, we have dropped its use. This most often happens with the subordinating conjunction *that*.

> **Example:** We all know school starts tomorrow.

In order for this sentence to be correct, the two clauses *we all know* and *school starts tomorrow* must be joined by a conjunction. We can almost hear the *that*: we all know *that* school starts tomorrow. Grammatically, we understand that it is there, but we don't include it because people don't use it in speech. Often we leave it out to avoid repetition.

> **Example:** We understand that she sings that song that she composed.

> **Revision:** We understand she sings that song she composed.

There are clearly three clauses in this example, but the clauses read more smoothly when the two conjunctions are left out.

Another Way To Subordinate

We can also subordinate by using **relative pronouns.** These clauses, though, are sometimes a bit more complicated to construct.

Subordinating Using Relative Pronouns

In Chapter Three we talked about personal pronouns, words used in place of a noun to avoid repetition. Another kind of pronoun, a relative pronoun, is also used to avoid repetition, but it is used to avoid repetition among clauses. We use relative pronouns as subordinating conjunctions. They are relatively easy to identify because there are only five of them.

Who	Whom	Whose	Which	That

Each of these pronouns is used for slightly different reasons. A careful writer observes these distinctions.

Who is used when the antecedent (what the pronoun refers to) is a *person;* unlike *whom,* it is used for a subject.

That is used to refer to either *persons* or *things.*

Which is used to refer to anything *except persons.*

Whom refers to a person and is used for an object; it is a form of *who.*

Whose refers to either persons or things and is also a form of *who.*

Relative pronouns always introduce a subordinate clause, and they tell us more about some aspect of the information in the independent clause. The following examples come from Russell's essay:

> **Example:** I couldn't help laughing and he looked hard at me with
>
> sharp blue eyes past the hand **that** was holding his nose,
>
> in a way **that** shut me up.

Note that the clause with the first *that* provides more information about the hand so that the reader knows which hand the author is talking about. With the second use of *that* we are given more information into the particular *way* that the character was looking at him.

> **Example:** Sometimes this promotes scours, **which** can be a virulent
>
> intestinal infection **that** will kill calves.

In this example, *which* introduces the clause that gives more information about scours, and *that* introduces more about the infection.

Example: It is good to pause once in a while to contemplate how much we owe those oldtimers **who** blazed the trails and showed the way.

Here, *who* tells us more about the oldtimers.

The thing to note is that the relative pronoun related directly back to a noun in a previous clause. If *that, which, who, whose, whom* do not appear to be introducing a subordinate clause, then they are likely performing some other pronoun function in the sentence, either as an *interrogative pronoun*, or as a *demonstrative pronoun*.

Interrogative Pronouns

Interrogative shares its meaning with the word *interrogate*. When we interrogate, we ask questions. Interrogative pronouns, *who? which? what? whose?*, are used to ask questions.

Example: *Who* brought in the snake?

In this example, *who* is an interrogative pronoun. *Who* serves as the subject of the sentence.

Example: *Which* of the films was the most interesting?

Here, *which* is the interrogative pronoun and it introduces the phrase *which of the films*. This phrase appears in place of the subject of the sentence.

Demonstrative Pronouns

Demonstrative pronouns, *this, that, these, those*, are used to point out some particular person or object.

Example: *That* was an x-rated movie.

That is a demonstrative pronoun: it refers to a particular movie. It also serves as the subject of the sentence.

Example: Martyn should not have brought *those* books.

Here, *those* is a demonstrative pronoun. *Those* indicates a particular set of books. *Those books* serves as the object of the verb.

Exercise S7-4

Indicate whether each of the following italicized pronouns is relative, interrogative, or demonstrative.

1. The man *who* telephoned was Dr. Werier.
2. *This* dress is not the right size.
3. *What* she tells me is great news indeed.
4. The window *which* you ordered just arrived.
5. *Which* of these two pieces of fruit do you prefer?
6. I think *that* I would like to go to *that*.
7. *That* hat looks smashing!
8. Pardon me, but *whose* idea was this anyway?
9. *Those* gloves look great with *that* dress.
10. *Who* brought *these* lovely daffodils?

Sometimes when we use relative pronouns in a sentence it is easy enough to figure out the subordinate clause that they introduce, but the independent clause is much trickier to identify. This is because the subordinate clause might appear in the middle of the independent clause, or because it appears to be sharing some words with the independent clause.

Example: My boss, **who is generally punctual**, was an hour late for work.

In this example, the subordinate clause introduced by the relative pronoun is easy to identify, but the whole clause appears after the subject and before the verb of the independent clause. In effect, the subordinate clause appears in the middle of the independent clause.

Example: What we can expect is a mystery to me.

Here, the sentence begins with the subordinate clause introduced by the relative pronoun *what*. The subject of the independent clause, however, is not so clear. In fact, the whole subordinate clause can be considered as the subject of the independent clause.

Points To Remember

- A sentence must contain an independent clause to be complete.
- A simple sentence contains one independent clause.
- A compound sentence contains two independent clauses joined by a coordinating conjunction.

- A complex sentence contains an independent clause and one or more subordinating clauses.

- Every subordinating clause is introduced by a subordinating conjunction.

- The conjunction *that* might be implied.

Exercise S7-5

Fill in the blanks with either a dependent or independent clause to produce complex sentences.

1. _____, call your mother. (dependent clause beginning with *before*.)

2. When you signed up for this class, _____? (independent clause)

3. Mrs. Benson, _____, won the lottery and moved to Victoria. (dependent clause beginning with *who*)

4. We will probably stay home tonight _____. (dependent clause beginning with *since*)

5. Whenever Dana's face turns red, _____. (independent clause)

6. Until my boyfriend arrives, _____.

7. I have cancelled the tickets _____ .

8. Several of my friends, _____, have left for Halifax.

9. The books, _____, look very interesting.

10. I have a passion for cookies, especially _____.

Exercise S7-6

Write a paragraph containing five original complex sentences, making sure that each sentence contains at least one independent clause.

 COLLABORATIVE WORK

After you revise your analyzing essay, exchange papers with a classmate and do the following tasks:

A. Mark each sentence that does not contain an independent clause with an X.

B. Look through each sentence. Mark each sentence that is missing a conjunction with an asterisk (*).

Then return the paper to its writer and use the information in this section to edit your draft.

CHAPTER EIGHT

Persuading

Remember, no one is obligated to take your word for
anything.

—M. L. Stein

LEARNING OUTCOMES

This chapter will help you:
- Understand and write an essay to persuade an audience;
- Understand and document sources you use; and,
- Recognize and use dramatic sentence techniques.

When was the last time you had to persuade someone? Most likely, it was just a few
moments ago. Persuading is one of the most common kinds of communication in our
daily lives: we try to persuade our friends to go to the movie we want to see; we try
to persuade our parents to let us borrow the car; we try to persuade a police officer
that we don't really deserve a ticket; we try to persuade the bank to loan us money
for a new car. We use persuasion all the time when we talk with others, so it is no
wonder that persuading plays an important part when we write essays.

Your research skills can help you as you write this kind of essay, too. Think about
a recent argument you won. What helped you win the argument? Could you have
won the argument without sounding like you knew what you were talking about?
Probably not. You have to sound like you know what you are talking about. That
doesn't mean you can fake it. You've probably heard a know-it-all try to win an argument by pretending to know what he or she was talking about. If you try to fake you
know a subject but you don't, you lose your audience's respect. You have to know
your stuff. That means if you don't know your subject from personal experience, you
have to do research.

How can you persuade people to share your viewpoint? How do you win an argument? There are three main ways to win an argument: you can appeal to your
reader's emotions with a story or an argument; you might try to win your audience

with impressive research and a strong logical argument; or, if you're an expert on your subject, you might try and persuade your audience based on your expertise.

Let's say we're writing on the subject of child poverty in major Canadian cities and we're trying to persuade our audience that child poverty is a serious problem. We could try to persuade him or her by attempting to sway his or her emotions. If we're writing on child poverty and we want to make our reader feel emotion, we might choose to relate the story of a child struggling with poverty:

> Willy gets up every morning with an ache in his belly and goes to school without eating and without a shower. As he sits through math, his first class of the day, he finds it hard to concentrate on the lesson. The math teacher notices that he can't concentrate and believes Willy just isn't motivated. The math teacher doesn't like what he sees. He tries to get Willy to do his work by threatening him, but it doesn't work. During recess, Willy has a hard time finding others who want to play with him. He is poorly dressed and others laugh at him for his poor hygiene. Is it any wonder why Willy doesn't like school?

We could use a logical argument and research to help make the same point in a different way:

> In the 1990s, child poverty was a growing problem. A study done in 1994 showed that one child out of every five lives in poverty (Lochhead, 9, 1996). Being poor doesn't just mean that a child doesn't have money. It is a severe disadvantage in several ways:
>
> > Poor children have poorer health and lower levels of educational attainment, they live in riskier environments, and they partake in riskier behaviors. Over the long term, child poverty significantly endangers a child's opportunity to grow and to develop into a healthy, self-reliant adult. (Lochhead, 9, 1996)

The last way we could persuade our audience about child poverty is if we were experts. What would make us an expert? You're an expert if you have had a firsthand experience with your subject. You're an expert if you've been trained or have studied your subject. In this kind of persuasion, you have to let your audience know what it is that qualifies you as an expert. Here's an example of how to persuade an audience based on expertise:

> I understand the kind of devastation child poverty wreaks on a child's life. I suffered from child poverty. I had nothing in my life to be proud of. Everything I owned, the places I lived, the clothes I wore, and the things I did were worse than anyone else I knew. People never respected me: they felt sorry for me. I learned to accept that I was, and would always be, worse, cheaper, and less than anyone else. I can't imagine learning a worse lesson. It's a lesson I have struggled with all of my life.

Any of these three techniques will work in the right situation. Or, perhaps all of them might work well in one essay.

When you look at persuasive writing, you will often notice more than one technique being used at once. This is quite common. People use more than one technique to help move their audience to their point of view. If we were writing an essay on child poverty and we included all three kinds of arguments in our essay, the reader would almost certainly be persuaded by what we wrote.

LEARNING FROM PUBLISHED WRITERS

Before You Read

Focus Your Attention

Before you read this story, take a few moments to respond to the following questions and statements in your journal:

1. Recall the best class you've ever taken and try to remember what you were like as a student.

2. If you were trying to make a teacher dislike you, what would you do?

Expand Your Vocabulary

Spend some time and read the sentences around the following words and see if you can figure out what each word means without using a dictionary:

Motivation (paragraph 1)

Extravagantly (paragraph 1)

Sullenly (paragraph 2)

Coup de grace (paragraph 4)

Immortalize (paragraph 5)

Nell Waldman

Flunking With Style*

People often remark that succeeding in school takes plenty of hard work.   **1**
That remark implies that failure is a product of general idleness and zero
motivation. This is an opinion I'd like to challenge. My long and checkered
past in numerous educational institutions has taught me that to fail grandly,
to fail extravagantly, to go down in truly blazing splendour, requires effort
and imagination. To fail your year in the grand style, you must antagonize
your teachers, disdain your studies, and cheat on your work. Keep the following guidelines in mind.

The first step, antagonizing your teachers, isn't difficult if you keep in mind   **2**
what it is that teachers like: intelligent, interested, even enthusiastic faces in
front row centre. Show that you're bored before the class begins by slouching
in a desk at the back of the room. Wear your Walkman, and don't forget to
turn up the volume when the teacher starts to talk. Carry on running conversations with your seatmates. Aim an occasional snort or snicker in the
teacher's direction when she's putting a complex point on the board. Above
all, never volunteer an answer and respond sullenly with an "I dunno" if the
teacher has the nerve to ask you a question. Before long, you'll have that
teacher bouncing chalk stubs off your head. Once you've earned the loathing
of your instructors, you'll be well on your way to a truly memorable failure.

The second step, disdaining your studies, is easy to master. They're proba-   **3**
bly B-O-R-I-N-G anyway. First, don't buy your books until close to midterm
and keep them in their original condition; don't open, read, or note anything in them. Better yet, don't buy your texts at all. Second, never attempt
to take notes in class. Third, stop going to class completely, but have lots of
creative excuses for missed assignments: "My friend's aunt died;" "My ger-
bil's in a coma;" "My boyfriend was in another car wreck;" "My dog ate the
lab report;" "I've got mono." You can bet your teachers will be really amused
by these old standbys. By now you are well on your way to disaster.

The third step, cheating, will deliver the *coup de grace* to your academic   **4**
career. Should an instructor be so sadistic as to assign a research paper, just
copy something out of a book that the librarian will be happy to find for
you. Your instructor will be astonished at the difference between the book's
polished professional prose and your usual halting scrawls; you're guaranteed
a zero. During your exams, sit at the back and crane your neck to read your
classmate's paper. Roll up your shirtsleeves to reveal the answers you've tat-
tooed all over your forearms. Ask to be excused three or four times during

the test so you can consult the notes you've stashed in the hall or the wash-room. Be bold! Dig out your old wood-burning kit and emblazon cheat notes on the desk. If you want to ensure not just failure, but actual expul-sion, send in a ringer—a look-alike—to write the exam for you!

If you follow these guidelines, you will be guaranteed to flunk your year.   **5** Actively courting failure with verve, with flair, and with a sense of drama will not only ensure your status as an academic washout but will also immor-talize you in the memories of teachers and classmates alike. The challenge is yours. Become a legend—pick up the torch and fall with it!

 ## Questions For Critical Thinking

Thinking Critically About Content

1. Does this essay use humour? How do you know? What kind of humour do you see?

Thinking Critically About Purpose

2. What do you think Waldman's purpose is with this essay? Explain your answer.

Thinking Critically About Audience

3. What type of audience do you think would most understand and appreciate this essay? Why?

Thinking Critically About Perspective

4. Does it sound like a teacher or a student is saying these words? Why?
5. How would the essay change if the perspective were reversed?

LEARNING FROM YOUR PEERS

There is no doubt that persuading others is a skill we all would like to have, and that successful people have strong persuasive skills. To see how one person writes a per-suading essay, we are going to follow the writing process of a student named Martin Whitman.

Martin's Writing Assignment: Persuading

This is the topic Martin's instructor assigned:

Think of a situation you would like to change, or an issue you disagree with related to your school or community. Your goal is to make readers feel sympathy for your position and to provide enough evidence and logical argument to convince them that your position is the correct one.

Martin went through his own writing process, covering some of the techniques in each of the sections in Chapter One: thinking, planning, developing, organizing, drafting, revising, and editing.

Thinking

Martin's class spent almost an hour brainstorming for topics. Some of the students had some big ideas. They wanted to write about national politics, the current international crisis, and environmental concerns. They decided that they did not have enough information to write about most of these topics unless they went to the library to do some research. Some of the students were willing to go to the library because they had other projects to work on. Most students, however, wanted to write about a topic that would not require them to spend hours reading in the library.

Martin left the class discouraged because he does not enjoy writing, and he does not see how doing this assignment will help him accomplish his goals. He is focused on his long-term goals: he wants to finish college, become an accountant, and marry his childhood sweetheart. This writing class seems to get in the way.

Martin pulled out his journal because his instructor told him that was a good place to write about his feelings. He recorded this entry:

> I am sick of idiotic assignments. I am sick of school. I just want to get out of here and graduate. Why do we have to do all these dumb assignments anyway. My adviser said there's no way I can graduate without taking this boring art history class I'm in. I can learn about art on TV if I want to. Heck, I can get a CD-ROM that takes me on tours of all the art museums in the world. I'm sure my future clients are more interested in what kind of software programs they should use in their business than "Who is Monet?" I don't care who Monet or Manet or any other nay is.

Martin felt better after he wrote. And as he wrote, he began to get an idea for his essay topic.

Planning

Martin looked at his notes again a day later. As he read them, he thought of all the courses he had taken that he felt he hadn't needed. He realized that there were too many required courses not related to his future goals. He scribbled this down in his journal. His disappointment turned to excitement: he had discovered his topic. As he reread his journal entry, he decided that his point about CD-ROMs was a valid one.

Martin listed all the courses he had to take to graduate. He put X's by the courses he wanted to take and asterisks by the ones he didn't want to take. There were a few courses he didn't want to take, but might be useful in his career—like statistics, for instance. So, of the asterisked courses, Martin underlined the courses that wouldn't help him with his career.

This is what his list looks like:

1.	Introduction to Accounting	X
2.	Intermediate Accounting	X
3.	Advanced Accounting	X
4.	Tax Accounting	X
5.	Office Accounting Systems	X
6.	Statistics for Business Majors	*
7.	<u>Art History</u>	*
8.	Math for Business Majors	X
9.	<u>Writing for Business and the Professions</u>	*
10.	<u>Physical Sciences for Non-majors</u>	*
11.	Introduction to Information Systems	*

Developing

Martin thought about family members who were accountants: his father, one aunt, and two uncles. He helped his dad and his aunt at the office, and he had a good sense of what they do every day. He realized his audience wouldn't be persuaded if he told them his own opinion without any support, so he decided to get the opinions of the accountants in his family that afternoon.

Martin wasn't very familiar with how colleges decide to require certain courses for graduation, but he thought that he could write about his topic without doing any library research. He spent some time looking through the catalogue and decided that this was a problem other students faced as well, so he asked students in some of his other classes. He discovered that many students objected to art history and writing course requirements as well. He made notes on their complaints.

Martin decided that his audience would be the policymakers at his college. They would be the group who could change the program requirements for accounting students. Then he tried to think of other things to help convince his audience:

1. There will always be a need for good accountants.

2. If I waste my time in art history, I will not be able to take courses that I need, like entrepreneurial skills.

3. My father never writes anything longer than a short note; he has a secretary to write letters.

4. Some of these courses might have been good for people a hundred years ago, but we have television, and we have more general knowledge of the world than people used to have.

5. Accountants do not need the same education as art historians. I want to be an educated person, but I do not think that everyone needs the same education.

Organizing

Martin struggled to begin his essay. He tried to imagine what would set his audience up to listen to his views. As he contemplated how to begin, he realized that he and the college shared the same desire: both he and the college wanted him to be successful. So, it made good sense to argue his case from this common ground. He decided to list his main points and to draft his essay according to these points:

1. I am in college because I want to be an accountant.
2. I have to take too many courses that don't have anything to do with accounting.
3. Some courses, like art history, are better learned from television or CD-ROMs.
4. My relatives, who are all accountants, say: "Don't take anything except business and accounting courses." They know the business.
5. I should be allowed to take the courses I think will help me, not someone else's ideas.
6. I will take as many credits as the school requires, but I want to take the courses I think will be useful for me.
7. I need a specialized education that fits my needs, not someone else's.

Martin examined his list and decided to begin writing his essay.

Drafting

Martin kept the list in front of him while he wrote because it helped him focus on his main point. As he finished writing one point, he developed the next point. Martin's first draft follows.

Martin's Essay: First Draft

Main idea: I shouldn't have to take college courses that have nothing to do with my goal in life.

My goal in life is to be an accountant. The only way that I know to become one is to graduate from a college or university and then take exams to become certified. My father, his sister, and his two brothers are all accountants, and I would like to carry on the family tradition. I am planning to get married soon. I would like to be able to support my new family.

I have talked to my adviser about this, and there ain't no way out. I've been real upset. I just have to take the courses if I want to graduate. I am talking about courses in art history, literature, and stuff like that. It just dose not interest me at all, and I think courses like that are a big blow-off. Plus, I don't do good in courses I don't like. I can't hardly follow this advise, because my graduation requirements are clearly stated.

Usually, you get to choose how you spend your money. All of these courses cost money. Time and money concern me a lot. I can't afford the tickets or spend the time at school basketball games. At my age, I need to be out of school and earning a living, not in school running up debts for stuff I can't use.

I think I may develope some of these same interests later in life, but right now I need to concentrate on getting ready for a job, for bringing in the bucks. My adviser, whose worked in business and education for over 25 years, says that if I just want a job, I should go to a school that don't require all these extra courses. I say that this school has top-notch accounting instructors. Their the best, and I oughta be able to come here and learn from them. I should also be allowed to take the courses that seems useful to me.

I would like the people who make the rules here to understand that I want to become an educated person and learn from the best minds, but I don't want to take courses I don't need. I don't think that's to much to ask. I am perfectly willing to take a lot of credits that are required, but I think I should be able to take those credits in math or computer science or marketing or business trends or entrepreneurship. I don't necessarily want to take less courses, just useful ones. In this age of push and shove, I need all the extra advantages I can come up with. I don't think that I will be able to persuade a client to do business with my accounting firm because I can tell the difference between an Expressionist and an Impressionist painting. A client may be impressed, however, if I can tell them how to use the latest software program to cut expenses. I am willing to become an educated person, but the days when we all needed the

same education are long gone. The world changes to fast, and I've got

to change with it. I don't no weather I can wait.

Revising

Martin felt that he wrote a worthwhile essay. Instead of just going through the motions to complete this assignment, he spent his time writing about something he believes in.

Now his instructor wants the class to focus their revising efforts on their paragraph structure—paying special attention to topic sentences in each and adding some dramatic effects to their essays.

Martin reviews the Focus on Sentences section in this chapter (p. 246), and he begins to put the finishing touches on his essay. He notices that several of his paragraphs are missing topic sentences (see p. 28) so he writes topic sentences for his paragraphs. Martin rewrites some of his topic sentences using dramatic techniques. He reads the Focus on Paragraphs (p. 237) section and does the exercises his instructor assigns.

 ## Collaborative Work

Peer Group Activity

After you read the portions of the Focus on Sentences section your instructor assigns, turn to Martin's first draft (pp. 229–231) and complete the following tasks in small groups:

A. Underline the topic sentence (for a definition, see p. 28) in each body paragraph. If a paragraph has no topic sentence, write one. If a topic sentence does not capture the main idea in its paragraph, put a line through it and rewrite it.

B. Add a dramatic technique to every paragraph except for the opening and closing paragraphs.

C. Are there too many dramatic sentences? Are there too few?

Look at the work your instructor will show you. How many techniques did he or she use? What do you need to review before writing your own essay?

Class Activity

As an entire class, look at the underlined portions of Martin's revised draft (pp. 232–234) to see how he changed each sentence.

A. Did you identify the revision problems that Martin corrected?

B. Do you think his changes are good ones? Discuss his changes.

Editing

Now that the sentences say what Martin wants them to, he needs to do some final proofreading and editing before handing in his essay. The instructor mentioned a few techniques students could use to dress up their essays. So Martin shifts his focus from the structure of his paragraphs to dressing up a few key sentences in his essay. He reads the Focus on Sentences section in this chapter. After he finishes the exercises his instructor assigned, he goes over the questions in the Checklist for Dramatic Sentences one by one (p. 246) and makes changes to his draft.

 ## COLLABORATIVE WORK

PEER GROUP ACTIVITY

After you read the portions of the Focus on Sentences your instructor assigns, turn to Martin's first draft (p. 229), and complete the following tasks in small groups:

A. Underline any sentences that could use a dramatic technique (see p. 246).

B. Suggest a technique that would suit the sentence and the writer's point.

C. Rewrite the sentence using the technique to give your classmates a clear sense of what you have in mind.

Compare your changes with those your instructor shows you. Did you identify similar topic sentences? Where do your changes differ from your instructor's? What do you need to review before writing your own essay?

Martin's Revised Essay ....

What About My Goal in Life?

Everyone has a goal in life. My goal in life is to be an accountant. My goal requires education. My goal is in danger. I do not believe my university's graduation requirements will help me achieve this goal. The only way that I know to become one is to graduate from a college or university and then take exams to become certified. My father, his sister, and his two brothers are all accountants, and I would like to carry on the family tradition. I am a veteran, and I am planning to get married soon. I would like to be able to support my new family.

I looked at my schedule and my first reaction was this: "why do I have to take all the courses that don't have anything to do with my

goal?" I have talked to my adviser about this, and there ~~ain't no~~isn't
~~any~~ way out. I've been real~~ly~~ upset. I just have to take the courses if I
want to graduate. I am talking about courses in art history, literature,
and stuff like that <u>sociology</u>. It just ~~dose not~~ doesn't interest me at all,
and I think courses like that are a big ~~blow-off.~~ waste of time and
money. Plus, I don't do ~~good~~ well in courses I don't like. <u>If I want to
learn about art history, I can go visit a museum somewhere or even
tour one with a CD-ROM program. Or I can watch public television and
learn about all the endangered species. I know about geography
already—all about isthmuses, estuaries, peninsulas—because I was in
the navy. I talked to my father and relatives, and they say the same
thing: "Don't bother to take those courses if they don't help you in
your goals."</u> I can't~~hardly~~ follow this ~~advise,~~advice, because my
graduation requirements are clearly stated.

<u>The university treats us the way a preschool teacher treats
children. Universities need to realize that all students are not kids
just out of high school as they used to be and allow students to spend
their tuition dollars and their time on courses that advance their
goals.</u> Usually, you get to choose how you spend your money. All of
these courses cost money. Time and money concern me a lot. I can't
afford the tickets or spend the time at school basketball games. At my
age, I need to be out of school and earning a living, not in school
running up debts for ~~stuff~~things I can't use.

<u>Even though</u> I think I may develop~~e~~ some of these same
interests <u>an interest in art, nature, or literature</u> later <u>on,</u> in life, ~~but~~
right now I need ~~to concentrate on getting ready for a job, for bringing
in the bucks.~~a job. I need bucks. Show me the money. ~~My advisor,
whose worked in business and education for over~~ 25,~~says~~ that if I
~~just want a job, I should go to a school that don't require all those
extra courses. I say that~~Since this school has ~~top notch~~ excellent
accounting ~~instructors. Their~~instructors, ~~They are the best, and~~ I

~~oughta~~should be able to come here and learn from them. I should also be allowed to take the courses that ~~seems~~ seem useful to ~~me.~~me. I would like <u>to be able to substitute extra courses in computer science, finance, and economics for the required courses.</u>

<u>I want to talk to </u>the people who make the <u>rules. The people who make the</u> rules ~~here to understand that I want to become an educated person and learn from the best minds, but I don't want to~~<u>are some of the best minds around. The best minds around make me</u> take courses I don't <u>think I </u>need. I don't think that's ~~to much to ask.~~<u>an unreasonable position or request.</u> I am perfectly willing to take ~~a lot of~~<u>the number of </u>credits that are required, but I think I should be able to take those credits in math or computer science or marketing or business trends or entrepreneurship. I don't necessarily want to take ~~less~~<u>fewer </u>courses, just useful ones. In this age of push and shove <u>competition</u>, I need all the extra advantages I can come up with. I don't think that I will be able to persuade a client to do business with my accounting firm because I can tell the difference between an Expressionist <u>painting </u>and an Impressionist painting. A client may be impressed, however, if I can tell ~~them~~<u>him or her </u>how to use the latest software program to cut expenses. I am willing to become an educated person, but the days when we all needed the same education are long ~~gone~~<u>past.</u> The world changes ~~to~~<u>too </u>fast, and I've got to change with it. I don't ~~no weather~~<u>know whether</u> I can wait.

WRITING YOUR OWN PERSUADING ESSAY

So far, you have seen a professional writer and a fellow student at work trying to persuade you to share their views. As you read the published essay and followed the writing process of another student from first to final draft, you absorbed ideas and ways of giving those ideas a form of their own. These reading and writing activities have prepared you to write your own persuading essay on a topic that is meaningful to you.

What Have You Discovered?

Before you begin your own writing task, let's review what you have learned in this chapter so far:

- In a persuading essay, you present an argument to convince your readers to adopt your position.

- To persuade your audience you should try to sway their emotions, present a well-researched, logical argument, or convince them of your own expertise. Or, use all three techniques to move the reader to take your view of your subject.

- To present your persuading essay effectively, you need to organize your ideas.

- To help you shape your essay, you should learn as much as possible about your readers.

- Before you write a draft, you need to decide on a point of view toward your subject.

- After you write a draft, you should revise your essay for meaning and organization.

- After you revise your essay, you should edit its grammar, usage, and sentence structure.

Your Writing Topic

Choose one of the following topics for your persuading essay:

1. Consider a time in your life when you were required to do something that did not achieve the intended results and perhaps even caused you discomfort or serious unhappiness. In a letter to the person in charge of the institution that imposed the requirement on you, try to persuade the person or institution to stop the practice. Be certain to offer evidence in the form of details, examples, and explanations; these elements are crucial to successful persuasive writing.

2. Write an essay that persuades an administrator at your college or university to change something about your program or your school.

3. Write an essay that persuades your classmates to devote some of their time to doing volunteer work in your community.

4. Create your own persuading essay topic (with the assistance of your instructor), and write a response to it.

When you have selected one of these topics, you may begin your writing process in the same way Martin did. If some tasks occur out of order, that adjustment is probably part of your personal writing ritual. Follow your instincts, and let them mold your own writing process. But make sure you've worked through all the stages to your final draft.

When you're finished, turn in your revised draft to your instructor.

Some Final Thoughts

When you have completed your own essay, answer these four questions in your journal:

1. What was most difficult about this assignment?
2. What was easiest?
3. What did I learn about persuading by completing this assignment?
4. What did I learn about my own writing process from this assignment—how I prepared to write, how I wrote the first draft, how I revised, and how I edited?

Reading Aloud

One of the ways you can tell if your writing is interesting is to read it aloud or have someone read it to you. If the sentences create a repetitive pattern, you're likely going to bore your reader. If your sentences sound interesting when they're read aloud—the rhythm of each sentence changes—then your writing will be more interesting to your reader. Break into groups of two. Here is a boring paragraph. Either you or your partner should read it aloud:

> He was a fair man. He liked to help the homeless. He liked to walk his dog, too. He would often walk to the river with his dog. He also liked to scrape gum. He scraped it from the bottom of chairs and tables. He kept the gum he found in a special jar. He would feed the gum in his special jar to his dog.

This paragraph sounds dull when you read it out loud. Why? The paragraph uses the same sentence pattern over and over again. The sentences are all fairly short. There is nothing exciting about the way these sentences are written. Readers appreciate variety, even in sentence structure. Read this paragraph out loud:

> He was a big man, and he loved his dog. The dog often needed a walk, so he would take the dog to his favourite place: the river. A special jar he had held a collection of chewed gum, his findings from the undersides of chairs and tables. He tenderly fed these chewed morsels to his dog.

This second paragraph varies the sentence pattern, sentence length, and choice of words. This writing is much more interesting, and it sounds better, too.

Documenting Your Sources

Checklist For Documenting Other People's Words

✓ Do you use an "in-text" citation every time you quote, paraphrase, or reword a source?
✓ Is every source you use listed on the Works Cited page?
✓ Have you removed any sources that you didn't cite in your paper from your Works Cited list?

When you document your sources, you have to document the sources in two places. First, you have to include a documentation reference right after you use the other person's words or ideas in your essay. This is called an **in-text** citation. Second, you have to build a list of all the sources you included in your essay. The list is called Works Cited, and you include it as the last page of your research essay. First, we'll learn how to document a source right after you use it. Then, we'll learn how to make a Works Cited page.

How To Document A Source Within Your Essay

If you include anyone's ideas or words, taken from another source, you need to tell the reader who and where you borrowed from. When you tell your reader where you borrowed words from, it's called *documenting your sources*. There are at least 20 different documentation styles. The most common one in English departments is a system called the Modern Languages Association (MLA) documentation style. It's the documentation style used by people who write essays for composition classes.

Documenting your sources is essential for a couple of reasons. First, if a person writes an essay and uses someone else's words but doesn't tell the reader that those words weren't his/her own, that person is guilty of a criminal offence called *plagiarism*.

Second, documenting your sources is important for convincing your reader and demonstrating you understand the field. The documentation system you use tells your reader you understand the field and work within it. Glitches in the documentation of sources demonstrate that the writer doesn't know what he/she is doing.

To document your sources properly with the MLA system, you include some short references to books right in your essay. We call these references **in-text** citations. Then, at the end of your essay, you include all the details of your sources in the **Works Cited list**.

The bottom line is this: documenting your sources has to be done and done right to be an effective part of your essay. Below you'll find the details of the MLA documentation style for each of the following sources.

How To Do An In-Text Citation

After you've paraphrased, restated, or quoted from a source you need to include an *in-text* citation with enough information that the reader can identify which source you used from your Works Cited list. All the information needed to identify the source is put in parentheses right after you use the source.

The kind of in-text citation you use depends on the sources you're including in your essay. If you're using several sources, and none of them has the same title or author, you can use the **standard in-text citation**. If you're using two or more sources with the same author, you'll want to use the **alternate in-text citation** format.

Standard In-Text Citations

If you only use one book by an author, then usually the author's name and the page number are enough for the reader to locate the source. When you cite the author, you only need to include his or her last name, dropping the first name.

If The Author Is Named In The Introduction To The Source Then Include The Page Number After You Cite The Source

In Chapter Six we learned different techniques to introduce quotes. One of those techniques uses the author's name to introduce the source. If you do introduce the source with the author's name, then just put the page number in parentheses after you finish the paraphrase, restatement, or quote. Here's an example:

> As Heather-Jane Robertson concludes, technologies "have their own politics" (235).

Notice that the word "page" or the letters "p" or "pp" don't go in front of the page number. That's because the reader will expect it to refer to a page in the text they are reading.

If The Author Is Not Named In The Quote's Introduction Then Include The Author's Name First Followed By The Page Number

If you don't name the author when you introduce your source, then you need to add the author's name to the information in parentheses after you use the source. Put the author's name before the page number. Here's an example:

> Even something as banal as a tomato harvester carried social conse-quences: "the development of the mechanical tomato-harvester was not a political statement, but its introduction dramatically shifted power rela-tions nonetheless" (Robertson 235).

Variations On The Standard In-Text Citation

If Your Book Has Two Or Three Authors

If you're using a source with two or three authors, you must either include the author's last names in the introduction or put them in parentheses at the end.

> Robertson, Davis, and Ford note that while the car ushered in a new conception of the world, the "radical shift in thinking altered the social fabric in a way that most people weren't even aware of" (235).

> While the car ushered in a new conception of the world, the "radical shift in thinking altered the social fabric in a way that most people weren't even aware of" (Robertson, Davies, and Ford 235).

If Your Book Has Four Or More Authors

If your source has more than four authors, use the first author's name and the words "et al." Et al. is a Latin phrase that means "and others." Here are some examples:

> While the car ushered in a new conception of the world, the "radical shift in thinking altered the social fabric in a way that most people weren't even aware of" (Robertson et al. 235).

> Robertson, et al., note that while the car ushered in a new conception of the world, the "radical shift in thinking altered the social fabric in a way that most people weren't even aware of" (235).

If You Have A Corporate Author

Many sources don't mention an author's name as the originator of the material. If an institution or an agency claims authorship, then treat the name of the agency or corporation as you would treat the author's name.

> The Society for the Preservation of the Horse suggests that while the car ushered in a new conception of the world, the "radical shift in thinking altered the social fabric in a way that most people weren't even aware of" (235).

> While the car ushered in a new conception of the world, the "radical shift in thinking altered the social fabric in a way that most people weren't even aware of" (Society for the Preservation of the Horse 235).

If The Author Of A Source Is Part Of A Bigger Source, Written Or Edited By A Different Author

Some books include articles that are written by people other than those who wrote or edited the book. Newspapers, magazines, Web sites, and edited works can do the same thing. This book, for instance, uses essays that were written by other people. In this instance, use the specific article's author as the author of the source. So, if you wanted to quote from the professional essay in this chapter, you would cite the author of the essay, not the authors of this textbook:

> As Waldman notes, "the first step, antagonizing your teachers, isn't difficult if you keep in mind what it is that teachers like: intelligent, interested, even enthusiastic faces in front row centre" (225).

> Failing in style means the student needs to remember what teachers like. They like "intelligent, interested, even enthusiastic faces in the front row centre" (Waldman 225)

Alternative In-Text Citations

If you use several sources in your essay and two or more of the sources share the same author, you'll need to use an alternative in-text citation format. The point of the in-text citation is to help the reader identify the source in your Works Cited list. If the author wrote two or more of the sources you're using, then the reader can't identify the quote if the citation only uses the author's name. Instead of using the author's name to identify the source, use the title of the source.

Referring To The Title And Author In The Introduction

If you're using two or more sources by the same author, then include the book titles in your in-text citation. If you use the title of the book to introduce the quote, then just include the page number in parentheses:

> In *No More Teachers, No More Books*, Heather-Jane Robertson concludes that technologies "have their own politics" (235).

If the source's introduction doesn't use the name of the source or the author, then include a slightly abbreviated name of the source with the page number in parentheses after using the source. Here's a sample:

> Even something as banal as a tomato harvester carried social consequences: "the development of the mechanical tomato-harvester was not a political statement, but its introduction dramatically shifted power relations nonetheless" (*No More Teachers* 235).

Quoting Someone Who Quotes Someone Else

If you quote a source and that source is quoting another source, you're using an **indirect quote**. Use the original author's name, but attribute the quote properly to the source you found it in. Notice the addition to the information in parentheses: "qtd. in." It means "quoted in." Here are some samples:

> Frank Davies insists that while the car ushered in a new conception of the world, the "radical shift in thinking altered the social fabric in a way that most people weren't even aware of" (qtd. in Robertson 235).

> While the car ushered in a new conception of the world, the "radical shift in thinking altered the social fabric in a way that most people weren't even aware of" (Davies qtd. in Robertson 235).

How To Build A Works Cited Page

Once your in-text citations are in place, you can put together your **Works Cited** page. This list provides your readers with all the detail they need to locate the sources you've used.

Works Cited is different than a bibliography. In a bibliography, you can include books you looked at but didn't use in your essay; the Works Cited page includes only the sources you use in your essay. If you don't use an in-text citation to refer to the work, you can't include it in your Works Cited list.

There are specific techniques to help you document every possible situation and source you might come across. The following is a selection of the most common techniques and sources.

Documenting Books

If you're documenting books, most of the information you'll need to include in your list of works cited is on the title page, inside the front cover. On the front of the title page, you'll often find the complete title of the book and the publisher. On the back of the title page, you'll find the details of the publication: the date, the place of publication, the edition, etc.

Most citations include the following bits of information: the name of the author(s), last name first; the name of the work; the name of the publisher; the city and province or city and state the book was published in; and the date of publication.

Books With One Author

List publication information in the order shown in the example. Remember to put the last name of the author first, followed by his/her first name.

Pura, Murray. <u>Mizzly Fitch</u>. Simon & Pierre: Toronto, Ontario. 1988.

Books With Two Or Three Authors

If you have a book with two or three authors, include each author's name in the citation listing. Remember to put the last name of each author first.

Downing, L., Carter, J.C., and McManus, T. <u>Students In Our Midst</u>.

Toronto, Ontario: Doubleday. 1995.

More Than Three Authors

If your book has three authors or more, then you can abbreviate the list of authors. Write down the name of the first author, last name first, and afterward include the abbreviation "et al.," a Latin phrase meaning "and others."

Everest, Beth, et al. <u>Mosaics: Sentences in Focus</u>. Pearson Education:

Toronto, Ontario. 2000.

Books With An Editor

If, instead of an author, your book has an editor, include the editor's name the way you would an author's; after the editor's name include the abbreviation "ed." for "editor."

McArthur, Murray, ed. <u>Contest: Essays by Canadian Students, Third</u>

<u>Edition</u>. Harcourt Brace: Toronto, Ontario. 1998.

Books With Corporate Authors

Sometimes books and other publications produced by institutions and corporations don't have a person's name associated with the text. In cases like this, use the name of the corporation or institution.

City of Calgary. <u>Our Future Through Diversity.</u> Calgary, Alberta: City of

Calgary. 1996.

Documenting Articles Within Books

Edited books often include works by other authors. When you list these kinds of books in your list of citations, you need to recognize the author of the piece and the editor of the book.

Signed Article/Edited Book

If the article is signed, include the author and name of the article first, and the book title and editor(s) afterward:

> Plato. "Phaedrus." *Readings in Classical Rhetoric*, Benson, Thomas, and
>
> Prosser, Michael, eds. Hermagoras Press: Davis, California. 1988.

Unsigned Article In A Dictionary, Almanac, Or Encyclopedia

Though many of these books don't have a named author or editor, they're not the same as an institutional author. These books differ from books with corporate authors in that they aren't representing an institution or agency. Instead they are products intended to supply information to readers.

Sometimes dictionaries and other reference-type books don't have an author. Just include the name of the entry in quotation marks, or if it's an entry in an encyclopedia or dictionary, include the name of the listing as the article title:

> "Grace." Webster's Third New International Dictionary of the English
>
> Language, Unabridged. G. & C. Merriam Company: Springfield,
>
> Massachusetts. 1976.

Multivolume Work

Encyclopedias and other kinds of books come in sets of multiple books called volumes. If you use one book from a set, you need to let your readers know that the book comes from a set. Include the volume number in the title of the source. Here's an example:

> "Peterson, Oscar" The Guinness Encyclopedia of Popular Music, *Vol. 4.*
>
> Middlesex, England: Guinness Publishing. 1995.

Documenting Magazines, Journals, Or Newspapers

Newspaper Article

Citing a newspaper is much the same as citing a book with different authors writing in it. The author of the specific article goes first with the name of the article afterward in quotes. The name of the newspaper is underlined as the title of a book would be, followed by the date of publication, and the section/page number:

> Nicholson, Blake. "Wind Power Works for Benedictines." The Chronicle-
>
> Herald. August 21, 1999. A16.

Newspaper Article With No Author

Some articles in newspapers have no named authors. The listing is much the same as listings with an author, except the name of the author isn't included. Begin with the name of the article in quotes, then the name of the paper, underlined, followed by the date of publication, and the section/page number:

"Refugee Status Based on Specific Criteria." <u>The Vancouver Sun.</u>

September 7, 1999. A6.

Documenting Internet Pages Or CD-ROMs

A listing of a CD-ROM includes the name of the CD in quotes. After the name, comes the name of the medium, in this case, CD-ROM. Finish the listing with the name of the company or organization releasing the CD-ROM and the date of release:

"Ban Landmines! The Ottawa Process and the International Movement to

Ban Landmines." CD-ROM. Department of Foreign Affairs and

International Trade. 1998.

Documenting Lectures Or Conversations

If you're documenting a lecture, put the name of the lecturer or speaker first, as you would the name of the author, then the name of the lecture, or if there isn't a name for the lecture, then include the topic of the lecture as the title. The name of the class is underlined. End the listing with the place and date of the lecture or speech:

Everest, Beth. "Signs, Symbols and Myth." <u>Introduction to Creative</u>

<u>Writing.</u> Mount Royal College, December 3, 1999.

If you want to quote from a personal conversation you've had with someone, put the name of the person you're quoting first, followed by the words "Personal Interview," followed by the date of the conversation.

Patterson, Diana. Personal interview. October 31, 1999.

Documenting TV And Radio Programs

To quote from radio or TV shows, begin with the name of the episode or specific show first. If the show spotlights individuals, include the names after the show title. Underline the name of the series followed by the producers' information and the date of the airing.

"My Healing Journey: Seven Years with Cancer." With Joe Viszmeg.

<u>Witness.</u> CBC. National Film Board. Dec. 3, 1999.

Documenting Films, Videos, Or Musical Recordings

To cite a movie, begin with the director's name, followed by the abbreviation "dir." Underline the title of the film and include the names of the principal actors. Include the name of the company that released the movie as well as the date it was released.

Duvall, Robert, dir. <u>The Apostle.</u> With Robert Duvall, Farah Fawcett, and

Miranda Richardson. Universal, 1997.

If you're watching a video, the listing needs to inform the reader that it came from a video. The listing is similar to citing a film: it begins with the director's name and the abbreviation "dir." The title of the video is underlined. After the title, include the name of the medium, in this case "videotape." The listing ends with the name of the company releasing the video, the place and date of release, and the length of the video:

Jhally, Sut, dir. <u>Peter Elbow on Writing: A Conversation With America's</u>

<u>Top Writing Teacher</u>. Videotape. Media Education Foundation:

Northampton, MA. 1995. 43 min.

For a musical recording, the name of the group or musician performing the music is listed first. The name of the recording is next, followed by the names of the companies that released it. Almost every musical recording has a unique number assigned to it. Include the recording's number at the end of the listing with the year of release.

Jars of Clay. <u>Much Afraid</u>. Essential/Silvertone, 01241-41612-2, 1997.

 ## COLLABORATIVE WORK

PEER GROUP ACTIVITY

After you read the portions of the Focus on Sentences section your instructor assigns, your instructor will put you into groups and send you to the library. When you get there:

A. Locate at least one source from each category of citation listing.

B. Document each source.

C. Compile a Works Cited page.

Return to class and trade your Works Cited page with another group. Check their listings to make sure they're done properly.

Dramatic Sentences

Checklist For Dramatic Sentences

✓ Are your dramatic sentences in the right place?
✓ Did you use the dramatic technique correctly?
✓ Did you use too many (too few) of these techniques in your essay?
✓ Do the dramatic techniques improve your essay or add clutter?

Most people have too much to read and don't like reading things that don't present ideas well. So, we have to work hard to make our writing interesting to our audience. One of the ways to hold your reader's interest in your essay is to add variety and excitement to your sentences. It's just a matter of learning a few different techniques and then using them to polish the draft of your essay.

These techniques don't guarantee you'll have a wonderful essay. But, if you have a good essay already, these techniques add some nice finishing touches to your writing. Like any good thing, these techniques can be used too often. One technique per paragraph is the maximum for most situations. Remember, when you use one, use it in the right place.

Where To Use Dramatic Sentences

What is a good place to use a dramatic sentence? These sentences attract your reader's attention. So, make sure you ask your reader to focus on the right material in your essay. You should use these kinds of techniques to emphasize your main points or material in your essay. Often, your paragraph's topic sentence is a good candidate for one of these techniques because the topic sentences should be your main points (see Focus On Paragraphs, Chapter Two). You can also try one of these techniques on support sentences in your paragraph, if you think that attracting extra attention to these sentences helps you make your point. Finally, these techniques are often used to open or end an essay. Introductions and conclusions are places where you want to help focus the reader's attention on what you're trying to say.

The following techniques are commonly used in essay writing.

Include A Piece Of Conversation

For some reason, people are more interested in reading words that someone has actually spoken than words committed directly to paper. So, you can help your reader keep his/her attention focused on your essay and add a little variety if you use bits of conversation to help you make your point.

I said, "It couldn't be possible!" But it was.

If you're going to use a piece of conversation, be sure the quotation marks and commas are in the right place.

Write Three Staccato Sentences

A staccato is a musical term for a short, sharp sound. When you write, put three short sentences together in a row for a fast action, punchy effect:

He jumped. The shot exploded. It was over.

Compare Your Idea To Something Else The Reader Understands

If you compare what you're trying to explain to something else, you can sometimes make your point more clearly and better draw your reader into your essay.

That man treated me the way couriers treat a parcel.

Choose Words That Begin With The Same Letter

Try to begin as many words as you can in a particular sentence with the same letter or sound.

Foul, cried the fair-faced fellow.

Open Two Or Three Sentences With The Same Words Or Phrase

Several of the sentence techniques in this section have been around since writing was invented. Just use the words you use to open a sentence to open the next one or two sentences.

I didn't like what I saw. I didn't like what I ate. I didn't like what I paid.

End Two Or Three Shorter Sentences With The Same Word

To create this type of sentence, repeat a word at the end of several clauses or short sentences:

He did nothing but eat healthy, dream healthy, and live healthy.

Begin A Sentence With The Words That Ended The Previous Sentence

This technique is quite subtle, so some of your readers won't notice it. It involves starting a sentence with the last word of the previous sentence for three or four sentences:

He struggled to pound the spike into <u>the ground</u>. <u>The ground</u> crumbled as he pounded the spike with <u>his hammer</u>. <u>His hammer</u> had all it could take, and as he raised it, <u>the handle broke</u>. <u>The handle broke</u> at the worst possible time.

Use The Same Word To Start And End A Sentence

This technique requires you to begin and end a sentence with the same word.

Blood begets blood. Power calls to power.

Reverse The Order Of The Words In The First Half Of The Sentence To End The Sentence

With this technique, you reverse the phrase you used to start the sentence to end the sentence:

One should eat to live, not live to eat.

Use More Conjunctions

Try using more conjunctions than normal in a sentence. Most often, this technique is used in a list. Look for a list and try it. It draws attention to the sentence:

There were donuts <u>and</u> ice cream <u>and</u> bagels <u>and</u> cheese.

End Two Sentences Or Clauses With A Rhyme

This kind of sentence uses rhyming words at the end of two clauses or sentences:

He stopped on a <u>dime</u>, though he wasn't on <u>time</u>.

Use A Rhetorical Question

A rhetorical question is a question your readers should be able to answer without you having to answer it for them.

Aren't politicians always honest?

Exercise S8-1

Look at Martin's revised essay (p. 232) and complete the following tasks:

1. Identify the dramatic technique Martin used in each paragraph. Is each in the right place? Did the technique replace the topic sentence or does the topic sentence go before or after the dramatic technique?

2. What effect do the techniques have on Martin's essay? Does the essay seem more serious or less so? Does Martin sound less confident when he uses the dramatic sentences?

3. Change three of the techniques that he uses.

Using Strong Verbs

Verbs are the muscle of the sentence. If you choose weak verbs, your writing might seem a little boring. For example, if you write "Kiona walked down the street," your reader doesn't learn as much as if you were to write "Kiona sauntered down the street." The second verb gives us a sense of Kiona's mood and identifies her actions with greater accuracy. When you are trying to improve verbs, look for two things: first, look for weak verbs that you can strengthen; second, look for linking verbs that you can replace with action verbs.

Replace Weak Verbs With Strong Ones

If you replace weak and vague verbs with strong, precise verbs, your writing gains a lot of power and your readers will be more interested in what you have to say. Here are some examples:

Instead of	You could write
Jeremy cut the orange.	Jeremy slashed the orange.
I cried when I remembered her.	I wept when I remembered her.
Everything smelled like fish.	Everything reeked of fish.
Frank is going to succeed in life.	Frank plans to succeed in life.

Use Action Verbs, Not Linking Verbs, As Often As Possible

If you replace linking verbs with action verbs when you can, your sentences become more lively. Take a look at these sentences:

Instead of	You could write
Violet was in the middle of the road.	Violet froze in the middle of the road.
The car was hanging over the edge.	The car teetered over the edge.
City Hall was changed forever.	City Hall changed forever.

Exercise S8-2

Find as many alternatives to the verb "walk" as you can. Then group the verbs by the impression or mood each creates.

 ## COLLABORATIVE WORK

PEER GROUP ACTIVITY

After you read the portions of the Focus on Sentences section your instructor assigns, trade drafts of your paper with a classmate and complete the following tasks:

A. Identify the topic sentence of every paragraph.

B. Did the writer use dramatic techniques? Have they been used properly?

C. Evaluate the effects of the dramatic techniques. Do the techniques help or distract you from the writer's topic? Could the writer use more or fewer dramatic sentences in his/her essay?

Problem Solving

I write to discover what I think. I don't think and then write. If
you think and then write you often get propaganda.
                    —W. D. VALGARDSON (JOHN ROBERT COLUMBO,
                              DICTIONARY OF CANADIAN QUOTATIONS)

LEARNING OUTCOMES

This chapter will help you:
- Understand and write an essay that offers a solution to a problem;
- Write effective introductory and concluding paragraphs; and,
- Write successful and varied sentences.

That we encounter problems in our lives is a given. Some are no more than minor annoyances: a car that won't start, a person who is rude or inconsiderate, too much homework over the weekend. Other problems, however, are far more serious: not enough money to pay bills, a sick child, a painful or unhappy relationship. Even larger problems trouble our society, our country, and our world: poverty, mass starvation, war, racism, disease.

Just as soon as we experience a problem, most of us begin to look for a solution. In fact, **problem solving** is a particularly satisfying form of essay writing because it helps us identify what is wrong in our lives; it helps us determine solutions to these problems; and it enables us to present solutions so that others can benefit from them. As we go through the process of writing a problem-solving essay, in a sense, we are also going through a process to discover what we think.

In *Second Sight*, a memoir about going blind, Robert Hine explores his thinking about losing his vision. When he lost his vision soon after becoming a college history professor, the problems he faced seemed insurmountable. How would he continue to do research? How would he read and grade his students' essays? And—the most serious problem of all—how would he be able to get to know his students and keep track of them in class? Hine discovered that the answer to many of his problems was Braille, a form of writing produced on a machine that leaves imprints on the page for each letter, enabling blind people to read with their hands rather than with their eyes. Hine described how his learning to write and read Braille helped him to overcome the obstacles faced as an unsighted teacher:

> For lectures . . . I held packs of three-by-five cards with brief Braille notes, [containing] the structure and ideas of the lecture and specific statistics when needed. Another pack of cards identified the students, so I could unexpectedly call them out and ask for comments at any time. Since I asked them to keep the same seats during the term, voice identification was not hard. . . . The whole system gave me the feeling of being in charge. I think it also kept the students on their toes and minimized their taking advantage of my blindness.

Robert Hine was not able to solve all the problems that arose as the result of his blindness—just as in our own lives we can solve many but not all of our problems. As you write your problem-solving essay, ask yourself the following questions: Does the problem have a solution? Is the solution one that will work, or is it so complicated, expensive, or farfetched that it is not practical? Will the solution create more problems beyond the original one?

LEARNING FROM PUBLISHED WRITERS

The published problem-solving essay in this chapter was written by Quade Hermann and published in *The Globe and Mail*. In the essay, she deals with the problem of not liking one's own name, and finds that the solution is not as simple as it seems. Here she explores how she goes about finding a new name, and the associated problems of changing it.

Before You Read

Focus Your Attention

Before you read this problem-solving essay, take a few moments to respond to the following questions. Jot down your thoughts in your notebook.

1. Think about a problem that you recently solved. How did you go about solving the problem? Did you have to change your lifestyle or behaviour in some way, or did you have to convince other people to behave and think differently? Were you happy with the solution, or was it not as satisfying as you expected it to be?

2. In the essay you are about to read, the writer describes her experience of changing her name. Think about your own experiences with your name. Have you ever been teased or bullied because of it? Have you ever wished it were different?

Imagine that you changed your name. What would you name yourself? Why? What do you expect would be the problems associated with changing your name? How would you solve these problems?

Expand Your Vocabulary

Find each of the listed words in the following essay. Without looking up dictionary definitions, jot down a definition for each. Compare your definitions with those in a dictionary. When you feel confident that you know the meanings of the words, write an original sentence for each that use the words in context.

Enigmatically (paragraph 2)

Prevarication (paragraph 2)

Conspiratorially (paragraph 3)

Moniker (paragraph 4)

Irredeemably (paragraph 6)

Appropriated (paragraph 7)

Epochs (paragraph 7)

Hybrid (paragraph 7)

Quade Hermann

Are You Talking to Me?*

"Quade. What kind of a name is that?" 1

I usually just smile and shrug enigmatically. When pressed, or if I'm feeling 2
cheeky, I'll roll my eyes and invoke the inexplicable excesses of the decade when I was born. "Blame it on the sixties," I say. It's a shameless prevarication, because most of what my parents—a practical young woman from small-town British Columbia, and a German immigrant who barely spoke English—knew about the swinging sixties came from watching the Ed Sullivan show.

Nevertheless it works, every time. People laugh conspiratorially and drop 3
the subject, especially older people who probably have a couple of historical excesses of their own tucked under their belts. And this little white lie has inspired the best guess so far on the origin of my name: "Oh, it must be from Quaalude!"

*From *The Globe & Mail*, "Facts & Arguments," Wednesday, August 11, 1999, A22.

The truth is even more mind-blowing: I'm living under an assumed name. I never liked my given name, a moniker so coy and girlish it made my teeth ache. It is a name that put the femme in feminine, the sugar in sweet. For a girl who preferred violent games of tetherball to Barbie dolls, it was something of a cross to bear. It did the job—I came when called—but it never felt right. Perhaps it represented my parents' idea of who the tiny bundled stranger might become, but, unfortunately, did not in any way reflect who I turned out to be.   **4**

I'm not sure when exactly intermittent musings gathered speed and became serious consideration, but eventually choosing a new name for myself seemed as natural and obvious as my best friend giving me a nickname.   **5**

I set about developing a list of criteria. It had to be androgynous and unique, but not so unique that I would be obliged to spell it out every time (as it is the odd person calls me "Quad"). I wanted a name that didn't automatically refer to a celebrity or a movie character (sadly, that let out Yoda and Cher). Most importantly, I wanted a name that hinted at complexity, shadows, and maybe even something of a dark side. My given name was irredeemably bright-and-sunny-not-a-storm-cloud-in-sight—and therefore nothing like me.   **6**

I kept a list of candidates in the back of my Daytimer and tried them out in disposable conversations with taxi drivers and hairstylists. I appropriated from all cultures, considered all historical epochs. I cut-and-pasted hybrid creations and one-by-one discarded them. In desperation I bought a baby-naming book, but found the lists of designated characteristics, mythic in proportion and invariably split along gender lines, depressing.   **7**

I was down to two finalists when Quade dropped from the sky. The first time I said it out loud, I knew it was right. The long "a" felt good in my mouth. It was unusual. It sounded good when my lover whispered it in my ear.   **8**

Changing my name seemed to be a very personal consideration, and I was surprised when others had something to say about it. A few people questioned my decision and declared themselves unable to change the habit of a lifetime. Strangers began leaping across the social distance to compliment my new name, and I heard several shy confessions from those who have always wanted to change their names, but never did. One friend hugged me in sheer relief, finally able to reveal that she had always hated my old name.   **9**

I put off telling my mother until the paperwork was done. I figured if anyone had a right to be attached to my name she did, and I didn't want her response to sway my decision. I was afraid she'd interpret the change as a rejection of her best parental intentions. All things considered, I thought it went very well; she didn't take it personally at all.   **10**

"Quade? *Quade?*" she shrieked, "What kind of weirdo name is that?"   **11**

My Uncle Jim, who has a charming (if perverse) sense of humour, likes to bestow silly nicknames. He got to work right away and within days announced my new one: Kumquat McQuade. My brother was a bit of a harder sell. A year after the fact and he still refers to me both by my old and new name, often in the space of one breath, with "Sorry" inserted like a hyphen in between.   **12**

June 11, 1999 was the first anniversary of the change. Though it took **13**
some time to begin reliably responding to Quade (I strained a few friend-
ships breezing past people on the street) I was surprised at how effortlessly I
shrugged off the old name, which I identified with for nearly 30 years, and
adopted Quade. These days when I hear my given name it barely registers,
and I find it remarkable that it ever had any association to me at all. You
probably would too, if you knew what it was.

 ## QUESTIONS FOR CRITICAL THINKING

THINKING CRITICALLY ABOUT CONTENT

1. What do you think the writer means when she uses the term "historical excesses"
    (paragraph three)? What exactly is she referring to?

2. She says that her name "was something of a cross to bear." What does she mean
    by this, and why does she use the word *cross*.

THINKING CRITICALLY ABOUT PURPOSE

3. What is Quade Hermann's purpose in this essay? Why would an audience find
    this interesting?

4. What does the author not tell us here? What purpose does this serve?

THINKING CRITICALLY ABOUT AUDIENCE

5. Who do you think is Hermann's intended audience for this essay? Why do you
    think she sent it to *The Globe and Mail* for publication?

6. What other groups would benefit from reading this essay? Why?

THINKING CRITICALLY ABOUT POINT OF VIEW

7. Why do you think the author provided us with the responses to her name change
    by members of her family? What effect does it have on her argument?

8. What parts of this essay would change if someone else had written it, i.e., her
    mother, her brother, or Uncle Jim?

LEARNING FROM YOUR PEERS

Some of the problems we face every day have obvious solutions, and we handle them
quickly. Others are more complicated, and sometimes we cannot find a solution unless someone helps us. As the saying goes, "If you always do what you've always
done, then you'll always get what you've always got." This may not be the most elegant phrasing in the English language, but it makes an important point: learning to

analyze and solve problems is a valuable skill that we can develop throughout life if we are open to new possibilities. In the following pages, we follow the process of one student, Sandy Bliss, to see a possible approach to a problem-solving essay.

Sandy's Writing Assignment: Problem Solving

This is the topic Sandy's instructor assigned:

Most of us will never find the solutions to overwhelming social problems or the cures for devastating diseases, but we often solve smaller problems in our lives. Think of a problem that you have successfully solved. Then, in a carefully crafted essay, explain the problem and its solution to your class.

Generating Ideas

Sandy's class spends some time brainstorming and comes up with a list of possible topics:

- Managing study time
- Compromising with a roommate about visitors
- Solving a misunderstanding with a co-worker
- Reaching an agreement with parents about using their car
- Exchanging childcare with a neighbour for an evening out
- Managing money on a student budget
- Trading routine car care for house-cleaning services
- Car-pooling with a classmate so driving time is study time

Several students realize that they have been solving complicated problems for several years, but others are still looking for topics, so the class spends about 15 minutes freewriting to explore and develop ideas. It is here that Sandy comes up with a general topic—the stress of holiday celebrations.

By the end of the class period, Sandy has begun to narrow her topic. She has decided to write about holiday celebrations at her house. Because everyone in her family has a different picture of the ideal holiday, no one is ever happy with holiday preparations or celebrations. Recently, the family reached a compromise that was satisfactory to all concerned.

Planning

Clustering is a favourite creating technique for Sandy. She takes a large piece of drawing paper and scribbles her ideas all over it. Sometimes she doodles and draws until ideas come to her. For this essay, she finds herself drawing Christmas trees and poinsettias and pine boughs, even though Christmas is several months away. She writes the words "Merry Christmas" in the centre of her paper and then starts drawing more decorations. They remind her of the jumble of her house before the holidays. She writes the following phrases on her paper:

Mom's search for the perfect holiday

Artichokes and persimmons

Evergreens everywhere

After writing these phrases on her paper, Sandy laughs out loud at the essay that is forming in her mind. She knows that she can use many visual details to explain the problem to her readers. She remembers exactly what her mother's large collection of holiday ornaments looks like, and she thinks about the stress of holidays in her house.

Developing

Sandy wants to introduce her mother to her readers, but she does not want them to conclude that her mother is a close relative of Ebeneezer Scrooge. She hopes she can capture her readers' interest by comparing her house to the colourful magazines that always seem to be everywhere during the holidays. She also wants to explain the conflict clearly, because it has caused endless complaints, accusations, and arguments over the years. She wants her readers to know that she has always dreaded holidays and why, but now she looks forward to them with enthusiasm because of the solution her family devised.

Sandy takes out a piece of notebook paper and draws a line down the middle. She heads the two columns: "Before the Great Compromise" and "After the Great Compromise." Then she lists several differences in her house that she has observed over the years. This is how her list looks:

Before the Great Compromise	After the Great Compromise
Refrigerator full of holiday food.	Simple foods.
Cleaning frenzy, arguments.	Regular housekeeping okay.
Seasonal decorations in every room.	A few nice touches.
Cinnamon everywhere.	Normal, clean smell.
Clutter, clutter, clutter.	Room to move around.
No storage space, too much holiday stuff.	Room to store winter clothes.

Sandy is satisfied with her list and decides to start arranging her ideas.

Organizing

Sandy writes out her main ideas for the essay:

Problem: stress of the holidays.

Cause of the problem: too much needless preparation.

Solution: simplify, and mom has her perfect holiday.

Sandy looks over her "before" and "after" lists and decides to outline her essay in a way that emphasizes the differences. She also takes out her original doodling sheet with the clusters on it and tacks it to the bulletin board over her desk. As she maps out her essay, she moves back and forth between the list and the doodles, adding bits here and there, and modifying what she has until she sees that she is ready to make a rough outline in her notebook. Here is what the rough outline looks like.

1. Main problem: when I was growing up, Mom wanted every holiday to be the perfect holiday.
2. Thanksgiving and Christmas were the worst. She would start bringing in foods that were yucky as soon as she started reading those holiday magazines. Things like candied cherries and persimmons when we just wanted peanut butter and jelly.
3. Then came the cleaning frenzies. And her need to have baking bread smells in the air at all times.
4. She would go nuts with the decorations—evergreen everything.
5. And dishes—she would buy every plastic Santa Claus cup on the market.
6. There was a turning point—my sister and I decided to tell Mom to quit doing this—simplify!
7. Conclusion: life got more peaceful and we enjoy holidays now.

That evening, Sandy shares the outline with her sister. They spend some time laughing about the arguments they used to have, and talk about how they felt then compared to now. They realize that much of the family tension has been lifted by this simple solution. Sandy makes a few suggestions for details to add to the outline, and now feels ready to write up a first draft.

Drafting

When Sandy decides to write her essay the next day, she sits at her desk with the doodles on the bulletin board in front of her and her list and outline close at hand. She puts some Christmas music on the stereo to get in the holiday mood, and she starts writing her essay. This is the draft she wrote.

Sandy's Essay: First Draft ....

Main Idea: Mom always wanted the perfect holiday but it was too stressful; we wanted to simplify.

When I was growing up, holidays at our house were always dreadful. Mom always wanted things to be just like they are in the magazines. The problem was obvious. We do not live in places like the ones we saw in magazines. We never ate the kinds of foods that she found in the women's magazines or that we saw on television commercials. She wanted to make it a perfect holiday. It was too much stress. We didn't want it. My sister and I hated it. We always ended up fighting. I hated holidays.

The tension would start about a week before Thanksgiving usually. She would start buying stuff and bringing it in the house. Buying all sorts of groceries, the kitchen began to look like an overstocked supermarket. The refrigerator was so full of holiday food, packed that there was no room for anything like peanut butter and jelly. We would have to dig around the dates and candied cherries and the thawing turkey and the artichokes and the persimmons—Mom's boss gave it to her—to find something to pack into our lunch boxes. Clipping bizarre recipes out of the Sunday paper, the refrigerator would be filled with ingredients. We always say, "Yuck, what is that? When you saw the latest concoction of cranberries, whipped cream, and walnuts. I don't care what you do to cranberries, it always tastes sour to me.

Also every year, at about the same time as the strange food started coming into the house, she decided we all needed to go on a cleaning frenzy. Now remember that we did not have any relatives within a thousand miles. No one was likely to drop in on us. But she had this idea that everything had to be clean and organized so that no one would think she was a slob. I think that she thought that the scent of persimmon bread baking in the oven was going to draw in curiosity seekers from miles around to tell her how domestic she was.

Once the house was clean, she would decide that we needed to have seasonal decorations in every room in the house. One year there was so much stuff that smelled like cinnamon in our house that you would have dreams about cooking in a bakery or working in a spice warehouse. During another year, she would decide that everything should smell like evergreens, that our house would look like a pine forest. We would have evergreen wreaths on every door, evergreen candleholder rings on every table, evergreens in baskets with pine cones, evergreen printed table cloths and napkins and dish towels. This really got on our nerves. I mean no one like their entire house taken over by evergreens. It was crazy.

Then there was the matter of dishes. First, it was just plastic dishes with Santa Claus on them. Then it was punch bowls. We didn't even like punch! Then coffee mugs with cute little elves on them. Then china. Every year, she would go to the sales after Christmas and buy anything that was at least 50% off. You should always try to save money, but enough is enough! By the time I was 15 and my sister was 17, we decided that she had to quit buying so much holiday stuff. So we decided on Labour Day to have a talk with her before school started and then suddenly we would be into it,.

Laura and I knew that Mom wanted our holidays to be perfect. But she didn't have to keep buying all those decorations and strange foods. In a couple of magazine articles, it even said that people should not overdo things at holidays and feel pressure to spend money just because everyone else is. We told her so, and she acted really surprised. Of course, we also told her we didn't believe in Santa Claus anymore and that we really did not care for persimmons and pomegranates. We wanted to help her make the holidays fun, but not crazy. After talking things out, we agreed to buy some convenience foods that we really liked, things that are your timeless favorites. Also, we each offered to make some cookies, quick breads, and other simple foods, so we could save time and money that we could spend on gifts. To help matters even more, we would buy a turkey breast and roast it so that we would not have all those leftovers. One of us had to tell their side of the story. Think about it. Doesn't our compromise solution sound much better?

We started following this major plan for all the major holidays. It is much more relaxing and peaceful. And my sister and I do agree to taste one new recipe that she prepares every holiday. However, we don't promise not to say, "Yuck, Mom, what is this?"

Revising

Now that Sandy has written her draft, she faces the task of revising. During the next class period, the instructor asks the students to look at their essays as a whole this time, paying special attention to **introductory** and **concluding** paragraphs. The instructor spends a lot of time talking about the importance of strong thesis statements.

Sandy reviews the Checklist for Writing Introductory and Concluding Paragraphs at the beginning of the Focus on Paragraphs section in this chapter. She now knows from the checklist and from class that revising involves checking the contents of the thesis sentence, then checking to make sure that each paragraph after the introduction is fully developed and directly related, through its **topic sentence** and its related details, to the essay's thesis. She reads the Focus on Paragraphs section in this chapter, which explains more about how to shape introductory and concluding paragraphs and how to write a strong thesis statement.

Sandy uses the checklist to review the entire structure of her essay. She pulls out her main ideas from her introductory paragraph and formulates them into a single, bold thesis sentence. She writes this at the top of a separate piece of paper. Then she takes out each topic sentence and writes them below the thesis to make sure that each is related to her thesis and is developed as fully as possible. She discovers several problems in logic and begins moving sentences around. After she makes her changes, she rereads her essay and feels that it fulfills the revision guidelines as she understands them.

 ## COLLABORATIVE WORK

PEER GROUP ACTIVITY

After you read the portions of the Focus on Paragraphs section that your instructor assigns, turn to Sandy's first draft and complete the following tasks in small groups:

A. Highlight the main ideas in the introductory paragraph with a coloured marker. Formulate them into a thesis statement.

B. Underline the topic sentence of each body paragraph.

C. Put an X by any paragraph that lacks a topic sentence or has a topic sentence that is not directly related to her main ideas (thesis).

D. Put in brackets any details that do not support their topic sentences.

E. In the margin, make suggestions for improving the introductory and concluding paragraphs.

Compare the marks your group recorded with those your instructor shows you. Where do your marks differ from your instructor's? What do you need to review before writing your own essay?

Class Activity

As an entire class, look at the underlined portions of Sandy's revised draft to see what changes she made.

A. Did you identify the revision problems that Sandy corrected?

B. Do you think her changes are good ones? Discuss her changes. What else would you change to make the essay stronger?

Editing

Now that Sandy's supporting paragraphs are fully developed, and she has written a strong thesis statement and strategically arranged materials in her introductory and concluding paragraphs, she is ready to do some final proofreading and editing before handing in her essay. The instructor explains that all the students in the class should have a similar understanding of **sentence structure** and **variety**. So Sandy shifts her attention from the content of her paragraphs to specific points of grammar. She reads the Focus on Sentences section in this chapter to learn more about writing sentences that are parallel, consistent, and varied in structure and type. After she finishes the exercises her instructor assigns, she rereads her essay and immediately finds a couple of problems with inconsistent tenses. These errors put her on the alert for more problems with consistency. She decides she had better slow down and approach her revision more systematically, so she goes over the questions in the Checklist for Writing Successful Sentences one by one and makes changes to her essay so that her revised draft fulfills all the requirements on the checklist.

 ## COLLABORATIVE WORK

Peer Group Activity

After you read the portions of the Focus on Sentences that your instructor assigns, turn to Sandy's first draft and complete the following tasks in small groups:

A. Put an X through any pronouns that are remote, unclear, or broad.

B. Use an arrow to show where a modifier should be moved in a sentence so that the word(s) it modifies are clear to the reader.

C. Mark with a wavy line any part of a series that is not parallel in structure to the other items in the series.

D. Circle any words that are not consistent in tense, person, or number.

E. Put brackets around any sentences that are monotonous in their structure or type and should be varied.

Compare your marks to those your instructor shows you. Where do your marks differ from your instructor's? What do you need to review before writing your own essay?

CLASS ACTIVITY

As an entire class, look at the underlined portions of Sandy's revised draft to see how she changed each sentence.

A. Did you identify the editing problems that Sandy corrected?

B. Do you think her changes are good ones? Discuss her changes. What else would you change?

Sandy's Revised Essay ....

Inventing The Perfect Holiday

 Persimmons, pine boughs, and cinnamon. This was what our holidays were made of, and every kind of thing that my mother found in magazines. When I was growing up, holidays at our house were always dreadful and filled with stress. Mom always wanted things to be just like they ~~are~~ were in magazines. The problem was obvious. We ~~do~~ did not live in places like the ones ~~we saw in magazines~~ that were featured. Also, she was not a very good cook, and w~~We~~ never ate the kinds of foods that she found in the women's magazines or that we saw on television commercials. ~~She wanted to make it a perfect holiday. It was too much stress. We didn't want it. My sister and I hated it. We always ended up fighting. I hated holidays.~~ It took us several years, but we finally found a solution that ended Mom's search for the perfect holiday.

 The tension would usually start about a week before Thanksgiving ~~usually~~. Mom ~~She~~ would start buying stuff and bringing it in the house. Buying all sorts of groceries, <u>my mom filled</u> the kitchen <u>until it</u> began to look like an overstocked supermarket. The <u>packed</u> refrigerator was so full of holiday food~~, packed~~ that there was no room for anything like peanut butter and jelly. We would have to dig around the dates and candied cherries ~~and the thawing turkey~~ and the artichokes and persimmons <u>and the thawing turkey</u>—mom's boss gave it to her—to find ~~something~~ <u>some bologna</u> to pack in our lunch boxes. Clipping bizarre recipes out of the Sunday paper, <u>my mom</u> <u>would fill</u> the refrigerator ~~would be filled~~ with ingredients. We always ~~say~~ <u>said</u>, "Yuck, what is that?" when ~~you~~ <u>we</u> saw the latest concoction of cranberries, whipped cream, and walnuts. I don't care what you do to cranberries~~; it~~ <u>they</u> always ~~tastes~~ <u>taste</u> sour to me.

Also every year, at about the same time as the strange food started coming into the house, she decided we all needed to go on a cleaning <u>and organizing</u> frenzy. <u>First, my sister and I would have to</u> <u>help her take everything out of the kitchen cabinets and hall closet.</u> <u>Then, we had to sort, clean, and pack all the holiday china,</u> <u>decorations, and candles from preceding years along with everyday</u> <u>dishes and utensils. One year, we even had to clean the edges of the</u> <u>tiles with Q-tips dipped in ammonia. After that, we had to take down</u> <u>all the curtains, wash them and hang them back up, and shampoo the</u> <u>carpet, which then stayed damp for days and got dirtier than ever</u> <u>from pine needles and spills.</u> ~~Now remember that~~ <u>Since</u> we did not have any relatives within a thousand miles, no one was likely to drop in on us. But she had this idea that everything had to be clean and organized so that no one would think she was a slob. I think that she thought that the scent of persimmon bread baking in the oven was going to draw in curiosity seekers from miles around to tell her how domestic she was <u>and to compliment her on her cooking</u>.

Once the house was clean, she would decide that we needed to have seasonal decorations in every room in the house. One year there was so much stuff that smelled like cinnamon in our house that ~~you~~ I would have dreams about cooking in a bakery or working in a spice warehouse. During another year, she would decide that everything should smell like evergreens, that our house would look like a pine forest. We would have evergreen wreaths on every door, evergreen candleholder rings on every table, evergreens in baskets with pine cones, evergreen printed table cloths and napkins and dish towels. ~~This~~ All these evergreens in the house really got on our nerves. I mean, no one likes ~~their~~ his or her entire house taken over by evergreens. ~~It~~ Mom's overdecorating was crazy.

Then there was the matter of dishes. First, it was just plastic dishes with Santa Claus on them. Then it was punch bowls. We didn't even like punch! Then coffee mugs with cute little elves on them. Then china. Every year, she would go to the sales after Christmas and buy anything that was at least 50 ~~%~~ percent off. ~~You~~ People should always try to save money, but enough is enough! By the time I was 15 and my sister was 17, we decided that she had to quit buying so much holiday stuff. So ~~we decided~~ on Labour Day, we decided to have a talk with her before school started ~~then suddenly we would be into it.~~ and the whole cycle would begin again.

Laura and I knew that Mom wanted our holidays to be perfect~~.~~ ~~B,~~ but she didn't have to keep buying all those decorations and strange foods. ~~In a~~ A couple of magazine articles~~, it~~ even said that people should not overdo things at holidays and feel pressure to spend money just because everyone else is. We told her so, and she acted really surprised. Of course, we also told her that we didn't believe in Santa Claus any more and that we really did not care for persimmons and pomegranates. We wanted to help her make the holidays fun, not crazy. After talking things out, we agreed to buy some convenience foods that we really liked, things that are ~~your~~ some of our timeless favorites. Also, we each offered to make some cookies, quick breads, and other simple foods, so we could save time and money that we could spend on gifts. To help matters even more, we would buy a turkey breast and roast it so that we would not have all those leftovers. One of us had to tell ~~their~~ her side of the story. Think about it. Doesn't our compromise solution sound much better?

We started following this <u>more relaxing and peaceful</u> plan for all the major holidays. ~~It is much more relaxing and peaceful.~~ <u>Mom went through all her holiday decorations and saved only the prettiest ones; the others went into a yard sale. Now, even though she enjoys the pictures in holiday magazines, she no longer believes that her house must look like them.</u> And my sister and I do agree to taste one new recipe that she prepares every holiday~~.~~<u>, even if it has black walnuts, cranberries, persimmons, cream cheese, and fake frozen whipped cream in it.</u> However, we <u>did not</u> promise to <u>stop saying</u>, "Yuck, Mom, what is this?"

PRACTISE OUTLINING

As a class, spend some time generating ideas, planning, developing, and organizing a potential problem-solving essay:

1. Spend five minutes writing a list of problems that might make a good essay topic. Choose your best three to write on the chalkboard.
2. When all members of the class have added theirs to those on the chalkboard, choose the best two to practise outlining.
3. Divide the class in half. Choose which of the two topics to outline.
4. Choose a group leader to monitor discussion, and another person to record your ideas. Spend five minutes talking about the problem and possible solutions.
5. Write a possible thesis statement for the proposed essay.
6. Write five possible topic sentences that relate directly to the thesis.
7. Arrange the topic sentences in the order that would best bring across the topic.
8. Suggest some ideas for a concluding paragraph.

WRITING YOUR OWN PROBLEM-SOLVING ESSAY

So far, you have seen a professional writer and a fellow student at work trying to solve a problem. As you read the professional essay and followed the writing process of another student from first to final draft, you absorbed ideas and ways of giving those ideas a form of their own. These reading and writing activities have prepared you to write your own problem-solving essay on a topic that is meaningful to you.

What Have You Discovered?

Before you begin writing, review what is necessary to a problem-solving essay:

- Problem-solving essays identify a problem and present a possible solution if one can be determined.

- Ask yourself the following questions as a guide for your essay:

    Does the problem have a solution?

    Will the solution work, or is it so complicated, expensive, or farfetched that it is not practical?

    Will the solution create more problems beyond the original problem?

- To present your problem-solving essay effectively, organize your ideas.

- To help you shape your essay, learn as much as possible about your readers.

- Before you write a draft, decide on a point of view.

- After you write a draft, revise your essay for meaning and organization.

- After you revise your essay, do a final edit for grammar and sentence structure.

Your Writing Topic

Choose one of the following topics for your problem-solving essay:

1. Have you ever run into problems with your name? Write an essay in which you describe the problem as Quade Hermann does in "Are You Talking to Me?" Be certain to include enough facts, details, and examples for your reader to have a full understanding of the problem. Then suggest possible solutions. Be as precise and thorough as possible.

2. Consider a possible problem that one or more people might have: it could be caused by a physical or mental disability; by discrimination, poverty, illness, or injustice; or by lack of caring and concern. Write an essay in which you describe the problem and the way it could be solved.

3. Imagine your college newspaper is running a special edition on proposed solutions to important campus problems. Write an essay for the paper that identifies such a problem (i.e., a problem in the cafeteria or with parking), and suggest how this problem might be successfully solved.

4. Write a letter explaining a problem that you had with a business or organization to the CEO of that business or organization; then, offer your solutions to this person.

5. Create your own problem-solving topic (with the assistance of your instructor), and write a response to it.

When you have selected one of these topics, you may begin your writing process in the same way that Sandy did if her writing methods suit you. By now, though, you have probably found your own personal style to begin an essay. If some tasks occur out of order, trust that adjustment as part of your own way of thinking. Follow your instincts, but make sure you have worked through all of the parts of the process by the time you write up the final draft of your essay.

Writing Introductory And Concluding Paragraphs

Checklist For Paragraphs

✓ Does your introductory paragraph contain a **hook** that leads into your essay's main idea?

✓ Does your introductory paragraph contain a **strong thesis statement** that leads into your essay's major points?

✓ Does each supporting paragraph have a **topic sentence** that relates to the essay's thesis statement?

✓ Is the topic sentence of each supporting paragraph **fully developed**?

✓ Does the essay's concluding paragraph **summarize** the main ideas, **highlight** the most important issues, and **conclude** the essay?

A skilled artisan making a fine wooden table understands the importance of constructing a sturdy base. The legs or pedestal must support the top so that it does not collapse or even wobble. Only after the foundation is firm does the artisan supply a fine finish to enhance and protect the beautiful wood. Building an essay is like building a table. Once you are satisfied with the foundation (your title, introduction, and thesis), you need to add supporting paragraphs and a fine finish for your conclusion. Without any one of these parts solidly established, your essay (table) will wobble.

Introductory Paragraphs

First impressions are important, whether you are showing off a piece of furniture you built or meeting an employer for the first time. In the same way, the introductions to your essays should give a great first impression to capture your readers' attention, set the tone for the essay, and explain your purpose for writing. Introductions often have a funnel effect; they typically begin with general information, then narrow the focus to your position on an issue. To justify your purpose for writing, you may need to cite some facts or statistics, tell a story related to the issue, or ask some questions that the essay will answer. Regardless of your method, your introduction should "hook" your readers by grabbing their attention.

Quade Hermann immediately *hooks* her readers in her essay "Are You Talking To Me?"

"Quade. What kind of name is that?"

She captures her readers' attention with a question in the second sentence. The name "Quade" is unusual enough for the reader to want to know more. The rest of the essay answers this question about the name, but more importantly shows why her given name was a problem, how she felt about it, and the problems of changing it.

Andy Russell, in his essay in Chapter Five, takes another approach. He begins "A Way of Life" with a factual statement:

"There have been changes."

The essay that follows this fact develops the statement by analyzing what those changes are and how they have influenced the way of life for a cowboy in Canada today.

There are innumerable ways to hook your reader, but the most important thing to remember is that your hook must lead into your thesis statement, and consequently the rest of your essay.

Once you have hooked your reader, you need to let your reader know where you are going with your essay. In "Are You Talking to Me," Hermann provides her readers with her typical response to her opening question, and some personal anecdotes. Then, she sets out her main idea, how her given name was always a problem, and how the name *Quade* is in fact the solution.

In "A Way of Life," Russell provides us with a brief overview of some of the changes, and then shows us by personal anecdote what life used to be like so that we can visualize the changes.

An introduction is not complete, however, without a thesis statement, your reason for offering the product. A good **thesis statement** furnishes the controlling idea for your essay, focusing and directing the essay's development. Your thesis statement should narrow a broad subject into a topic that can be developed in 500 to 700 words (or the length of the essay that your instructor assigns). Your thesis statement is a sentence (or sentences), usually at the end of your introduction, that tells your audience what the focus of your paper will be.

Here is an example from a problem-solving essay that narrows to the thesis statement in the last sentence of the introductory paragraph:

> It happened so quickly. One minute I was riding my bicycle to my baseball game, and the next I was trying to force my eyes open. It seemed that fast, although supposedly there were days in between. I completely skipped the events in the middle, or at least I don't recall them, even though much has been explained time and time again. Everyone keeps asking what I remember: A warm evening in early June. I am on my bike. I am whistling. Opening my eyes. Seeing Clare. And now **I live inside a body that I cannot move.**

The opening line here works to *hook* readers, partly because readers don't immediately know what the *it* is. Gradually we are made aware that there was some kind of accident involving the narrator on his bicycle, and this is the *it*.. The author provides only enough details to make us curious, and then provides us with the thesis. The *thesis*, then, states the problem that will be worked through in the space of the essay. Because the paragraph is set up this way, with the thesis positioned as it is at the end of the introductory paragraph, we as readers expect that the author is going to talk about some of the struggles of learning to live with a paralyzed body.

FOCUS ON PARAGRAPHS

As Sandy reads over her first draft, she realizes that her introductory paragraph is weak. It lacks a hook, and the thesis is not clearly stated; the focus was on what she hated, rather than setting out the problem and suggesting that the family found a solution. Sandy sets out to make some changes to her essay.

First Draft: When I was growing up, holidays at our house were always dreadful. Mom always wanted things to be just like they are in the magazines. The problem was obvious. We do not live in places like the ones we saw in magazines. We never ate the kinds of foods that she found in the women's magazines or that we saw on television commercials. She wanted to make it a perfect holiday. It was too much stress. We didn't want it. My sister and I hated it. We always ended up fighting. I hated holidays.

Revision: **Persimmons, pine boughs, and cinnamon. This was what our holidays were made of, and every kind of thing that my mother found in magazines.** When I was growing up, holidays at our house were always dreadful <u>and filled with stress</u>. Mom always wanted things to be just like they ~~are~~ <u>were</u> in magazines. The problem was obvious. We ~~do~~ <u>did</u> not live in places like the ones ~~we saw in magazines~~ <u>that were featured</u>. <u>Also, she was not a very good cook, and w</u>~~W~~e never ate the kinds of foods that she found in the women's magazines or that we saw on television commercials~~. She wanted to make it a perfect holiday. It was too much stress. We didn't want it. My sister and I hated it. We always ended up fighting. I hated holidays.~~ **It took us several years, but we finally found a solution that ended Mom's search for the perfect holiday.**

With the addition of an opening hook, and a new final statement, Sandy's introductory paragraph now introduces the problem she is focusing on and its causes, then clearly states her thesis. Now she turns her attention to the other paragraphs.

Exercise P9-1

Read Sandy's revised introductory paragraph. What other effective ways might she use to hook her readers? Does she supply sufficient information to move the reader to the thesis? Can you suggest an alternative thesis statement?

Exercise P9-2

Read the sentences below and decide which ones cover broad subjects and which might serve as thesis statements. Rewrite each broad statement as a clear thesis that might introduce an essay of 500 to 700 words in length.

1. My school's core curriculum is unrealistic.
2. The best study methods combine reading, note taking, and repetition.
3. I do not believe that we should allow illegal immigrants to stay in Canada.
4. Athletics should be supported because they teach discipline, encourage competitiveness, and aid physical development.
5. Astronomy is the oldest of the sciences.
6. Skateboarding should be outlawed.
7. Today a new significance has been attached to word games by educators and psychologists.
8. Universities need to be more sensitive to the needs of their students.
9. Both high schools and prisons are institutions based on rules with built-in punishment for any sort of disobedience.
10. Environmentalists have done a heroic job trying to save our Earth from any more pollution, but some regulations that they have lobbied for go too far in restricting property owners' freedom.

Exercise P9-3

Compose a vibrant hook and a clear and detailed thesis statement for the essay you might write in response to each of the following assignments. (You do not have to write the essay).

1. Describe the positive contributions one invention has made to modern life.
2. Select a controversial campus issue that you have a definite opinion about. Write a thesis statement for a letter to the editor of your school's newspaper presenting your point of view.
3. Describe either the best or the worst teacher you had in high school.
4. Write a letter to a manufacturing company in which you describe your dissatisfaction with one of its products.
5. Write an essay in which you offer a solution to a problem in your community.

Exercise P9-4

Revise the following paragraph so that it opens with a hook, introduces its subject, and contains a clear thesis statement focusing on the main idea.

I am a second-year student in the School of Engineering. There are only a few of us girls in my class. We really have a lot of problems because of this. There should be ways to help this situation.

Concluding Paragraphs

The **concluding paragraph** is the final paragraph in an essay. Although concluding paragraphs can be structured in several ways, usually a conclusion summarizes the main ideas in an essay and highlights the most important issues the writer has discussed. Two other ways to end a paper on a strong note are to leave the reader with a further question on the topic or to make a prediction or recommendation. The most important responsibility of the last paragraph is that it actually conclude the essay.

Hermann concludes her essay with some parting comments about how easy it was for her to adapt to her new name, and rounds out the essay with a reminder to us that we still don't know what her original name was.

> June 11, 1999 was the first anniversary of the change. Though it took some time to begin reliably responding to Quade (I strained a few friendships breezing past people on the street) I was surprised at how effortlessly I shrugged off the old name, which I identified with for nearly 30 years, and adopted Quade. These days when I hear my given name it barely registers, and I find it remarkable that it ever had any association to me at all. You probably would too, if you knew what it was.

With this ending, the author again teases her readers and keeps them curious about her given name. It also allows readers space to contemplate their own, and indirectly asks if we too are satisfied with what we have been called.

Andy Russell (in Chapter Five) takes a different approach. In his final paragraphs he sums up the changes that have taken place in the ranching way of life, and offers a generalization of what has not changed. His final two lines of the conclusion tell us why he has written the essay, to honour those who have come before and made the changes possible.

> Above all, ranchers have to be practical. Their spirit has not changed even though the vast, open ocean of grass has gone forever. It is good to pause once in a while to contemplate how much we owe those oldtimers who blazed the trails and showed the way. They worked hard and played hard and through their sacrifices made it easier for their great-grandchildren.

This ending is a very satisfying conclusion to the essay. It asks readers to pause, to contemplate, and to recognize a few of the people who have been instrumental in making Canada what it is today.

As Sandy studies the conclusion of her first draft, she decides it needs strengthening in two ways.

First Draft: We started following this plan for all the major holidays. It is much more relaxing and peaceful. And my sister and I do agree to taste one new recipe that she prepares every holiday. However, we don't promise not to say, "Yuck, Mom, what is this?"

Revision: We started following this **more relaxing and peaceful** plan for all the major holidays. ~~It is much more relaxing and peaceful.~~ **Mom went through all her holiday decora-**

tions and saved only the prettiest ones; the others went into a yard sale. Now, even though she enjoys the pictures in holiday magazines, she no longer believes that her house must look like them. And my sister and I do agree to taste one new recipe that she prepares every holiday, even if it has black walnuts, cranberries, persimmons, cream cheese, and fake frozen whipped cream in it. However, we did not promise to stop saying, "Yuck, Mom, what is this?"

Sandy's revised conclusion summarizes the main points in her essay and ends with a question. The conclusion takes the reader back to the beginning by repeating some of the actual words from the introduction, but then goes one step further. The final sentence, in particular, could have taken the final thoughts in a number of different directions. Sandy's choice lightens the tone of the entire essay and brings closure to her story as well.

Exercise P9-5

Rewrite an alternative concluding paragraph for Hermann's essay: "Are You Talking to Me?"

Exercise P9-6

Suggest another way that Sandy could have concluded her first draft. Write a new conclusion based on your suggestion.

Exercise P9-7

Using one of the thesis statements that you composed for Exercise P9-3, write a final paragraph that might serve as a conclusion to this potential essay.

Exercise P9-8

Write an alternative conclusion for one of the essays that you have written during this school term. Hand your essay in with your revised conclusion.

 ## COLLABORATIVE WORK

After writing a draft of your own problem-solving essay, exchange papers with a classmate, and do the following tasks:

A. Read the hook. Does it capture your attention and lead to the thesis? If not, suggest an alternative.

B. Read the thesis. Is it strong, clear, and does it lead into the essay's main points? If not, suggest an alternative.

C. Put a line through any topic sentences that are not directly related to the essay's thesis.

D. Put an X by any paragraphs that do not have enough supporting details or that include details that do not develop the topic of the paragraph. Suggest improvements in the margins.

E. Decide whether the conclusion is effective. If not, suggest revisions.

Then return the paper to its writer, and use the information in this section to revise your draft.

Successful Sentences

Checklist For Writing Successful Sentences

✓ Is each **pronoun** located near its **antecedent**?
✓ Does each **pronoun** clearly refer to just one antecedent?
✓ Are pronouns and antecedents **specific**?
✓ Do **modifiers** describe or refer to the **correct word**?
✓ Do **modifiers** clearly refer to only **one word**?
✓ Are sentences grammatically **parallel**?
✓ Are sentences **consistent** in tense, person, and number?
✓ Do sentences **vary** in structure and type?

At one time or another, you have probably been a member of a team. You may have actively participated in sports at school or in your community recreation leagues. Perhaps your part-time job at a fast-food restaurant depends upon your interaction with other people. Or maybe you have taken part in classroom discussion groups or special projects that required your interaction and cooperation with your peers. Whatever the situation, teamwork is important in many everyday situations. To be a good team member, you must perform your individual duties and work with others.

Sentences also require good teamwork. Each individual sentence must function independently, possessing all the necessary elements to form a complete thought. But expressing ideas is not enough. To be truly successful, sentences must connect with each other and express similar ideas, working toward the common goal of communicating their meaning.

In this section, you will learn to compose successful sentences that work in harmony. You will learn to isolate and correct the errors that keep sentences from fulfilling their communication goals: you will encounter problems with pronoun reference, modifiers, and parallelism, as well as unnecessary shifts in tense, person, and number. You will also learn more about sentence variety. Incorporating specific sentence-building strategies will help your writing become more engaging and cohesive as you achieve your goals of clarity and unity.

Pronoun Reference

Each pronoun must have an **antecedent**, a noun or another pronoun it refers to. (See Chapter Three for more information on pronouns). Usually the antecedent is in the same sentence. Sometimes, however, the antecedent appears in a previous sentence. Look at these examples from Sandy's revised problem-solving essay.

Antecedent   Antecedent   Pronoun

My mom always wanted **things** to be just like **they** are in the magazines.

Pronoun

Also, **she** was not a very good cook, and we never ate the kinds of foods

Pronoun

that **she** found in women's magazines or that we saw on the television
commercials.

The pronouns and antecedents in Sandy's sentences are easy to spot. Sometimes, however, problems with pronoun reference arise, particularly when antecedents are remote, unclear, or vague.

Remote Reference

In some sentences, words, phrases, or clauses separate a pronoun from its antecedent. In fact, the two words may be so far from each other that the pronoun's antecedent is unclear. Look at this example from Sandy's first draft:

Remote: We would have to dig around the dates and candied cherries and the thawing **turkey** and the **artichokes** and the **persimmons**—mom's boss gave **it** to her—to find something to pack in our lunch boxes.

The pronoun *it* refers to *turkey*. However, because artichokes and persimmons separate it from *turkey*, the sentence is confusing. Here is Sandy's revised sentence with the pronoun and antecedent as close together as possible:

Revision: We would have to dig around the dates and candied cherries ~~and the thawing turkey~~ and the artichokes and the persimmons and the thawing **turkey**—mom's boss gave **it** to her—to find some bologna to pack in our lunchboxes.

Sometimes words even have to be shifted from one sentence to another.

Remote: The **shelves** in the refrigerator had not been cleaned out for weeks, and the **cupboards** had not been rearranged for months. So **they** were pretty crowded with life forms of their own flourishing in the cold.

Revision: The shelves in the refrigerator had not been cleaned out for weeks, so they were pretty crowded with life forms of their own flourishing in the cold. The cupboards had also not been rearranged for months.

Rearranging the sentence so that the pronoun *they* is closest to the word *shelves* makes the reference clear to the readers.

Unclear Reference

Sometimes a pronoun seems to have more than one antecedent. **This unclear reference** causes problems for readers because they do not know what is intended. Consider the following sentences:

> **Unclear Reference:** Sandy told Laura that **she** would have to talk to their mother.

Who will talk to their mother—Sandy or Laura? As the sentence now stands, we can't tell which person the word *she* refers to. Such sentences must be rewritten to make the intended message clear, even if it means eliminating the pronoun.

> **Revisions:** Sandy and Laura agreed that **Sandy** would have to talk to their mother.
>
> Sandy and Laura agreed that **Laura** would have to talk to their mother.

> **Unclear Reference:** Sandy likes to clean house more than Laura does. Sometimes **she'd** rather do **her** homework.

> **Revision:** Sandy likes to clean house more than Laura does.
>
> Sometimes Sandy would rather do her homework.

Here is another unclear pronoun reference from Sandy's first draft:

> **Unclear Reference:** We would have evergreen wreaths on every door, evergreen candleholder rings on every table, evergreens in baskets with pine cones, evergreen printed table cloths and napkins and dish towels. **This** really got on our nerves. I mean no one likes their entire house taken over by evergreens. **It** was crazy.

In this paragraph, the antecedents for the words *this* and *it* are unclear. We don't really know what they refer to. What got on Sandy's and her sister's nerves? What was crazy? This paragraph lists many causes of the frustration in the household, but these two pronouns need to refer to a specific issue.

Revision:	All these evergreens in the house really got on our nerves. Mom's overdecorating was crazy.

If you think a pronoun is unclear, a good rule is to substitute a specific noun for the pronoun, like Sandy did here.

Broad Reference

Writers often use the pronouns *you* and *it* to refer to general groups of people or things. Such examples of **broad reference** should be avoided; *you* and *it* are personal pronouns that should refer to specific persons, places, ideas, or items. Look at these examples from Sandy's essay:

Broad:	**You** should always try to save money, but enough is enough!
Revision:	**People** should always try to save money, but enough is enough!
Broad:	In a couple of magazine articles, **it** even said that people should not overdo things at holidays and feel pressure to spend money just because everyone else is.
Revision:	**A** couple of magazine articles even said that people should not overdo things at holidays and feel pressure to spend money just because everyone else is.

Both of these examples illustrate a different type of broad reference. Sentences should always be rewritten to clear up these problems.

Exercise S9-1

List the pronouns and their antecedents in paragraphs 9 through 12 of Quade Hermann's essay "Are You Talking to Me?"

Exercise S9-2

List each pronoun and its antecedent in paragraphs two and six of Sandy's first draft.

Exercise S9-3

Correct the faulty pronoun references in the following paragraphs.

One September morning my sister Connie woke me from a deep sleep. "It says right here in the paper that tickets go on sale next week for the first of two Pearl Jam concerts at the Pyramid. We've got to get some!" she screamed in my ear.

That's how our ticket-buying adventure began. We made plans to arrive outside the ticket window at least 12 hours before tickets went on sale. That meant midnight. When we got there, several security guards were there and about 30 people, including some of our friends. We showed them our identification and settled down for the night.

We had brought sleeping bags, several bags of snacks, two ice chests, a boom box, pillows, extra clothes, and a flashlight. We had borrowed them from my boyfriend, who goes camping a lot. We also had plenty of batteries for the boom box and flashlight. You need to buy a good brand so they will last a long time. Anyway, Connie turned it on as soon as we got settled down, but I made her turn it off because we didn't really need it.

We talked to the people around us in line. Two guys—Zack and Frank—were ahead of us. Zack kept making goofy noises, and Frank said he was going to have to move. They were really funny and entertained us. The girls behind us were Alice, Carrie, and Chris. They weren't too friendly because Alice and Carrie had been in an argument, so it seemed. Alice told Carrie that she was going to pay for all of their tickets. That's what they kept fighting about until she said she would. This kept us up for a while.

About 4:00 a.m. we finally dozed off to sleep. We woke up about 8:00 shivering from the cold. On the news that night it had said it would be pretty warm. Connie dug a sweatshirt and a jacket out of a paper sack and gave it to me. I was still cold, but one of the security guards brought me some coffee. His kindness made me smile because it really warmed me up.

Exercise S9-4

Write a paragraph (six to eight sentences) in which you describe a significant "first" in your life—your first day of college, your first date, your first day driving a car. Underline each pronoun and circle its antecedent.

Modifier Problems

Modifiers are words that describe, limit, or explain other sentence elements. When we hear the word *modifier*, we usually think of adjectives, which describe nouns and pronouns, and adverbs, which modify verbs, adjectives, and other adverbs. (See Chapter Three for more information on modifiers.)

Single words, phrases, and clauses can function as modifiers and should be as close as possible to the words they describe. What word the modifier refers to should also be clear. You can easily correct problems with modifiers by shifting and adding words to clarify the sentence.

Misplaced Modifiers

For a sentence to function effectively, every word must be in its correct place. Sometimes modifiers are far away from the words they describe. When modifiers are misplaced, you should rewrite the sentences, moving the modifiers to their correct locations.

Look at the following examples from Sandy's first draft:

Misplaced Modifier:	The refrigerator was so full of holiday food, **packed** that there was no room for anything like peanut butter and jelly.
Revision:	The **packed** refrigerator was so full of holiday food, ~~packed~~ that there was no room for anything like peanut butter and jelly.
Misplaced Modifier:	The tension would start about a week before Thanksgiving **usually.**
Revision:	The tension would usually start about a week before Thanksgiving ~~usually.~~

Sometimes entire phrases and clauses are in the wrong position in a sentence. Like words, phrases, and clauses should be located near the words they modify.

Misplaced Modifier:	Sandy's mother served a holiday punch to the guests in **red plastic cups**.
Revision:	Sandy's mother served a holiday punch **in red plastic cups** to the guests.
Misplaced Modifier:	We found the magazine and put it in a safe place **that had an article about clipping coupons.**
Revision:	We found the magazine **that had an article about clipping coupons** and put it in a safe place.
Misplaced Modifier:	When she arrived at the concert, Sandy told her mother that she would call home.
Revision:	Sandy told her mother that she would call home when she arrived at the concert.

You can see that after putting words and phrases in clusters that logically go together, you can easily solve most problems caused by misplaced modifiers.

Dangling Modifiers

If something dangles, it hangs, like a worm wiggling on the end of a fishing line or a colourful piñata swaying at the end of a string. **Dangling modifiers** are incorrectly placed in a sentence without any noun or pronoun to modify. Look at this sentence from Sandy's first draft:

| **Dangling Modifier:** | **Buying all sorts of groceries,** the kitchen began to look like an overstocked supermarket. |

Buying all sorts of groceries appears to modify the word *kitchen.* We know this is not logical. The kitchen was not buying groceries; Sandy's mother was, but she isn't even in the sentence. Simply reword the sentence, adding *my mom* as close to the modifier as possible.

| **Revision:** | **Buying all sorts of groceries,** my mom filled the kitchen until it began to look like an overstocked supermarket. |

Another option is to make the dangling modifier a clause.

| **Revision:** | **As my mom bought all sorts of groceries,** the kitchen began to look like an overstocked supermarket. |

Here are two more examples:

| **Dangling Modifier:** | **Before going to the store,** the car needed gas. |
| **Revision:** | **Before going to the store,** we put gas in the car. |

| **Dangling Modifier:** | **To enter the contest,** the application must be submitted by Friday. |
| **Revision:** | **To enter the contest,** you must submit the application by Friday. |

As these examples illustrate, introductory phrases and clauses usually modify the main subject. Therefore, to correct a dangling modifier, simply rewrite it to make it a clause, or supply the correct subject.

Squinting Modifiers

Squinting modifiers are not as common as misplaced or dangling modifiers. Nevertheless, they can still cause problems when they appear. Because squinting modifiers are sandwiched between other words, determining which words they modify is difficult.

Squinting Modifier: Sandy decided **today** to paint her room.

It's unclear whether Sandy *decided today* or whether Sandy *will paint her room today*. Simply move the adverb *today* to the location in the sentence that sends your intended message.

Revision: **Today** Sandy decided to paint her room.

Revision: Sandy decided to paint her room **today**.

Squinting Modifier: The teacher told the students **after the bell** to begin their tests.

Revision: **After the bell**, the teacher told the students to begin their tests.

Revision: The teacher told the students to begin their tests **after the bell**.

The revisions in both of these examples send different messages depending on the placement of the modifier in bold type.

Exercise S9-5

Underline the modifier problems in the following sentences adapted from Sandy's first draft.

1. Clipping bizarre recipes out of the Sunday paper, the refrigerator would be filled with ingredients.
2. Now remember that we within a thousand miles did not have any relatives.
3. She would decide that we needed to have seasonal decorations in every room of the house once the house was clean.
4. So we decided on Labour Day to have a talk with her.
5. Saving only the prettiest ones, the holiday decorations made Mom a little money at her yard sale.

Exercise S9-6

Correct the misplaced, dangling, and squinting modifiers in the following paragraph.

Skimming the newspaper the other day, an article caught my interest. It was about dieting. According to the latest research, people who count fat grams and calories consistently lose more weight than people who only count fat grams. That makes sense because some low-fat foods are high in calories. The article gave a couple of examples. Testing some 200 overweight teenagers, results showed that those who counted both fat grams and calories lost an average of five pounds more than those who counted only fat grams. Researchers conducted the study over a six-month time period. Having completed an additional study with adults, the results convinced researchers that fat-gram and calorie counting was the best way to lose weight. This is something that nutritionists and scientists have always suspected. After reading this article, my eating and dieting habits have changed.

Exercise S9-7

Correct the modifier errors you found in Exercise S9-5.

Parallelism

When you think of parallelism, you probably remember geometry class and a discussion of lines that run side by side and never intersect. **Parallelism** in writing has a similar meaning: ideas of equal weight should appear in equivalent forms. Simply put, in a series or comparison, words should be used with words, phrases with phrases, and clauses with clauses. Moreover, the words, phrases, and clauses in parallel structures should follow the same grammatical form. These examples of parallel structures are from Sandy's revised essay:

Words:	We always said, "Yuck, what is that?" when we saw the latest concoction of **cranberries, whipped cream**, and **walnuts**.
Phrases:	One year there was so much stuff that smelled like cinnamon in our house that I would have dreams about **cooking in a bakery** or **working in a spice warehouse**.
Clauses:	During another year, she would decide **that everything should smell like evergreens, that our house would look like a pine forest**.

Sometimes words, phrases, and clauses in a series or in comparisons are not in a similar form within sentences. When this happens, we call the error faulty parallelism. To correct faulty parallelism, simply replace the word, phrase, or clause in question so that all constructions are equal in structure and form, as in the following examples:

Faulty:	Jill likes skiing, cooking, and crossword puzzles in her spare time.
Revision:	Jill likes skiing, cooking, and doing crossword puzzles in her spare time.

Faulty: During our trip to New York City, we have many things to do, people to visit, and sights that should be seen.

Revision: During our trip to New York City, we have many **things to do, people to visit,** and **sights to see.**

Faulty: Lori signed up for judo **because she wanted to exercise** and **because of the boys in the class.**

Revision: Lori signed up for judo **because she wanted to exercise** and **because she wanted to meet the boys in the class.**

In the revisions, each item in a series begins with the same part of speech, and each item is equivalent to the other items. Parallelism helps make the message clear and straightforward.

Exercise S9-8

Underline the parallel structures in the following sentences from Sandy's essay. Then write whether each structure is composed of words, phrases, or clauses.

1. We never ate the kinds of foods that she found in the women's magazines or that we saw on the television.

2. She would start buying stuff and bringing it in the house.

3. I think she thought that the scent of persimmon bread baking in the oven was going to draw in curiosity seekers from miles around to tell her how domestic she was and to compliment her on her cooking.

4. Of course we also told her that we didn't believe in Santa Claus any more and that we really did not care for persimmons and pomegranates.

5. Also, we each offered to make some cookies, quick breads, and other simple foods, so we could save more time and money that we could spend on gifts.

Exercise S9-9

Correct the sentences in the following paragraph that contain faulty parallelism.

This past spring I attended a convention in Jasper. I had always wanted to go to one of our nation's National Parks seeing all the famous sights. The first day I was there I took a tour bus to the Ice Fields, the Athabasca Falls, and viewed the Sunwapta Falls. Every stop was impressive. Like most people, I prefer sight-seeing rather than to read about historic places. During another afternoon, I toured the museum. Our group watched a film that was very informative about the town and its history. Jasper Hawes, who the town was named after, was influential because he survived harsh winters, prospered, and becoming a fur trader for all people in the area. Then we got back to the hotel, and I rushed to the Information Centre. I was upset after running down the street, pushing people out of my way, only to find the Centre was closed. Anyway, my trip to Jasper was great, and I plan to go back again to see more things that I missed.

Exercise S9-10

Compose five original sentences using parallel constructions to satisfy the following conditions.

1. Use three parallel verb forms in a sentence.
2. Write a sentence containing two parallel phrases.
3. Write a sentence using two parallel clauses.
4. Use three prepositional phrases in the same sentence.
5. Write a sentence using neither/nor.

Unnecessary Shifts

Unless they are reading a mystery or suspenseful story, most readers dislike surprises. They prefer to follow a smooth path, anticipating what comes next in the sentence. Sometimes sudden changes within sentences throw readers off course, making the sentences misleading and confusing. We call these stumbling blocks **unnecessary shifts**: changes that usually occur in *tense*, *person*, and *number*.

Shifts In Tense

Tense refers to the time of the verb's action, mainly present, past, and future. Verbs in sentences usually keep the same tense unless expressing action that occurs at different times is logically necessary.

          Present   **Present**

While Bill **sits** at home studying, Robin **parties** with her friends from

work.

          Future   **Present**

The college **will send** your transcript after you **complete** a request form.

Sometimes writers shift tenses unnecessarily, producing sentences that are misleading and illogical. Usually the shift occurs from present to past or from past to present. Correcting unnecessary shifts in tense is easy: simply make the verbs "match up," as in the following examples.

          Present   **Past**

Shift in Tense: Sandy **tends** to get upset when she **got** writer's block.

          Present   **Present**

Revision: Sandy **tends** to get upset when she **gets** writer's block.

Past · Past

Revision: Sandy **tended** to get upset when she **got** writer's block.

Past

Shift in Tense: Last semester Sandy **had** allowed enough time to study but

Present

finds it hard to concentrate because of noise in the dorm.

Past

Revision: Last semester Sandy **had** allowed enough time to study but

Past

found it hard to concentrate because of noise in the dorm.

The actions in all the revised sentences take place in the same time frame.

Shifts In Person

Basically, English makes use of three **persons**: first person (*I*), the person speaking; second person (*you*), the person spoken to; and third person (*he*, *she*, *it*), the person spoken about. The most common shift occurs when a sentence starts out in the first person (*I*) and changes to the second person (*you*). When this shift occurs, the writer is usually trying to make a generalization by referring to a large group of people, whether specifically identified or unidentified. The simple rule to follow is to keep your person references consistent, as in the following sentences:

Shift in Person: I took a driving course where **you** learned how to parallel park and how to change lanes correctly.

Revision: I took a driving course where **I** learned how to parallel park and how to change lanes correctly.

Shift in Person: Relaxing is a simple thing for **me** to do, if **I** allow myself the time. First, **you** find a quiet place and lie down. Then **you** shut your eyes and let **your** body go limp.

Revision: Relaxing is a simple thing for **me** to do, if **I** allow myself the time. First, **I** find a quiet place and lie down. Then **I** shut my eyes and let **my** body go limp.

F
O
C
U
S

O
N

S
E
N
T
E
N
C
E
S

Shifts In Number

When it comes to grammar, **number** refers to whether a noun or pronoun is singular or plural. Shifts in number are probably the most difficult to correct. We hear these mistakes so often that they readily find their way into our writing. Shifts in number usually occur when indefinite pronouns (all, everyone, somebody, etc.) appear in a sentence. Learn which indefinite pronouns are singular, which are plural, and which can be either singular or plural. Then read the sentence closely, making sure that singular nouns are paired with singular pronouns and that plural nouns agree with plural pronouns.

Shift in Number: **Someone** left **their** keys in the copy room.

Revision: **Someone** left **his or her** keys in the copy room.

Shift in Number: **All** the bystanders told **his** own version of the accident.

Revision: **All** the bystanders told **their** own versions of the accident.

Exercise S9-11

List any shifts in person, tense, and number in Sandy's first draft, and label the shifts by type.

Exercise S9-12

Correct the unnecessary shifts you found in Exercise S9-11.

Exercise S9-13

Rewrite the following paragraph, correcting any unnecessary shifts in tense.

My cat Louise wears two faces. When she is inside, she is really well behaved, but when she got outside she went wild! Basically, she's a killer, destroying any bird or small animal that crosses her path. Anyone walking through our backyard should watch their step. It's a minefield of animal carcasses. Sometimes she places her kill near the back door, while on other occasions she put her prey behind a tree near the house. I have tried to control her by letting her out at night, but you really can't teach a cat not to kill birds and mice. It's their instinct. Everyone has their own opinion about Louise. Some think I should have her declawed, while others thought I should have given her away. But she's my cat, annihilator that she is!

Sentence Variety

A good writer always strives for sentences that flow smoothly, allowing readers to follow the ideas easily. Well-written prose should be an almost effortless ride without jarring changes or unexpected detours. But being too effortless can be a problem. The readers should be able to anticipate what comes next while being carried along by writing that is informative and engaging. But when readers cease anticipating and begin predicting repetitious writing patterns, the writer is in trouble. Prose that is boring and monotonous causes sentences, paragraphs, and entire essays to lose their impact.

One of the best ways to keep readers interested in your writing is to vary sentence structures. Often, writers rely too heavily on the standard subject-verb pattern, as in the following paragraph:

S   V   **S   V**

We decided last weekend to take a spur-of-the-moment trip. We didn't

V   **S   V**

want to go very far. We wanted to save some of our money for a

S   V   **S   V**

concert next month. We went to a nearby forest preserve. It was only

S   V   **S**

45 miles away. It had a creek for tubing and many hiking trails. We

V   **S   V**   **S**

took our camping supplies and spent one night. It was too hot. We

V

went home the next day.

Notice that every sentence begins with a subject and a verb. You probably began to be bored or irritated with the "choppy" effect of the repeated pattern after a few sentences. With just a little effort, we can add sentence variety to produce a much more interesting paragraph.

S   V   **S**

Last weekend we decided to take a spur-of-the-moment trip. We

V   **V**   **S   V**

didn't want to go very far because we wanted to save some of our

                                                 S   V

money for a concert next month. So we went to a forest preserve that

      V   S   V

was only 45 miles away. It had a creek for tubing and many hiking

            S   V   S   V

trails. We also took our camping supplies, but we spent only one night

            S   V   S   V

because it was too hot. The next day we went home.

    The main subjects and verbs appear not just at the beginning but at different points in the sentences.

    On the following pages, you will learn how to add words, phrases, and clauses to sentences and how to shift sentence elements to improve sentence variety. You will also learn how to combine sentences to make more complex structures that will keep your readers anticipating, but not predicting, what comes next.

Varied Structure

Often the best way to tell someone how something works or to give directions is to keep your words simple. The same principle generally holds true in writing. In terms of sentence structure, however, we certainly don't want to restrict ourselves to simple sentences. As you learned in previous chapters, there are three other sentence forms: compound, complex, and compound-complex. Good writing displays a variety of sentence structures that keep thoughts flowing smoothly.

    Look closely at this paragraph from Sandy's revised problem-solving essay. Notice how Sandy uses a variety of sentence structures.

> 1. **Laura and I knew** that **Mom wanted** our holidays to be perfect, but **she didn't have** to keep buying all those decorations and strange foods. 2. **A couple** of magazine articles even **said** that **people should** not **overdo** things at holidays and **feel** pressure to spend money just because **everyone** else **is**. 3. **We told** her so, and **she acted** really surprised. 4. Of course **we** also **told** her that **we didn't believe** in Santa Claus anymore and that **we** really **did** not **care** for persimmons and pomegranates. 5. **We wanted** to help her make the holidays fun, but not crazy. 6. After talking things out, **we agreed** to buy some convenience foods that **we** really **liked**, things **that are** some of our timeless favorites. 7. Also, **we** each **offered** to make some cookies, quick breads, and other simple foods, so **we could save** more time

and money that **we could spend** on gifts. 8. To help matters even more, **we would buy** a turkey breast and roast it so that **we would** not **have** all those leftovers. 9. **One** of us **had** to tell her side of the story. 10. **Think** about it. 11. **Doesn't our compromise solution sound** much better?

The sentences are structured as follows:

1. Compound-complex
2. Complex
3. Compound
4. Complex
5. Simple
6. Complex
7. Compound-complex
8. Complex
9. Simple
10. Simple
11. Simple

Not only has Sandy provided a variety of sentence structures, but she has also included sentences that begin differently. Notice that the main subject and main verbs appear in different places.

Using varied structures takes concentrated effort. When you write, try to allow sufficient time to work with your sentences to ensure that you don't overuse any one structure. Sometimes you may rely on the same structure several times in succession, but try to use different sentence beginnings to vary the basic pattern. Just remember that a good mix of sentence structures will refine your writing as you communicate with confidence.

Exercise S9-14

Label the structure of each sentence in paragraphs two and four of Quade Hermann's essay "Are You Talking to Me?" (p. 253)

Exercise S9-15

Label the structure of each sentence in the first paragraph of Sandy's revised draft (p. 263) as simple, compound, complex, or compound-complex.

Exercise S9-16

Rewrite the following paragraph using different sentence structures. Then identify the structure you used for each new sentence.

I decided to move out of my parents' house last month. My parents had too many rules. My friend Jules decided to move in with me. We looked at several apartments. We also looked at a couple of small duplexes. We even looked at one mobile home. We decided to move into a small apartment complex. It is near the college that we both attend. The apartment has two bedrooms and one and a half baths. It also has a kitchen and a separate living room. We have a small patio. It has room for a grill and a couple of lawn chairs. We have made it just fine so far. We don't foresee any problems, as long as we keep paying our bills.

Exercise S9-17

Select one of the following topics and write a short paragraph (six to eight sentences), making sure your sentences vary in structure. After you complete your paragraph, label the structure of each sentence.

1. Explain the advantages of attending college.

2. Describe your best friend or your boyfriend or girlfriend.

3. Tell about a memorable trip you took.

4. Explain why you like living in your hometown.

Varied Types

When you think of a sentence, you probably think of a series of words, including a subject and verb, that begins with a capital letter and ends with a period. The sentence expresses a complete thought or declares an idea. This is called a **declarative sentence**. But complete thoughts can also be expressed by other sentence types: questions, commands, and exclamations.

A sentence in **question** form seeks an answer and ends with a question mark. Usually a question begins with one of the following words: *who, what, when, where, why, or how.*

> **Questions:**   When did Sandy finish her paper?
>
> How much does she make at her part-time job?
>
> Who was your guest last night?

A **command**, sometimes called an **imperative** sentence, asks someone or something to perform an action. Unless a subject is specified, the understood *you* serves as the main subject.

> **Commands:**   (You) Turn off the stereo.
>
> (You) Call home before it gets too late.
>
> Sandy, please remember to call the phone company.

An **exclamation** is a statement that expresses a strong feeling—anger, surprise, fear, disappointment, disgust. An exclamatory sentence always ends with an exclamation point.

Exclamations: I won!

    If you lie to me again, I'll leave!

    Sandy, look out for the bee!

Usually, your sentences will be declarative statements ending with periods. For variety's sake, however, try to use questions, commands, and exclamations every now and then. It's not difficult either to add different types of sentences to your paragraphs or to convert declarative statements to questions, commands, and exclamations.

Exercise S9-18

Find five declarative statements in "Are You Talking to Me?" (p. 253). Then rewrite the sentences you found, making each a question, a command, or an exclamation.

Exercise S9-19

Sandy's revised problem-solving essay, "Inventing the Perfect Holiday," uses mainly declarative statements. List the sentences in her essay (p. 263) that are either questions, commands, or exclamations.

Exercise S9-20

Rewrite each of the following sentences from Sandy's early draft using a different sentence type.

1. When I was growing up, holidays at our house were always dreadful and filled with stress.
2. No one was likely to drop in on us.
3. We didn't even like punch!
4. Doesn't our compromise solution sound much better?
5. We started following this plan for all the major holidays.

Exercise E9-21

Rewrite the paragraph you wrote in Exercise S9-17 varying the sentence types. Include at least one question, one command, and one exclamation. You may have to add sentences to accomplish this task. Add transitions as necessary.

COLLABORATIVE WORK

When you revise your problem-solving essay, exchange papers with a classmate and do the following tasks:

A. Underline any antecedents that are not close to or do not agree with their pronouns.

B. Circle any errors in modifier usage.

C. Put brackets around any example of faulty parallelism.

D. Put an X through any shifts in tense, person, or number.

E. Choose one paragraph and identify each sentence according to structure and type.

Then return the paper to its writer and use the information in this section to edit your draft.

Afterword

One of life's quiet excitements is to stand somewhat apart from yourself and watch yourself softly becoming the author of something beautiful.

—NORMAN MACLEAN

You spend a great deal of time in this course practising your writing.

Understanding Yourself

If you ask most people what they need when they write, they'll tell you that they need a computer and word-processing software, or they'll ask for pen and paper. Both requests overlook the most important writing utensil you have: you. You feed words to your computer or pen. Even with a pen in hand, and paper lying patiently in front of you, the words may not come. But once you, the primary ingredient of the writing process, find something to write about, writing begins.

It makes a good deal of sense, then, that you should understand something about yourself, how you write, how you like to write, and how to make yourself happy, in order to get the best work out of yourself.

What Have You Discovered?

Writing is about you: knowing a bit about yourself and knowing how you like to write. This next activity is about collecting what you've learned about yourself and your writing process and putting it all together into a more complete picture.

You've written several assignments for this class. You've gone through your writing process several times. Use the following questions to profile your own writing process:

- What was your most successful essay? What steps did you take to write it?

- What was your least successful essay? What steps did you take to write it?

- Were there any differences between how you wrote, when you wrote your best, and how you wrote when you weren't at your best?

- When do you like to write? Is there a time of day you found more productive than others?

- Where was your favourite place to write? Home? Outside? A restaurant? School?

- What did you have around you when you wrote? Chips? A cola? TV on and blaring? Quiet?

- How were you dressed? In your pajamas? Casually? In your underwear?

- Do you prefer to write with a pen and paper or on a computer? Or do you prefer alternate methods of writing like recording your essay on tape and writing it down?

- What techniques do you prefer to use to generate ideas?

- Which techniques helped you work through dead ends when you hit them?

To write well know yourself and know how you write best. After thinking through your writing process, write up a one-page description of your ideal writing process. The next time you need to write, try putting yourself in that ideal setting. It'll help your writing.

Get to know what you like, what works for you, and how your writing process happens. You are where the writing process begins.

Understanding The Writing Process

Many writers admit that some of their biggest barriers to writing came from what they thought the writing process was supposed to be, and how they thought essays were supposed to be written. When these writers discovered that they couldn't write the way they thought they were supposed to, they came to believe they were not writers. Nothing could be further from the truth.

As you've written over the past few weeks and months, we hope you've discovered for yourself how the writing process works and what works for you.

There Isn't One "Right" Way

One of the great myths of the writing process has been taught for years as the only way to write. It goes something like this: first you come up with a thesis statement; then you come up with an outline that clearly supports your thesis statement and includes an introductory paragraph, three body paragraphs, and a concluding paragraph; finally, you write out a draft of your essay and fill in your outline. To be fair, some writers do write this way, but most don't. Most writers can't come up with the thesis statement or the outline of the essay until they've written something. There is no one right way to write an essay. In fact, there are many different ways, and they all depend on how each writer likes to write.

The student essays in this book all demonstrate that no two people approach writing the same way. And your way is as good as any other way.

There Isn't One "Right" Structure

Many writers struggle with writing because of some mistaken beliefs about the writing process itself. For instance, many students believe that essays must always follow a set structure. Here's the classic structure: introductory paragraph, three body paragraphs, and a conclusion. Most of the professional essays in this book do NOT follow this particular structure. And many people struggle with their essay writing because they cannot work with this format. Good essays do not often follow the classic format. And, likely, your essay won't nicely fit this particular structure either. That's fine.

You Don't Need To Get It Right The First Time

Many writers have a sense that good writers are people who can write something well the very first time they set pen to paper. Instead, we've tried to show you that to write well you don't have to get everything right the first time. Writing is revising, fixing your essay after you've written a draft or two. It's about getting words onto the paper and rewriting them until you're happy.

The best writers don't get it right the first time. They revise. Here is a professional writer writing about the importance of revising an essay.

Donald M. Murray

The Maker's Eye: Revising Your Own Manuscript*

Donald M. Murray won a Pulitzer Prize in 1954 for his editorials in the Boston Herald. *He worked as an editor with* Time *magazine before accepting a position at the University of New Hampshire. The following essay appeared in 1973.*

*Donald M. Murray, professor emeritus of English at the University of New Hampshire, writes a weekly column for *The Boston Globe*, poetry, fiction, and non fiction following the instruction of Horace *nulla dies sine linea*, never a day without a line—well almost every day.

When students complete a first draft, they consider the job of writing done—and their teachers too often agree. When professional writers complete a first draft, they usually feel that they are at the start of the writing process. When a draft is completed, the job of writing can begin.

That difference in attitude is the difference between amateur and professional, inexperience and experience, journeyman and craftsman. Peter F. Drucker, the prolific business writer, calls his first draft "the zero draft"—after that he can start counting. Most writers share the feeling that the first draft, and all of those which follow, are opportunities to discover what they have to say and how best they can say it.

To produce a progression of drafts, each of which says more and says it more clearly, the writer has to develop a special kind of reading skill. In school we are taught to decode what appears on the page as finished writing. Writers, however, face a different category of possibility and responsibility when they read their own drafts. To them the words on the page are never finished. Each can be changed and rearranged, can set off a chain reaction of confusion or clarified meaning. This is a different kind of reading which is possibly more difficult and certainly more exciting.

Writers must learn to be their own best enemy. They must accept the criticism of others and be suspicious of it; they must accept the praise of others and be even more suspicious of it. Writers cannot depend on others. They must detach themselves from their own pages so that they can apply both their caring and their craft to their own work.

Such detachment is not easy. Science fiction writer Ray Bradbury supposedly puts each manuscript away for a year to the day and then rereads it as a stranger. Not many writers have the discipline or the time to do this. We must read when our judgment may be at its worst, when we are close to the euphoric moment of creation.

Then the writer, counsels novelist Nancy Hale, "should be critical of everything that seems to him most delightful in his style. He should excise what he most admires, because he wouldn't thus admire it if he weren't . . . in a sense protecting it from criticism." John Ciardi, the poet, adds, "The last act of the writing must be to become one's own reader. It is, I suppose, a schizophrenic process, to begin passionately and to end critically, to begin hot and to end cold; and, more important, to be passion-hot and critic-cold at the same time."

Most people think that the principal problem is that writers are too proud of what they have written. Actually, a greater problem for most professional writers is one shared by the majority of students. They are overly critical, think everything is dreadful, tear up page after page, never complete a draft, see the task as hopeless.

The writer must learn to read critically but constructively, to cut what is bad, to reveal what is good. Eleanor Estes, the children's book author, explains: "The writer must survey his work critically, coolly, as though he were a stranger to it. He must be willing to prune, expertly and hard-heartedly. At the end of each revision, a manuscript may look . . . worked over, torn apart, pinned together, added to, deleted from, words changed and words changed back. Yet the book must maintain its original freshness and spontaneity."

Most readers underestimate the amount of rewriting it usually takes to **9** produce spontaneous reading. This is a great disadvantage to the student writer, who sees only a finished product and never watches the craftsman who takes the necessary step back, studies the work carefully, returns to the task, steps back, returns, steps back, again and again. Anthony Burgess, one of the most prolific writers in the English-speaking world, admits, "I might revise a page twenty times." Roald Dahl, the popular children's writer, states, "By the time I'm nearing the end of a story, the first part will have been reread and altered and corrected at least 150 times . . . Good writing is essentially rewriting. I am positive of this."

Rewriting isn't virtuous. It isn't something that ought to be done. It is **10** simply something that most writers find they have to do to discover what they have to say and how to say it. It is a condition of the writer's life.

There are, however, a few writers who do little formal rewriting, primarily **11** because they have the capacity and experience to create and review a large number of invisible drafts in their minds before they approach the page. And some writers slowly produce finished pages, performing all the tasks of revision simultaneously, page by page, rather than draft by draft. But it is still possible to see the sequence followed by most writers most of the time in rereading their own work.

Most writers scan their drafts first, reading as quickly as possible to catch **12** the larger problems of subjects and form, then move in closer and closer as they read and write, reread and rewrite.

The first thing writers look for in their drafts is *information*. They know **13** that a good piece of writing is built from specific, accurate, and interesting information. The writer must have an abundance of information from which to construct a readable piece of writing.

Next writers look for *meaning* in the information. The specifics must **14** build to a pattern of significance. Each piece of specific information must carry the reader toward meaning.

Writers reading their own drafts are aware of *audience*. They put them- **15** selves in the reader's situation and make sure that they deliver information which a reader wants to know or needs to know in a manner which is easily digested. Writers try to be sure that they anticipate and answer the questions a critical reader will ask when reading the piece of writing.

Writers make sure that the *form* is appropriate to the subject and the audi- **16** ence. Form, or genre, is the vehicle which carries meaning to the reader, but form cannot be selected until the writer has adequate information to discover its significance and an audience which needs or wants that meaning.

Once writers are sure the form is appropriate, they must then look at the **17** *structure*, the order of what they have written. Good writing is built on a solid framework of logic, argument, narrative, or motivation which runs through the entire piece of writing and holds it together. This is the time when many writers find it most effective to outline as a way of visualizing the hidden spine by which the piece of writing is supported.

The element on which writers may spend a majority of their time is *development*. Each section of a piece of writing must be adequately developed. It must give readers enough information so that they are satisfied. How much information is enough? That's as difficult as asking how much garlic belongs in a salad. It must be done to taste, but most beginning writers underdevelop, underestimating the reader's hunger for information. **18**

As writers solve development problems, they often have to consider questions of *dimension*. There must be a pleasing and effective proportion among all the parts of the piece of writing. There is a continual process of subtracting and adding to keep the piece of writing in balance. **19**

Finally, writers have to listen to their own voices. *Voice* is the force which drives a piece of writing forward. It is an expression of the writer's authority and concern. It is what is between the words on the page, what glues the piece of writing together. A good piece of writing is always marked by a consistent, individual voice. **20**

As writers read and reread, write and rewrite, they move closer and closer to the page until they are doing line-by-line editing. Writers read their own pages with infinite care. Each sentence, each line, each clause, each phrase, each word, each mark of punctuation, each section of white space between the type has to contribute to the clarification of meaning. **21**

Slowly the writer moves from word to word, looking through language to see the subject. As a word is changed, cut, or added, as a construction is rearranged, all the words used before that moment and all those that follow that moment must be considered and reconsidered. **22**

Writers often read aloud at this stage of the editing process, muttering or whispering to themselves, calling on the ear's experience with language. Does this sound right—or that? Writers edit, shifting back and forth from eye to page to ear to page. I find I must do this careful editing in short runs, no more than fifteen or twenty minutes at a stretch, or I become too kind with myself. I begin to see what I hope is on the page, not what actually is on the page. **23**

This sounds tedious if you haven't done it, but actually it is fun. Making something right is immensely satisfying, for writers begin to learn what they are writing about by writing. Language leads them to meaning, and there is the joy of discovery, of understanding, of making meaning clear as the writer employs the technical skills of language. **24**

Words have double meanings, even triple and quadruple meanings. Each word has its own potential for connotation and denotation. And when writers rub one word against the other, they are often rewarded with a sudden insight, an unexpected clarification. **25**

The maker's eye moves back and forth from word to phrase to sentence to paragraph to sentence to phrase to word. The maker's eye sees the need for variety and balance, for a firmer structure, for a more appropriate form. It peers into the interior of the paragraph, looking for coherence, unity, and emphasis, which make meaning clear. **26**

I learned something about this process when my first bifocals were pre-   **27**
scribed. I had ordered a larger section of the reading portion of the glass because of my work, but even so, I could not contain my eyes within this new
limit of vision. And I still find myself taking off my glasses and bending my
nose towards the page, for my eyes unconsciously flick back and forth across
the page, back to another page, forward to still another, as I try to see each
evolving line in relation to every other line.

When does this process end? Most writers agree with the great Russian   **28**
writer Tolstoy, who said, "I scarcely ever reread my published writings, if by
chance I come across a page it always strikes me: all this must be rewritten
this is how I should have written it."

The maker's eye is never satisfied, for each word has the potential to ig-   **29**
nite new meaning. This article has been twice written all the way through
the writing process, and it was published four years ago. Now it is to be re-
published in a book. The editors made a few small suggestions, and then I
read it with my maker's eye. Now it has been re-edited, re-revised, re-read,
re-re-edited, for each piece of writing is full of potential and alternatives.

A piece of writing is never finished. It is delivered to a deadline, torn out   **30**
of the typewriter on demand, sent off with a sense of accomplishment and
shame and pride and frustration. If only there were a couple more days, time
for just another run at it, perhaps then . . .

The Last Word

The course is almost over, and you've written a few essays. The essays you've written
aren't the best part of what you have learned: the best part is what you've learned
about yourself, how you write, and what you need to do to write your best. That's
what you can take from this course and apply to other writing situations in other
times and places. You may have even learned a few habits to feed your writing skills
and keep them well tuned. These insights are what we hoped to help you find, for
this is how great writers are born.

Index